CW01558734

Up in the Air

Contents

First published by Verso 2025
© Holly Smith 2025

The manufacturer's authorized representative in the EU
for product safety (GPSR) is LOGOS EUROPE, 9 rue
Nicolas Poussin, 17000, La Rochelle, France
contact@logoseurope.eu

1 3 5 7 9 10 8 6 4 2

Verso
UK: 6 Meard Street, London W1F 0EG
US: 207 East 32nd Street, New York, NY 10016
versobooks.com

Verso is the imprint of New Left Books

ISBN-13: 978-1-80429-737-7
ISBN-13: 978-1-80429-738-4 (UK EBK)
ISBN-13: 978-1-80429-739-1 (US EBK)

British Library Cataloguing in Publication Data
A catalogue record for this book is available from the British Library

Library of Congress Cataloging-in-Publication Data

Names: Smith, Holly, 1998- author
Title: Up in the air : a history of high-rise Britain / Holly Smith.
Description: London ; New York : Verso, 2025. | Includes bibliographical
   references and index.
Identifiers: LCCN 2025025916 (print) | LCCN 2025025917 (ebook) | ISBN
   9781804297377 hardback | ISBN 9781804297391 ebook
Subjects: LCSH: High-rise apartment buildings—Great Britain—History |
   Public housing—Great Britain—History |
Architecture and society—Great
   Britain—History—20th century | Architecture and society—Great
   Britain—History—21st century
Classification: LCC NA7863.G7 S65 2025
(print) | LCC NA7863.G7 (ebook)
LC record available at https://lccn.loc.gov/2025025916
LC ebook record available at https://lccn.loc.gov/2025025917

Typeset in Sabon by Biblichor Ltd, Scotland
Printed and bound by CPI Group (UK) Ltd, Croydon CR0 4YY

Up in the Air

A History of High-Rise Britain

Holly Smith

VERSO

London • New York

Introduction

A woman gazes out from the balcony of her high-rise flat in Merritt Point, over the East London borough of Newham. A gleaming tower block surges up in front of her. It makes for an arresting contrast with the surrounding urban landscape, which descends into a dark scramble of Victorian terraces in the distance, bordered by some newer maisonettes closer by – all shrouded by the murky haze of the Docklands. Her flat is very high up, on the seventeenth floor, so she is tightly holding her seven-year-old daughter, who peers over the open ledge. Inside are her husband and another daughter, aged eleven. It is the last time she will see this view, because her family are moving house today.

It is 20 January 1969. We might have guessed the period from the woman's fashionable, coiffed, peroxide-blonde hairdo. The sun was setting on the 1960s: a momentous decade that transformed Britain's conurbations into brave new worlds of modern architecture and infrastructure, ushering in New Towns, shopping centres, motorways, and power stations. Perhaps most conspicuous of all was the revolution in housing that spawned a wave of futuristic high-rise towers to replace miles of slums.

The tower block in front of her is Ronan Point. The year before, it had been the scene of Britain's worst high-rise disaster of the twentieth century. In May 1968, just two months after opening, a corner wing of this twenty-two-storey building collapsed. A gas leak had caused a small explosion, around which the flats above and below had crumpled like a house of cards. The Ronan Point disaster triggered a national scandal: it was discovered that the block had been structurally flawed and lacked an internal frame. It was not a one-off. A government inquiry into the collapse warned that reams of other blocks had been built with equivalent flawed designs. This included several identical neighbouring blocks which, together with Ronan Point, made up the Freemasons Estate in Newham. One of them was Merritt Point.

This lady from Merritt Point appears fleetingly in several news reports, although little trouble was taken to spell her name correctly. She is alternately named by journalists as Ingeborg Paine, Ingeboug Paine, Ingeburg Payne, or Ingebord Payne, and the same goes for her daughter, who is either Diana or Diane. The electoral register confirms that her actual name was Ingeburg Payne. She lived at Number 81 Merritt Point with her husband, Graham, and their daughters, Diana and Susan.[1] The couple had married in 1956 in West Ham (Graham's hometown but not Ingeburg's, who was born in Germany with the maiden name Hanke).[2] Graham was a soldier. It is possible that they met while he was posted abroad in the early 1950s.

Their family was the first in Merritt Point to be evacuated, so the block could be strengthened and the gas supply removed. We can see the scaffolding on Ronan Point's collapsed corner. It was patched up and soon filled with other households from Newham's colossal housing waiting list. The Paynes had endured bombing during postings to Cyprus and Aden for Graham's job. Even with this hardy experience, their sense of security in the East End was shaken by the Ronan Point disaster. 'It's all right in daylight,' Ingeburg told Vincent Mulchrone from the *Daily Mail*. 'But at night, when the wind gets up . . .' Many of her neighbours shared fears that the building would not stand up to high winds. Yet in spite of the risks that had erupted into view, they also nursed attachments to their homes in the sky. Mulchrone explained:

The big blocks are exciting. They burst free of the mean streets of Canning Town like a promise to coming generations. For most of the young couples in Merritt Point this is their first real home. They are desperately keen to hang on to it. As they show you the G-Plan in the living room, the second telly in the bedroom, they talk of the old place, the one-roomed flat, the claustrophobic years with the in-laws.[3]

If we look carefully at Ingeburg's photograph, we realise that she is not looking at Ronan Point. Her eyes are in fact focused beyond it, on her new home, which she can also see from her balcony: Ferrier Point, a twenty-three-storey tower block of more secure construction just half a mile away. Her daughters are excited, packing toys and appliances into crates with beaming smiles. Newham Council intended Ferrier Point to be a temporary home, from which tenants would return to their old block after refurbishment, but Graham had other plans for their future residence. 'I am determined,' he resolved, 'to stay put.'[4]

This snapshot of life at Merritt Point summons up the complicated feelings that emerged within the walls of high-rise Britain. High-rise housing has long been subject to blanket opprobrium in the form of sweeping cliché. As a result, we have lost sight of the people who have called these buildings home. This book presents a new history of high-rise council housing in twentieth- and twenty-first-century Britain, putting its residents at front and centre.

The state-powered mass housing drive that followed the Second World War was unprecedented in its scope and its ambition. It reached staggering new heights, quite literally: housing the working classes hundreds of feet up in the sky. It was a remarkable episode in British history. Yet the post-war welfare state had fundamental flaws, around which dissatisfaction would accumulate in the decades that followed.

Council housing was heavily paternalistic from its inception; it strove to forge model communities. Most of these modern homes provided light, clean, and well-equipped dwellings that far surpassed the dilapidated Victorian accommodation they replaced. Some were inspired feats of architecture, sculptural in form and attentive in detail – high, mid-, and low rise. Others, however, had shocking structural defects, which have since dogged residents in many thousands of atrociously constructed multistorey flats. Neglected by the state for decades, people are still living in blocks with unrectified faults today.

Walking through London in the 1990s, the writer Patrick Wright pronounced high-rise council housing to be the 'Tombstone of the Welfare State'. The tower block, he argued, had become 'a monstrous emblem of the futility of all State-led social reform'.[5] The historian Patrick Dunleavy similarly described high rise as instrumental to the 'delegitimisation of public housing' in post-war Britain, a symbol of 'the inherent inefficiency, bureaucratic indifference, and the unresponsiveness of state intervention compared with market provision'.[6] These readings definitely correspond to the narrative purveyed in much of the mainstream media over the decades. But do they really give us the full picture of high-rise Britain?

This book tells a different story. By exploring grassroots struggles on a range of estates, it shows how high-rise housing served as a crucible for reimagining the welfare state. Through crisis and difficulty, people have appealed for improved public housing and forged progressive models for its realisation. Inefficiency, indifference, and unresponsiveness have been cause for criticism, but many people have wondered how these aspects of British council housing management might be constructively resolved. Across the decades, an appetite developed for state-sponsored housing that was more consultative in production, more consensual in allocation, more participatory in administration, and more accountable in governance. This book illustrates the resilience of investments in public housing: throughout the last century, there have been communities who needed it, demanded it, and fought for it. This remains true today.

Public housing tenure has regularly been pathologised as a locus of passivity. However, these pages trace a history of local action that has proved creative, resourceful, and visionary. The historian Peter Shapely narrates the history of the British tenants' movement as a tale of 'dormant recipients' becoming 'active consumers', in reaction to the 'concrete nightmare' of council housing.[7] Shapely's labels of dormancy and consumerism do a disservice to the depth and dynamism of working-class consciousness. These categories are as binary and narrow as the 'concrete nightmare' trope is monolithic and unhelpful.

We will navigate through a number of places and periods, to discover a multitude of stories. The chapters that follow explore the scattering of a local community to make way for Sheffield's flagship estate, Park Hill, during the 1950s; the outrage that followed the Ronan Point disaster at the end of the 1960s; the formation of a pioneering tenants' co-operative to revive a crumbling estate in London's Docklands in the 1970s; the advocacy of a National Tower Blocks Network agitating for high-rise safety in the 1980s and 1990s; the excitement of early digital culture in a Liverpudlian pensioners' high-rise internet television show in the 2000s; and the fierce battle to defend estates from demolition in the 2010s. These cases illuminate a fascinating landscape of enormous variation in multistorey forms – covering inter-war tenements, daring brutalist complexes, skinny point blocks, and mammoth slab schemes. They also capture a spectrum of experiences, showing how residential responses to these buildings have ranged from affection, to ambivalence, to aversion.

Many of Britain's high-rise blocks have been demolished, some just a few decades into their life. This began in the late 1970s, gathering steam up to the millennium, and continuing in the 2010s. For those buildings with major structural flaws and unhappy inhabitants, this has been a happy conclusion. There are others whose hasty demolitions perhaps seem injudicious and wasteful in hindsight, especially now that green concerns about embodied carbon have incentivised retrofit.

Regardless of opinion on the rectitude of their destruction, it is imperative that these high-rise buildings do not disappear from the historical record. A pedestrian walking through urban Britain today has few clues about the lost blocks that once towered overhead – previously impossible to ignore – on sites that have been comprehensively remodelled and pasted over. Many never graced the pages of glossy architectural journals in the form of perspective drawings, photographs, or detailed reports. So they dissolve further from view. For many of Britain's multistorey blocks, the sole images that survive in the public domain are those taken by the historian Miles Glendinning, who had the foresight to start documenting them, just as the tide was turning towards dynamite.[8]

Many blocks that feature in these pages no longer exist. This text attempts to commit them to the record. Even more importantly, it tries to document the past lives of the people who lived in them – their trials and joys, their hopes and memories – with the dignity they deserve.

1

Why High?

AN END TO THIS PLANLESS SCRAMBLE

Out of the shadow of the Victorian city, out of its soot, squalor, and strife, emerged radiant new visions for the twentieth century. The embers took flame in unexpected places. At the turn of the century, a little-known, middle-aged shorthand writer and budding inventor named Ebenezer Howard published a manifesto for a new city form. It was titled *To-morrow: A Peaceful Path to Real Reform* (1898). His publisher, Swan Sonnenschein & Co., had low expectations and Howard was obliged to raise money to fund its publication. In spite of his relative obscurity, Howard's missive caught public interest. It was soon republished with the snappier title *Garden Cities of To-morrow* (1902), becoming a bestseller.

Ebenezer Howard proposed a vision for the Garden City. This new kind of settlement, he argued, resolved the twin issues of urban overcrowding and rural depopulation by forging a marriage of town and country. More than a suburb, the self-sufficient Garden City was supposed to provide the best opportunities of the city, including work, leisure, and shopping. Its residents were to enjoy low rents as well as high wages; nature as well as entertainment; peace as well as intercourse. Howard wanted these settlements to be developed for the community instead of individual profit. There were to be no private landlords. All land was to be owned co-operatively, and any surplus made from the Garden City's activities would be reinvested, allowing rates to be kept low. These cities were supposed to stimulate emigration by demagnetising the old cities. Howard hoped that the area governed by the London County Council would see its population reduced to a fifth of its existing level.

The first Garden City was established in 1903, at Letchworth in Hertfordshire. Its master-planners, Barry Parker and Raymond Unwin, suffused Letchworth with a folksy Arts and Crafts architecture, featuring heavy eaves, half-timbering, and creamy roughcast render, invoking a romantic sense of the English pastoral in times gone by. Parker and Unwin favoured spacious cottages, informally situated, at low density – the optimum being twelve houses to the acre. Unwin's treatise, *Nothing Gained by Overcrowding!* (1912), denounced the rows of terraced streets which had proliferated in the Victorian age not only for their monotony but for the expense incurred by building narrow road after narrow road in parallel. Unwin proposed that houses could be more pleasantly and economically arranged in quadrangles and cul-de-sacs.

Only two Garden Cities were ever established in Britain. The second was founded at Welwyn, fifteen miles south of Letchworth, in 1920. Here, the architect-planner was Louis de Soissons, who designed the town in a more formal, neo-Georgian manner, based on a Beaux-Arts layout of verdant axial streets lined with trees. Raising sufficient capital to create new Garden Cities proved incredibly difficult. The Garden City Association had to source funding from wealthy individuals to purchase land, who demanded a return on their investment. Letchworth battled to break even: it struggled to establish its target population, to attract significant industry, and to fulfil Howard's ideal of self-sufficiency. Welwyn, so close to London, became a town chiefly of commuters.

The rustic domestic architecture of Letchworth was widely replicated, however, in Garden Suburbs that sprang up across the country in the early twentieth century, budding in Bristol,

8

Wavertree, Romford, Sutton, and Barry. The most famous, Hampstead Garden Suburb, was designed by Raymond Unwin himself, to the dismay of many of his allies including the Letchworth pioneer Charles Purdom: 'I could not conceive how a man who believed in the garden city as he did could forsake it for a cause so inferior as that of a garden suburb.'[1] These were dormitory settlements on the edges of existing cities, a far cry from the independent towns engineered to delimit straggling growth which were imagined in Howard's original tract.

At the end of the First World War, central government set up the Tudor Walters Committee to decide upon the template for Britain's post-war housing programme. The committee gravitated towards Garden City principles (indeed, Raymond Unwin was a leading member). The Tudor Walters Report of 1918 recommended building two-storey, pitched-roofed cottages at low densities in a new housing drive. The Liberal Prime Minister David Lloyd George exclaimed upon visiting Letchworth in 1918: 'In five years we will have a million people living in houses like this.'[2]

Letchworth Garden City, 1912.

He promised a novel programme of 'Homes Fit for Heroes'. In 1919, the Addison Act was passed to subsidise their construction, which would proceed principally on the outskirts of existing cities.

The 1919 legislation was responsible for the construction of 213,821 houses, a figure that was deemed a paltry return on Lloyd George's promise. The programme was shelved during the economic slump of 1921. By 1923, the shortage of accommodation was even worse than it had been in 1919.[3] Dr Christopher Addison, the minister for health, resigned in outrage against the 'betrayal of the slums'.[4] The housing historian Mark Swenarton has characterised Homes Fit for Heroes as an 'insurance against revolution' – a palliative for the working classes, rather than a crusade for a reformed Britain.[5] Homes Fit for Heroes marked an important moment at which housing became a state responsibility in Britain, but the slum problem persisted on a nationwide scale.

In the 1920s, cheap mortgages and speedy commuting allowed for a spurt of private suburban development around existing cities. It was the suburban semi, notes the architectural historian Alan Powers, that ultimately 'went further towards solving the slum problem than any direct government intervention' in inter-war Britain, 'whatever the cost in amenity and aesthetics'.[6] To many contemporaries, however, this cost was unconscionable. Architect Julian Leathart wrote in 1940,

> It is fashionable to hurl abuse at the speculative house builder, and it is, without dispute, to his appalling vulgarity and ignorance that the despoliation of town and countryside during the last twenty years is attributable. But the jerry builder has fulfilled a public demand, and, in the sacred name of private enterprise, his depredations have been allowed to go unchecked by either Government or local authority.[7]

Local authorities were hamstrung between the options of building upwards or outwards in the inter-war years.[8] Dispersal was the driving force in urban policy but, all the while, whistles were being blown about the threat of formless sprawl gobbling up the countryside. This anxiety was captured in the Welsh architect Clough Williams-Ellis's call-to-arms, *England and the Octopus* (1928). Williams-Ellis branded several culprits: nineteenth-century industrialisation; the growth of the railways; ribbon-road development; and *laissez-faire* speculative building. 'Surely as human beings,' he appealed, 'we ought to demand an ordered, reasonable, humanistic setting for our lives and an end to this planless scramble that would scarcely do credit to the lower animals.'[9] A chorus of figures rallied behind him, including John Maynard Keynes, E. M. Forster, Patrick Abercrombie, and Thomas Sharp. 'A gimcrack civilisation crawls like a giant slug over the country,' warned the anti-slum campaigner Howard Marshall, 'leaving a foul trail of slime behind it.'[10] Clough Williams-Ellis's proposed solutions were Garden City planning and (less palatably) a strong measure of birth control to shrink the country's 'monstrously swollen population'.[11]

Garden City cottages may have been a viable approach for new satellite towns on virgin sites. In inner-city areas, where land values were high, it was simply not possible to rehouse residents from former slum property by building at such densities. Nor was the Garden City model entirely enticing. Non-Conformist Letchworth had one pub, the Skittles Inn, which served apple juice and cocoa instead of beer. It had an oddball reputation for housing teetotallers, vegetarians, theosophists, and Esperanto enthusiasts. Overcrowding and dereliction had made the old, inner-city lodgings unpopular, but many people equally resisted the prospect of being shipped out to distant places far from their communities and workplaces. In 1930, the Greenwood Act set up a subsidy system to encourage local authorities to clear slums and build flats on expensive inner-city sites, a condition of the subsidy being that new housing needed to be at least four storeys high. After the general housing subsidy granted by the Wheatley Act of 1924 was ditched in 1933, the Greenwood Act came into its own. The nation's urban skylines crept slowly upwards in a handful of cities: in London, Liverpool, Glasgow, and to a lesser extent Leeds.

Building upwards unlocked access to air and light, which were major public health priorities. As president of the Royal Institute of British Architects (RIBA), Giles Gilbert Scott stressed to the Ministry of Health in 1934 that balconies in flatted blocks could be used for babies' cots.[12] The idea that young children should drink in the open air to grow up strong, guarding against rickets, pneumonia, and bronchitis, was in vogue. Babies of the future, *The Times* reported, could look forward to being 'under the mother's eye and out of reach of the cat, in the open air: and, bounded in a balcony, they may count themselves kings and queens of infinite space'.[13] As early as 1884, none other than William Morris, notwithstanding his predilection for the medieval, had proposed: 'It might be advisable, granting the existence of huge towns for the present, that the houses for workers should be built in tall blocks, in what might be called vertical streets.' Morris thought that this solution could offer space, air, sunlight, privacy, and gardens to the poor.[14] Even John Betjeman, later known for his conservationism, was sympathetic to this sentiment as a young man. In an article of 1934, titled 'What Would Wren Have Built Today?', he proposed:

> Two dozen skyscrapers, though they would obviously dwarf St. Paul's, would not take away from its beauty if they were beautiful themselves. They would alter the skyline, certainly, yet we should not sacrifice health, time, and comfort to one skyline because we have not the courage to create another.[15]

Much of Britain's 1920s and 1930s multistorey council housing was built in a standardised neo-Georgian style, usually between five and six storeys high, with ruddy load-bearing brickwork, pitched roofs, tall chimneys, sash windows, and dormers. Such features, which provided charm and proportional balance in a traditional Georgian house, did not necessarily translate to buildings of a much larger scale. The tightly ordered façades of these long blocks of flats elicited comparisons with army barracks.

During the 1920s the RAF had constructed military quarters in a similar neo-Georgian idiom, cementing a resemblance that did not seem completely appropriate for domestic architecture. There were commanding concerns that these tightly packed new blocks offered limited improvement upon the slums which they had replaced.

Proposals were emerging for new modernist flats. The inter-war neo-Georgian revival and the rise of the modern movement spoke to mutual concerns about light, proportion, and regularity. Both were reacting against the Victorians. Many modernists held deep respect for the urbanity and decorum of Georgian architecture and planning, the influence of which has been testified across countless modern housing schemes. Ernö Goldfinger's three houses at Willow Road in Hampstead (1939) updated the Georgian terrace. Armstrong and MacManus's Regent's Park Estate (1960) was arranged around the layout of John Nash's original squares. Lewis Womersley took inspiration from the hillside curvature of Bath's Royal Crescent in his plans for Park Hill in Sheffield (1961) and Hulme Crescents in Manchester (1971). The municipal neo-Georgian flatted estate, however, garnered little affection. These homes were typically small, noisy, and poorly insulated.

In avant-garde quarters, there was an impulse to engineer something less parsimonious. New construction materials and methods beckoned; house-building might be fundamentally revolutionised. The tight frame of the traditional window, for instance, could be left behind. *The Flat Book* (1939), a snappy guide to modern design and furnishing by the married architects Leslie Martin and Sadie Speight, waxed lyrical about the potentialities of long windows with sliding and folding functions which could 'almost transform the room into the equivalent of an open air terrace'.[16]

Upmarket blocks of modern flats showcased tantalising possibilities. Highpoint, built on the crest of a hill at Highgate, provided the ultimate model. It was designed by the Tecton partnership, under the leadership of the cosmopolitan Eastern European émigré and Marxist Berthold Lubetkin. The pure white Highpoint I

(1935), of eight storeys on a double cruciform plan, was followed by the even more luxurious Highpoint II (1938), with a penthouse for Lubetkin himself. Highpoint II deployed allusive materials and symbols – brick render, bronzed doors, glazed bricks, and caryatids purchased from the British Museum – alongside its groundbreaking architecture of double-height rooms, a cantilevered entranceway, and box-frame construction.

Seaside spots offered excellent vantage points for flats. Marine Court (1938), on the St Leonards seafront, resembled a moored cruise liner. This complex had restaurants, shops, and a tea lounge. Strolling on its promenade deck on the thirteenth floor, residents could imagine they were steaming across the Channel. The accommodation was grand too: the largest flats had four bedrooms, a dining room, and a sitting room. Every flat had a sea view, most with a balcony. Wells Coates's Embassy Court (1935), by the beach in Brighton, had a comparable streamlined aesthetic and unbroken ocean views thanks to its elegant wrap-around windows. The twelfth floor had a roof terrace and each flat its own 'sun room'.

The lavish perks of these new residences were not necessarily transferable to municipal projects. Residents of the iconic Lawn Road flats in Hampstead (1934, also by Wells Coates) were provided with shoe-polishing, window-cleaning, bed-making, and laundry services, and were served gourmet meals at its chic Isobar restaurant, or by dumb-waiter if they fancied a night in. No local authority could provide this hotel standard, but various enriching amenities could be incorporated in council flats alongside the core benefits touted by modernist architectural design – space, light, and functionality.

This was verified at Kensal House (1936), a trailblazing estate of modern flats for working-class residents in Ladbroke Grove, co-designed by Maxwell Fry and Elizabeth Denby for the Gas Light and Coke Company. Kensal House, unlike many inter-war flats, was more than an exercise in space-saving. Its designers were trying to forge a more collective way of life. Its sponsors, on the other hand, as the historian Elizabeth Darling reminds us, were attempting to advertise the suitability of gas for mass housing schemes to see off competition from electricity.[17] The estate had two social clubs and allotments, plus a nursery and playground set upon the circular site of a former gas holder. It was set up to be tenant-managed, with a committee per staircase (although there were strict regulations about hanging washing outside and redecorating). The flats each had two to three bedrooms, a private balcony, a pram shed, and a labour-saving kitchen with up-to-date appliances. The bedrooms faced east, to catch the morning sun, and the living rooms west, for light in the afternoon. Kensal House was an inspiring project. Here was an example of genuinely modern flat living, completely unlike the tenements before.

Modern sky living might offer a radically different future. Such ambitions were trumpeted in *The Modern Flat* (1937) – a manifesto authored by two evangelistic young architects and (fittingly) one-time flatmates, F. R. S. Yorke and Frederick Gibberd, illustrated with photographs of new housing schemes at home and abroad. *The Modern Flat* held up multistorey housing as the logical step forward from the speculative building and Garden Suburb developments that were 'disfiguring the landscape in every direction'. Yorke and Gibberd believed multistorey, flatted development was the route by which 'the perfect home could be achieved', offering a model of communal living with shared in-block amenities and access to common green space. Residents would thus be liberated from domestic and gardening responsibilities, forging a brand-new collective way of life. Yorke and Gibberd advocated flat-building 'not as a means of crowding more and more people into a given area, but as a means of releasing more ground space for parks, roads and gardens'.[18]

Dazzled by Le Corbusier's unrealised Ville Radieuse of 1924, Yorke and Gibberd were entranced by the idea of the slab block in green parkland. Slab blocks are wide multistorey buildings: they pack a high density by virtue of both their height and breadth, often housing maisonettes across two levels. When slab blocks are constructed on pilotis (pillar-like stilts that raise the building from the ground), the pedestrian can enjoy an uninterrupted view of the vista stretching out beyond it. This benefit is negated when these spaces are used for car parking, as is typically the case today.

This arcadian vision of high rise amid nature was captured vividly by the landscape architect Christopher Tunnard, who drew upon the tradition of the eighteenth-century English landscape garden to devise a new 'common garden' for all. Tunnard proposed a scheme of slab blocks scattered through Claremont Park in Surrey, amid scenery fashioned by his heroes Lancelot 'Capability' Brown, William Kent, and John Vanbrugh. This plan was sympathetically illustrated by Gordon Cullen for the *Architectural Review*. 'Today the suburban plot,' Tunnard proclaimed, 'tomorrow the garden without limitation.'[19] The flat roofs of these buildings opened up more possibilities. Le Corbusier asked: 'Is it not really illogical that one entire superficies of a town should be unused and reserved for a flirtation between the tiles and the stars?'[20] They might be used for recreation, coffee drinking, and sun lounging.

Christopher Tunnard's vision for Claremont Park, 1938.

For all the breathless excitement surrounding them, exemplar modern flats had teething problems. Quarry Hill, in Leeds, was devised by the city's housing director R. A. H. Livett in the mid-1930s, to provide just under a thousand multistorey flats in a former slum clearance area. The estate was built to an innovative ferro-concrete design – a steel-framed system with precast slabs – patented by the Parisian engineer Eugène Mopin. Advanced new features were planned, including a Garchey waste-disposal system and (for the first time in English municipal housing) lifts to spare tenants from climbing endless stairs. The proposed housing at Quarry Hill seemed to embody the rationalised future of accommodation for the poor. A slick photographed model of the estate served as the cover for Anthony Bertram's Pelican paperback *Design* (1938). The real building fared worse than its model. Quarry Hill's experimental construction dragged on into the war, delayed by production-line hiccups and arguments with the contractor. Soon after completion, the buildings were beset with structural issues, including insecure wall slabs, corroding steelwork, and fractures along the refuse chutes. Quarry Hill would be demolished within just four decades.

Fervour for flat-building was far from universal in inter-war Britain. Heath Robinson and K. R. G. Browne's tongue-in-cheek guide *How to Live in a Flat* (1936) lampooned the lofty aspirations being touted. This book was filled with knowingly outlandish illustrations of flat-dwellers of the future enjoying a spot of golf across balconies, sunbathing by luxurious swimming pools in the sky, and fishing in a ground-level goldfish pond all the way from the top floor. Notwithstanding their modern accoutrements, a new flat-dweller faced a cramped domestic future. 'There will be no more cat-swinging for him,' the authors lamented, 'of course, no more jolly games of Hide-and-Seek, and no more privacy – or only about as much as is enjoyed by a tinned sardine.'[21] This shortage of space applied to municipal and private flats in the inter-war period.

The 1930s trend for compact luxury flats spoke to the decline of domestic service, leading the veteran architectural cartoonist Osbert Lancaster to joke that such a flat 'usually fulfils its claim

THE ROOF GARDEN

Heath Robinson's wry cartoon depicting the fantastical recreational possibilities available in new flats.

of saving labour by being so abominably ill-planned that no respectable domestic can be induced to work in it'.[22] He poked fun at 'the fantastic illogicality which prompts those who could well afford comfortable and dignified homes to live in a collection of centrally-heated match-boxes in a building resembling a pickle-factory'.[23] Lancaster had little time for 'that Bauhaus balls' – but nor did he relish the suburban alternatives, which he waspishly caricatured as 'Stockbroker's Tudor', 'Wimbledon Transitional', and 'By-Pass Variegated'.[24]

Elsewhere, there was bitter opposition to modernist incursions specifically. Reginald Blomfield, a prominent establishment architect who favoured the classically inspired 'grand manner' as executed in his remodelling of Regent Street, disparaged '*Modernismus*' as an invasion 'alien to the English tradition and temperament'. He saw this style as no more than a passing fad, a deleterious product of cosmopolitanism that would fail to take root. 'We are not likely to part company with our birthright for a mess of pottage,' he proclaimed.[25] Blomfield's xenophobia clouded his judgement. 'Why should I be an internationalist because I accept the structural outcome of materials in common use everywhere', bit back Maxwell Fry. 'As well call Wren an internationalist for casting eyes towards Paris and Rome. Wren, whose very work was personal and English. As well call the author himself an internationalist for his love of French classical architecture.'[26]

Meanwhile, the mouthpiece of the Garden City movement, *Town and Country Planning*, continued to maintain that the ideal home was 'the self-contained house with a garden'. Flat-building struck them as a 'retrograde' step back to the old tenement model of working-class housing.[27] Raymond Unwin castigated blocks of flats as 'concrete warehouses'. 'It may be that the modern family will like living in a few cells in a vast pile of biscuit boxes,' Unwin said to the RIBA in 1933. 'I do not know. That has never appealed to me as an attractive idea of a home.'[28] Happily for Unwin, tall blocks were still thin on the ground. Flats made up only 5 per cent of Britain's subsidised housing during the inter-war period.[29]

Beneath all this vituperative disagreement, however, lay a resolute point of consensus. In the course of the early twentieth century, a prevailing belief had taken root: the cities of the future must be planned. There could be no return to uncoordinated, speculative scramble.

LIFT-OFF

The Second World War reignited the landscape of high-rise possibility. Nearly half a million British homes were destroyed or extensively damaged during Luftwaffe bombing.[30] Huge swathes of the run-down stock that remained were deemed unfit for human habitation, the hangover of nineteenth-century urbanisation awaiting slum clearance. The British public – having endured not only the sacrifices of the war but the privations of the 1930s – expected a major programme of rehousing at higher standards than those of the past. Clement Attlee's Labour Party, elected on a landslide in 1945, promised to deliver over one million new homes by 1951, championing a new era of council house-building.

Post-war reconstruction was haunted by two spectres from the past: overcrowding and sprawl. Rural conservation and modernist development, the architectural historian William Whyte has pointed out, accordingly became allied causes.[31] The planner Thomas Sharp insisted that the distinction between town and countryside should be preserved so that both could flourish. He deplored the 'trivial romanticism' of the Garden City impulse and its degeneration into 'Neither-Town-Nor-Country' suburbia steamrolling across inter-war Britain. Towns should proudly be towns: dense, varied, dynamic, and unapologetically urban. In his popular wartime Pelican paperback *Town Planning* (1940), Sharp called for the construction of a variety of houses and flats to make post-war towns 'far more architecturally successful, far more visually exciting, than our low-scaled earth-crouching cottagey towns of to-day can ever be'.[32] By doing so, precious stretches of the British countryside could, moreover, be preserved.

Such concerns informed the establishment of the first Green Belt around London in 1938, which Patrick Abercrombie and John Henry Forshaw extended in their Greater London Plan of 1944. Abercrombie had been a founding member of the Council for the Preservation of Rural England in the 1920s (Clough Williams-Ellis helped to establish its Welsh version). In 1955, the Ministry of Housing and Local Government urged other large towns and cities in England and Wales to draw up Green Belts of their own.

Abercrombie and Forshaw sought to tackle overcrowding and sprawl through a twin strategy of inner-city redevelopment and managed dispersal to designated New Towns, twenty-eight of which were created in the post-war period. This was a compromise offering something to the advocates for density and to those for decentralisation. The upwards-or-outwards debate of the inter-war decades was still live. Now, however, the scope for urban conurbations to ooze outwards was curtailed, while land values within their boundaries remained steep. Building upwards was a clear solution. This dilemma has been described by the historians Miles Glendinning and Stefan Muthesius as 'the land trap'.[33] Alongside Simon Pepper and Peter Richmond, they attribute the ultimate ascent of high rise in Britain to local authority realpolitik, rather than the bombastic rhetoric of architectural modernism.[34]

Abercrombie and Forshaw championed mixed development, which combined houses, two-to-four-storey maisonettes, and high flats on each estate to accommodate households at different life stages. This became the defining logic of the early post-war years, when big patches of bomb damage freed up space for comprehensive redevelopment. Mixed development leapfrogged the old choice between what Elizabeth Denby described as 'the extremes of beehive building in the centre and chicken-coop building on the outskirts of the town'.[35] It was supposed to provide a variety of tailored responses to housing demand. 'There is infinite variety in people's needs and problems,' stressed the Central Housing Advisory Committee report *Living in Flats* (1952).[36] Mixed development was geared to enable large families with young children to be housed in dwellings close to the ground, with access to a garden, while building at high densities. High-rise housing would be interspersed throughout estates, to accommodate young couples, single people, and the elderly. The Ministry of Housing and Local Government recommended that high rise should only be used 'to the extent that it must be', because it was expensive and risked 'monotonous development' if used without variation.[37]

Post-war rehousing got off to a slow start. The Labour government of 1945 to 1951 was dogged by austerity, a balance-of-payments crisis, and a punishing winter in 1947, on top of steel, fuel, and labour shortages. House-building accelerated in the

1950s with Harold Macmillan's drive for higher quantities, although this often came at the expense of dwelling size and quality as well as prioritising private-sector building. Central government faced considerable pressure from local councils burdened with mammoth housing waiting lists. As a result, new staggered subsidy regulations were introduced in 1956 under Conservative Minister for Housing Duncan Sandys, granting flats in buildings of six storeys over twice the subsidy as houses and nearly thrice for buildings of fifteen storeys and above. Just afterwards, in 1957, the subsidy for general housing needs was withdrawn.

A decade-long high-rise boom followed across the period of 1958 to 1968. In its course, the earlier scriptures of mixed development were often superseded. Bunched groups of tower blocks proved an easier way to fill tricky gap sites and a quicker route for local authorities to depopulate their waiting lists. The products of this strategy were often less successful. Pleasant landscaping and improved amenities could fall by the wayside, since they were not eligible for subsidy, negating the benefits of building high hailed all those years before. This shift also coincided with an enthusiasm for system building among hard-pressed local authorities seeking to produce housing quickly and at economies of scale.

Almost half a million high-rise flats were built in Britain between 1955 and 1975. Greater London dominated the construction tallies, followed by Scotland and North West England.[38] Yet high-rise units represented a statistical minority of Britain's post-war housing. Flats made up only a fifth of the dwellings built in Britain from 1945 to 1976, most of them in blocks of four storeys or lower.[39] The radical form and conspicuousness of high-rise blocks have nevertheless made them a highly charged symbol of twentieth-century housing.

High rise was not the product of a socialist coup. This was a joint political venture for which responsibility is shared by the Labour and Conservative Parties, in both central and local government. Post-war reconstruction was powered by electoral promises – from both sides of the ring – to deliver huge tallies of new housing in response to insistent popular demand. High flats became a bipartisan solution. Contrary to popular opinion, high rise was no cheap hack. This was an expensive way to build. In 1961, average construction costs per square foot stood at forty shillings for houses, forty-five shillings for maisonettes, seventy-four shillings for flats of eight storeys, and eighty-three shillings for flats of twelve storeys. The cost to local authorities was eased by central government subsidies for high buildings (though of course this was still the public purse), but the overall cost to local councils remained higher than low-rise construction.[40] Their maintenance was costly, too.

Tower blocks are often dismissed as eyesores, but they were conceived as the polar opposite. These tall, modern buildings were supposed to break up the repetitive, sooty dreariness of Victorian low-rise vistas. The RIBA hosted a landmark symposium on high flats in 1955 at which Evelyn Sharp (deputy secretary and powerhouse at the Ministry of Housing and Local Government) elucidated this point in an invective against 'ghastly uniformity':

> from the point of view of the urban scene, high dwellings interspersed with low and middle-sized dwellings are really a thing of beauty. There is nothing it seems to me more appalling, more deadening in the urban landscape than a uniform mass of low buildings covering acres and acres ... from the point of view of what they look like, high dwellings – I think really very high dwellings – are an enormous enhancement of the scene.[41]

John Henry Forshaw had recommended that Sharp read Osbert Sitwell's *The Four Continents* (1954), a lush travelogue of the sights of post-war voyages. They were both captivated by Sitwell's rhapsodic tributes to towers, old and new, across the globe – from medieval San Gimignano to twentieth-century Manhattan. 'So let me now sweep the harp-strings with my hand and sing in honour of them,' Sitwell exclaimed. 'Of towers I sing: of towers, steeples, minarets, spires, turrets, cupolas, *campanili*, belfries, pagodas, pyramids and skyscrapers – this last a fine exaggerative term worthy of its significance.'[42] Sharp later regretted proclaiming such impassioned support for high flats, but these raptures give us insight into the logic behind their lift-off.[43] As the architect Ernö Goldfinger explained in defence of his own tower blocks: 'The whole object of building high is to free the ground for children and grown-ups to enjoy Mother Earth and not to cover every inch with bricks and mortar.'[44] High rise could offer valuable topographical variety and visual interest by exploiting the drama of juxtaposition. The early Mark One New Towns illustrate this with aplomb.

Take the Lawn in Harlow. This was the site of Britain's first tower block (completed in 1951), proudly shown off in model form at the Festival of Britain and in the flesh to a delegation of eminent foreign visitors from the Congrès Internationaux d'Architecture Moderne (CIAM). It was designed by Frederick Gibberd, who had announced his commitment to multistorey architecture in his single-minded design for Pullman Court in Streatham (1936) – a

Britain's first tower block: the Lawn flats in Harlow New Town, Essex.

commission he secured at the precocious age of twenty-three. The sharp white Pullman Court was a thoroughly functionalist building in the International Style, with square projecting balconies cribbed from Walter Gropius's Bauhaus school at Dessau. Gibberd's approach softened during the Second World War, when he leaned into a more picturesque English modernism, retaining faith in flats while thinking increasingly about the harmony of the total environment. His ten-storey, earth-toned Lawn flats in Harlow (where he was chief planner) were engineered to provide a quiet neighbourhood with a visual punch, their verticality counterbalancing the surrounding housing. The block was built for single people and small families. It was just one of a variety of dwelling types on offer in Harlow, where each area was designed by a different architect. Gibberd explained his motivations for building upwards to the RIBA:

> Of course, most architects like the idea. A tall building is a fascinating problem, but – I hate to say it – that they provide opportunities for architects to build monuments to themselves is not sufficient justification for building tall flat blocks. However, there is a justification, and like most truths, it is quite simple. It is this. *The building of tall flat blocks gives more pleasure to more people.*[45]

The Lawn block was not the handiwork of hard-nosed necessity; it was supposed to bring happiness to its residents and its neighbours. It was constructed on a butterfly plan, which ingeniously gave every living room and balcony a south-facing aspect. Their delightful views over town and countryside were advertised in a promotional film that featured Gibberd chatting with an interviewer on one of these balconies. They were evidently quite poky, though. The two men look rather squashed, standing almost belly to belly. The Lawn block was surrounded by tall leafy cousins; it was set among mature oak trees, relating the building to its landscape. Its flat top was supposed to serve as a roof garden. Nature was a major consideration at Harlow, where all the pubs were named after butterflies and moths. Gibberd was a keen gardener, and he hired the gifted landscape architect Sylvia Crowe to act as a consultant for over two decades. The masterplan for Harlow New Town fused a dual offering of landscape and urbanity: 'Skylines, trees, woodlands, ancient buildings and so forth are all incorporated into the design, with the result that the town grows quickly into graceful maturity.'[46]

Brooke House in Basildon, on the other hand, delivered a gutsy, urban accent bang in the centre of town. It was completed in 1962 to a design by Anthony B. Davies, advised by Basil Spence, for Basildon Development Corporation. This fourteen-storey block seems almost to float on eight tall and willowy pilotis, thrusting up as a focal point in the main pedestrian precinct. There is a wonderful effect when its projecting triangular windows catch the sun: from wherever you stand, the rippling, concertinaed façade of Brooke House looks a little different. It is by far the most striking domestic architecture in the whole New Town. The *Architects' Journal* admired how it 'pulls the surrounding buildings together' – 'from a distance, when one is approaching Basildon, it stands up refreshingly in a sea of seemingly endless housing roofs'.[47]

Point Royal in Bracknell is another testament to the value of vertical interest. This slim, eighteen-storey block was completed by Arup in 1964, on a distinctive hexagonal plan. Point Royal looks like a space rocket. It sits atop a raised launch pad on a grassy mound concealing a residents' car park underneath. The building cantilevers out from a squat base and shoots upwards, forming a distinguished landmark in a patch of low-rise suburbia.

MULTIPLE MODERNISMS

High-rise housing is routinely castigated as monotonous. If we take the time to look up – to actually *look* – we find otherwise. These blocks make up a fantastically varied part of Britain's built heritage. Modernism is marked in its multiplicity. This was no narrow architectural tract: it evolved, expanded, and pluralised across the course of the twentieth century. The architectural theorist Sarah Williams Goldhagen correspondingly proposes that we should understand modernism as a discourse rather than a style.[48] The approaches of architects could vary within their own lifetimes. Le Corbusier's early machine aesthetic at the Villa Savoye ripened into a mature organicism, drawing inspiration from nature, at Ronchamp and Chandigarh.

High rise has taken myriad inventive architectural forms. We might look, for instance, to Denys Lasdun's sixteen-storey cluster block Keeling House (1957) in Bethnal Green, made up of four fans of maisonettes on a pinwheel plan. The William Stone Building (1964) in Cambridge provides another high-rise surprise. This is the university's only tower block – erected, curiously enough, in its oldest college, Peterhouse, courtesy of the chutzpah of Leslie Martin and Colin St John Wilson at the neighbouring Department of Architecture. It is eight storeys high and structured as a laterally stepped ziggurat, with wrap-around ribbon windows on its western side, taking inspiration from the sinuous work of Alvar Aalto. In spite of its height and unusual design, the William Stone block manages to nestle quite unobtrusively into the south of the Peterhouse Deer Park, where it grants its residents views over the Fens.

Different local authorities had diverging approaches. Miles Glendinning reminds us that the production of council housing in Britain was (as its name suggests) 'bound up with local political and civic microecologies to an extreme degree', distinguishing it from equivalent projects in much of Western Europe.[49] Manchester was reluctant to build high, whereas Glasgow leaped towards multistorey development with gusto.

The London County Council's (LCC) 1950s showpiece, the Alton Estate at Roehampton, plainly demonstrates the heterogeneity of modernist conceptions of high rise within just one estate. Here we see the realisation of the dream of tall blocks in a rolling landscape, whose flats enjoyed views over Richmond Park and Wimbledon Common. 'Each era needs, and has, its own architectural symbol,' reported the *Architectural Review* in an appraisal of the Alton Estate in 1964. 'It would be difficult to find for the twentieth century a more compelling one than the image of the great apartment building towering over the grass and trees of its surrounding parkland, bathed in the air and sunshine of a summer's day.'[50]

This massive project was portioned up between different architects at the LCC. The team at Alton East looked to Sweden, the team at Alton West to Marseille. The former was led by Rosemary Stjernstedt. Born in Birmingham with the maiden name Owen-Smith, she had worked as an architect and town planner in Sweden during the Second World War, taking the surname of the husband she married there. Her team was enamoured with the groupings of slim, elegant blocks in the forested Stockholm neighbourhoods of Danviksklippan and Vällingby. Alton East transplanted the *punkthus* (translated as 'point block') from Scandinavia to South

Showpiece housing at Roehampton, photographed from Alton West.

London. Point blocks slotted neatly into the existing landscape, allowing the park's mature conifers to be preserved, and cast smaller shadows than slabs. This housing was enlivened by a mixture of cheery colours and tiling.

Point blocks were also used at Alton West, but this later phase was distinguished by five monumental, eleven-storey slab blocks inspired by Le Corbusier's extraordinarily influential Unité d'Habitation, completed in Marseille in 1952. Alton West's slabs formed an epic row in uncompromising concrete on a Zeilenbau pattern, launching out on pilotis from a sloping hillside, around which the designers sought to evoke 'a feeling of endlessness to the grass carpet'.[51] Led by Colin Lucas, this team pushed against the grain at the LCC, scorning the Swedophile approach. Four of them – Bill Howell, John Killick, John Partridge, and Stan Amis – would later break away to form the daring practice HKPA. When the architect James Gowan paid their team a visit at work, he recalled being 'escorted around endless corridors and then to a small long room where the Bill Howell group was secreted, nursing their elaborate drawings of Roehampton. They were as suspicious as Corsican firebrands.'[52]

Rival sensibilities would continue to jostle. The early post-war period saw the hegemony of a picturesque style championed by the *Architectural Review* as 'Townscape'. Townscape invoked a specifically English form of modernism, drawing upon historic quirks to create bustling but urbane places full of variety and coincidence. This school of thought maintained that interesting places needed to marry the fruits of modernity with the charms of idiosyncrasy. Tall blocks provided a valuable feature in the modern townscape: the 'twentieth century visual equivalent of a church spire', in the words of architectural historian John Gold.[53] This thinking owed much to the Austrian theorist Camillo Sitte, who exalted the layout of Europe's medieval towns. Sitte talked of creating street pictures, using variation, enclosure, and prominent vertical landmarks to produce an assemblage of interesting viewpoints throughout a city. This fed into illustrations by Townscape's prime draughtsman, Gordon Cullen, who admired urban planning that played with serial vision – where new scenes are revealed to pedestrians at every twist and turn. His mural of 1957, in Coventry's Lower Precinct, celebrated Basil Spence's famous modernist cathedral side by side with the point blocks of Tile Hill, rendered in Poole ceramic tiles.

Townscape enjoyed a high-water mark at the Festival of Britain in 1951, when the philosophy was made concrete at the 'live architecture' exhibit of the Lansbury Estate in Poplar. But it also met pushback. To Colin St John Wilson, this represented an architecture of 'cold feet': a capitulation to folksy quaintness instead of a forward-thinking urbanism. He was unimpressed by the six-storey flats at the Lansbury. Instead, Wilson demanded an intrepid architecture featuring flatted buildings of up to thirty storeys, to forge a thriving 'vertical city'.[54] The formidable architectural partners Alison and Peter Smithson called for a many-levelled 'cluster city' – tightly knit, concentrated, and vital – in their influential

Gordon Cullen's mural in Coventry's Lower Precinct.

pushback against picturesque principles. The swing towards densification was manifested at Cumbernauld, the Scottish Mark Two New Town designated in 1955 to take overspill population from nearby Glasgow. At Cumbernauld, the town centre and residences were brought together in a dramatic, mega-structural hilltop metropolis of imposing concrete, later echoed at Thamesmead and the Barbican, ringed by a mixture of high- and low-rise housing.

High-rise architecture could be slipshod. It could also be superb. Goldfinger's Trellick Tower (1972) in North Kensington is a superlative example of crafted modern architecture. Its exposed concrete was bush-hammered and incorporated careful mouldings to thwart staining. The entrance hall was lined with marble and the lobby doors were made of heavy hardwood. The circulation spaces made use of stained glass and coloured tiles. The flats had special photobolic window screens to maximise light diffusion, stylish light switches set into the door jambs, and fine cedar boarding on their balconies.

There is beauty to be found in these buildings all over Britain. Gosport's point blocks Seaward and Harbour Towers (1963) were both adorned with whopping abstract mosaics by Kenneth Barden stretching from base to summit. The façade of Thornfield House (1962), a slab block in Limehouse, was divided up by a chunky vertical mural designed by Antony Hollaway, positioned adroitly off-centre. The Faraday Building at the University of Manchester (1967) had subtle patterned reliefs cast into its external concrete. A number of blocks in Aberdeen were faced with silvery granite, the area's traditional building material, to invoke the *genius loci*. Berkeley House, a point block in Snow Hill, Bath (1957), was clad with warm Bath limestone ashlar for the same purpose.

When we look up at high-rise housing, we see only the edifice. We get little sense of the interiors, which provide a crucial dimension to our understanding of these homes. The cramped flats of the inter-war period, usually kitted out with fireplaces and chimneys, contrasted markedly with post-war high-rise homes in their facilities and floor areas. These new flats were equipped with indoor lavatories, modern kitchens, hot running water, and heating. Such features feel banal today, but they were unprecedented luxuries for most of their first residents.

The Parker Morris Report, *Homes for Today and Tomorrow*, set generous guidelines for public-sector space standards in 1961 (made mandatory in 1969) establishing minimum square footage for net floor areas and storage allocation in council housing. Central heating was required in all new homes, as were plentiful electrical sockets. Blocks of flats with four or more floors had to be equipped with a lift, two in a building with more than six floors. New housing estates needed at least one car-parking spot per dwelling. The Parker Morris Committee (on which a third of sitting members were women) affirmed that the modern home needed to do more than fulfil people's basic requirements of shelter: 'It must be something of which they can be proud; and in which they must be able to express the fullness of their lives.'[55]

Architectural modernism was not about functionalism alone. Le Corbusier has suffered a century of repudiation for his proclamation that the house should be 'a machine for living in'. This snatched quote only partially encapsulates the message of *Vers une architecture* (1923), a book that Reyner Banham described as 'one of the most influential, widely read and least understood of all the architectural writings of the twentieth century'.[56] Le Corbusier was deeply invested in the connection between architecture and human feeling:

Architecture goes beyond utilitarian needs . . .

You employ stone, wood and concrete, and with these materials you build houses and palaces. That is construction. Ingenuity is at work.

But suddenly you touch my heart, you do me good, I am happy and I say 'This is beautiful.' That is Architecture. Art enters in.[57]

Verdicts on beauty have been historically volatile; the cycle of taste is always turning. Many eighteenth-century homeowners covered up their timber-framed houses with brick casing, partly as a fire retardant but also to follow fashion. This trend was turned on its head in the early twentieth century when neo-Tudor homes, faced with wooden planks nailed atop brick walls, popped up all across commuter-land. Victorian architecture became deeply unpopular by the mid-twentieth century, when its heavy ornament crashed out of style to the point of ridicule. Students at Nikolaus Pevsner's 1950s Slade lectures at Cambridge collapsed into fits of laughter upon being shown William Butterfield's Keble College, Oxford (1870), an audaciously polychromatic product of the High Gothic Revival.[58] Pevsner himself held more balanced views on Victorian architecture. 'There is much, e.g. in Butterfield, that is unbeautiful and yet of value, thanks to such qualities as character, intensity, bite, guts,' he maintained.[59] Pevsner was an early member of the Victorian Society, founded in 1958 to reappraise the period's built heritage in the face of indiscriminating disapprobation.

In the late nineteenth century, architects of the Queen Anne Revival – such as Richard Norman Shaw, Edward Robert Robson, and Basil Champneys – flocked to red gauged brickwork and crisp architectural terracotta in pursuit of 'sweetness and light'.[60] By the mid-twentieth century, brick had accumulated contrary connotations. Proliferating across huge urban areas, now covered in layers of soot, this building material seemed 'the enemy of light and space', in the words of the historian Raphael Samuel. Yet in the 1970s, the Victorian stock-brick terrace and industrial warehouse enjoyed a rebound in popularity and have since become desirable real estate, as Samuel charted in his essay 'The Return to Brick'.[61]

The modern movement was electrified by the potential of new industrial materials, namely glass, concrete, and steel. Plate-glass windows and curtain walls could transform the appearance of buildings externally and the penetration of light internally. Raymond McGrath and A. C. Frost's extensively illustrated *Glass in Architecture and Decoration* (1937) showcased the material's recent technical advances and diverse applications. The modernist master Walter Gropius loved its 'sparkling insubstantiality, and the way it seems to float between wall and wall imponderably as the air'.[62] He described the Peckham Pioneer Health Centre (1937) – the exterior of which seemed more glass than wall – as 'an oasis of glass in a desert of brick'.[63]

The contrast of light over dark lit British modernists aflame. 'When you live in the North of England everything is dirty,' recalled Peter Smithson, the modernist architect from County Durham, 'and you think, modern architecture is wonderful.'[64] Modern developments appeared luminous among their blackened neighbours when first constructed, although feelings shifted after many of Britain's older buildings were sand-blasted and cleaned of polluted muck in the 1970s. The reverse is now true, as the maintenance of Britain's twentieth-century heritage has been deprioritised. Concrete needs to be looked after. So does stucco, which must be regularly washed and reapplied to keep treasured Regency buildings gleaming.

Few building materials have been more vilified than concrete. It is worth remembering the sculptural qualities for which it was valued: concrete was beloved by many twentieth-century architects because of its supreme plasticity. It opened up thrilling possibilities, creating shapes that seemed to defy gravity, like cantilevered projections or roofs in the shape of hyperbolic paraboloids. This malleability allowed Chamberlin, Powell, and Bon to crown the centrepiece of their Golden Lane Estate, the sixteen-storey Great Arthur House (1959), with a swishing concrete tick curving up from the roof into the sky. In practical terms, concrete is fire-resistant and can be incredibly strong when properly reinforced and loaded. Its surface can take on all sorts of textures, such as the imprinted laminar grain of wood boards or the ribbed effect of corduroy. Ribbing assists rainwater run-off, as concrete tends to streak and stain without drip mouldings.

The ascent of novel techniques posed challenges on building sites. The Barbican Estate – Golden Lane's neighbouring big brother, also by Chamberlin, Powell, and Bon – has become a modernist landmark on account of its towers, raised walkways, and coarse concrete. The realisation of this complex project took two decades, going to tender in 1962 and reaching completion in 1982, in a process delayed by construction difficulties, industrial-relations clashes, and lock-outs. Health and safety provision was poor, resulting in fatalities on site. The Barbican's architects stipulated a rough finish for its exposed concrete surfaces to bring out the aggregate. The poured in-situ concrete was cured, then battered with power tools. This notoriously unpleasant job was allocated to black Caribbean workers, who were rarely given appropriate protective equipment. The work caused a form of permanent nerve damage known as white finger, produced by the impact of forceful vibration through the hands.

The Barbican site saw multiple strikes by construction workers petitioning for improved conditions and a steady wage system,

Bush hammering in process at the Barbican.

while the contractors deployed union-busting tactics, bringing in subcontracted casual labour and blacklisting shop stewards. This illustrates a tragic contradiction that ran through the heart of post-war reconstruction. The labour historians Christine Wall, Linda Clarke, Charlie McGuire, and Olivia Muñoz-Rojas have excavated these dynamics in oral history interviews with construction workers: their project reveals how the British welfare state was built by a workforce whose own welfare was all too frequently denied.[65]

New materials facilitate new forms, but they can be fickle friends. Asbestos, which was regularly used in housing and elsewhere for its fire-retardant and insulating properties, was recognised as a dangerous carcinogen in the 1970s. Concrete has proved vulnerable to frost and humidity. If water penetrates reinforced concrete, the steel within can rust and expand, causing cracking and spalling. The production of concrete and especially cement in the post-war period generated heavy carbon dioxide emissions. Wood-shuttering created enormous waste, as strips of wood pressed into concrete become soiled and unusable. High embodied carbon should, on the other hand, encourage us to think twice before wanton demolition. Concrete structures can perform well with regard to operational carbon because this material has a high thermal mass, making it possible to maintain a consistent interior temperature, cutting heating and air-conditioning demand.

In recent years, it has become clear that many buildings containing reinforced autoclaved aerated concrete (RAAC) components require urgent remediation. First developed in 1929, RAAC was used in many British buildings constructed since the 1950s, before being phased out in the late 1990s. Its bubbly aerated structure made it an effective insulator and light in weight, so it was often used for flat roofs. This same structure makes it susceptible to moisture permeation if it is inadequately waterproofed, leading to damage of the metal reinforcement. In cases where RAAC planks were installed with deficient support at their ends, or are overloaded, there lies risk of collapse. RAAC failure has been identified even in esteemed, high-expense projects, including Arne Jacobsen's St Catherine's College Oxford (1962), and Denys Lasdun's ziggurats at the University of East Anglia (1968).

In mass house-building, the mid-century fervour for prefabrication and system building proved calamitous. The partial collapse of the structurally unsound Ronan Point, after a gas explosion in 1968, sounded the first warning. Over the decades, it would become clear that equivalent faults were present in many other high-rise buildings across the country.

BUILDING DEMOCRACY

During the Second World War, Mass Observation ran a popular investigation into the nation's 'Dream Homes of the Future'. If given complete free choice, 79 per cent of respondents reported that they would like to live in a small house or bungalow, whereas 8 per cent said their first choice would be a flat.[66] Contemporary surveying consistently mirrored these findings. Yet Mass Observation also discovered that there were nuances in public opinion that had been obscured during the flats-versus-houses debate, drowned out by the 'shrill grinding of axes'.[67] Surveying residents in a new block of flats, they found that although 60 per cent would have ideally chosen to live in a small house or bungalow, 84 per cent still reported that they liked their flats. For certain people, such as the elderly, singletons, and young couples, flats could provide 'exceptionally high levels of satisfaction'.[68]

The envisioned dream home was often weighed up alongside other factors. The overwhelming majority of surveyed wartime servicemen reported that, although few would choose to live in a flat, they wanted to return to urban heartlands with their pubs, clubs, and cinemas, rather than be shipped out: 'Vehemently they wish to return to Bermondsey, or Battersea, to the back streets of Leeds, or Birmingham, or Glasgow.'[69]

The year after the war ended, the RIBA held a conference to discuss the importance of surveying and sociology in post-war reconstruction. Even armed with contemporary social-scientific methodologies, the task ahead did not seem straightforward: 'Finding out what the public wants does not necessarily give a statement of what the public should have, because the public does not always know what it can get, or what it will like and want some years ahead.'[70] It was one thing to ask whether the public ideally wanted to be housed on the ground or in the air; it was another to consider whether it would be possible to accommodate everybody's preferences.

Flats represented a form of living with which many British people were unfamiliar. In 1935, the *Architects' Journal* published a special issue, *The Flat: Pride and Prejudice*, that stressed: 'Custom and prejudice then (reasonable or unreasonable) determine the opinion on this subject for the average person – not the cold arguments of logic; but progress in most things consists in the process of logic and expediency overcoming instinctive antagonism.'[71] Flat advocates continued to cling to the optimistic conviction that there would be an awakening to the advantages of these dwellings once their new residents had settled in. Margaret Willis, the London County Council sociologist present at the RIBA's 'High Flats' symposium of 1955, maintained that flat-dwellers would be able to shake their vertiginous fears after a two-to-six-week adjustment period.[72]

Many architects and planners in the mid-century were deeply invested in a specific conceptualisation of democracy, based upon the concept of egalitarian provision satisfying fundamental user needs, to eliminate underprivilege and want. The post-war mass housing drive was unprecedented in its redistributive ambitions. Yet truly participatory planning and management were withheld. In post-war Britain, mapping onto a widespread 'decline of deference' which the historian Florence Sutcliffe-Braithwaite has traced in national political culture, satisfaction with this power nexus would fracture – profoundly.[73]

2

Park Hill

Sheffield, 1953–67

In 1953, Sheffield's City Architect Lewis Womersley appointed two remarkably young architects to design the largest council housing development the city had ever seen: Park Hill. They were Jack Lynn, aged twenty-six, and Ivor Smith, twenty-seven. Sheffield was one of the most ambitious local authorities in the country, and Park Hill was its flagship post-war estate. It was a magisterial project: undoubtedly one of the most architecturally distinctive examples of post-war state planning in Britain. From its construction to the present day, Park Hill has garnered much attention for the radicalism of its architecture – particularly for its streets-in-the-sky design, which purported to preserve the street life of the slums that were razed during the post-war rebuilding of Britain's cities.

The first plans for Park Hill were presented to and approved by the City Council in 1955, and construction began in 1957. The first phase of tenants moved in at the end of 1959 and the scheme was completed in 1961, when it was officially opened by Hugh Gaitskell, the leader of the Labour Party. Within four years, just under a thousand homes had been built in a vast edifice interconnected with sky bridges, ranging from four to fourteen storeys high. All its units were flats and maisonettes.

Park Hill was built early in the brief boom in multistorey building in Britain that reached its peak between 1958 and 1968, under the acute pressure of post-war demands for public housing stock.

The estate housed a whopping 178 people to the acre, although this was a marked decrease from the site's former density of 400 people to the acre.[1] 'The aim is to secure this very high density whilst maintaining a good standard of amenity,' explained the city engineer, Henry Foster.[2] Park Hill boasted its own shopping precinct, laundries, a police station, a tenants' meeting hall, playgrounds, pubs, garages, a nursery, and a junior school. The flats themselves were served by a Garchey waste-disposal system and central heating.

Park Hill hunkers on the hillside to the east of the city centre, in a continuous, winding slab formation, exploiting Sheffield's dramatic position at the foot of the Pennines. This was a site, the architect Jack Lynn observed, full of 'what Mr Brown would have called "capabilities"'.[3] Interrelation with the existing landscape was a critical thread between the city's high-rise developments here and at Woodside and Netherthorpe.

'The careful exploitation of this topography – the building up of hill-top architectural compositions – is gradually producing something of the fascination of the Italian hill towns,' hailed the chairman of the Housing Development Committee. 'It is stimulating, exciting!'[4] The committee saw its programme in Sheffield as work of international interest. The promotional book in which their chairman was writing, *Ten Years of Housing in Sheffield* (1962), included translations into French and Russian. Its opening spread featured a drawing of Netherthorpe's new point blocks by John Piper – the artist who masterminded the abstract stained glass at Coventry Cathedral, where Basil Spence's modernist resurrection was laced together with the charred ruin of the Gothic building wrecked by the Blitz. At Netherthorpe, Piper captured the beauty of Sheffield's scruffy jumble of Victorian streets and its radiant, clean-cut tower blocks bursting up from the hills, delighting in the juxtaposition between the historic and the modern in this tough Yorkshire cityscape.

The influential magazine *Architectural Design* dedicated its September 1961 issue to Sheffield's reconstruction. At Park Hill, it regaled, 'solutions have been devised that are creating an exceptionally high density on a scale hitherto unknown in this country: in fact, a radically new proposition for living in Sheffield'.[5] Its self-consciously social approach was especially applauded. *Architectural Design* described Park Hill as 'one of the most remarkable buildings in England today', singling out for praise its designers' approach to the question of community:

It is not intending to be Architecture with a big abstract A; but more directly building which has arisen from observations and propositions to do with specific people in a particular place, and the environmental tools they need for life and community. It springs from an assessment – objective, compassionate, ideological – of the character of the community itself; its structure and its resilience; the terms of its stability weighed against those of change; and its significance for us is that these things have been taken by the designers as the key and stimulus to the social/environmental form which the buildings, and the people who now live in them, realize together as a whole.[6]

Park Hill, photographed from the air in 1960.

Writing in the *Architectural Review* in December 1961, Reyner Banham similarly commended the estate as a 'most imaginative and advanced community-building gesture'.[7]

Two years on, Park Hill was still attracting acclaim. In 1963, the RIBA organised a special appraisal at its headquarters in Portland Place, London. The event included the screening of a film about the estate, followed by a formal discussion in which architects quizzed Womersley and Smith about the details of their scheme (Jack Lynn was unwell, so could not attend). Many big names were there: Michael Brawne, Oliver Cox, John Darbourne, Eric de Maré, and Cyril Sweett. The discussion circled primarily around the sociological and community-oriented aspects of the estate's design. J. M. Austin-Smith, as vice-president of the RIBA, declared that Womersley and his team deserved 'the highest possible congratulations for taking such a bold concept and following it through to completion over a period of ten years'.[8]

The street decks that materialised for the first time at Park Hill have remained central to the estate's status in both architectural and popular culture. In 1998 English Heritage acknowledged its 'international importance' with Grade II* listed status. The estate is in the process of a controversial redevelopment by Urban Splash into mainly private housing (the first phase of which was completed in 2011), for which the phrase 'streets in the sky' has figured prominently in the marketing material, with the approval of Ivor Smith in his old age.[9] In the process, however, the street decks have been narrowed to create larger apartments with more storage space.[10]

Today, Park Hill's claims to progressive politics are frequently taken at face value. We need to reappraise the estate's primary mythology: its purported attempt to preserve a local community. Park Hill's streets in the sky did not derive from the local area's pre-existing morphology, nor its residents from the site's original inhabitants. Park Hill did not reconstruct an existing working-class community. Rather, the project endeavoured to forge a more respectable one.

STREETS IN THE SKY

A Yorkshireman by birth, Lewis Womersley trained at the Huddersfield School of Architecture. He served as borough architect for Northampton immediately after the Second World War. In 1953, after seven years in public service, he became city architect of Sheffield. His ambitious approach to post-war reconstruction drew attention from early on. He was named as one of the *Architects' Journal*'s 'Men of the Year' in the same year as his appointment in Sheffield.

During Womersley's period of office, Sheffield underwent extensive reconstruction. This included major slum clearance, the rebuilding

Looking down to the ground at Park Hill, photographed by Roger Mayne, 1961.

of the university, and the construction of a new retail complex in the city's old market area. Womersley also served as a member of the Parker Morris Committee, which in 1961 published the report *Homes for Today and Tomorrow*, setting new space specifications to raise standards of living for council tenants. After leaving Sheffield in 1964, Womersley set up a private architecture practice with Hugh Wilson in Manchester where he led the design of Hulme Crescents, which incorporated deck access like that of Park Hill. Following his death in 1990, the *Sheffield Telegraph* recognised his 'particular talent for spotting and nurturing able and innovative young architects', running his office on the principle of group practice, 'more like an atelier than the conventional local government department'.[11]

Park Hill was the pinnacle of Womersley's career, for which he was given the RIBA Bronze Medal and an award from the Ministry of Housing and Local Government. He first proposed a multistorey development for the Park Hill clearance site to the city's Housing Committee in 1955, with a design that drew on the findings of a recent European tour of inspection undertaken by himself and members of the committee. To investigate the viability of building vertically, the deputation visited and compared housing at forty-three schemes in Denmark, Germany, the Netherlands, Belgium, France, and Switzerland. Impressed by what they saw, the deputation concluded that multistorey building (by which they meant structures of more than two storeys) was highly appropriate for the Park Hill site, an area with the oldest outstanding slum clearance orders in the city.[12]

Central to the proposal was the architectural innovation of street decks. These would be spacious, ten-foot-wide walkways, heralding a diversion from the four-foot-wide access routes typical at the time. 'A new system of access by street decks has been designed which, it is felt, is particularly adapted to the City's topography,' explained Womersley:

The decks, off which the front doors to the dwellings open, are thus much more commodious than the normal balcony and fulfil the

44

function of 'streets' within the building along which prams can be pushed and milk trolleys wheeled. Being covered from the weather and free from vehicular traffic they form ideal places for daily social intercourse – for the conversation of adults and for small children's play.

The social scene Womersley painted was beguiling. Yet the Housing Committee will have been most convinced by his emphasis on the 'substantial potential savings' of his proposed design: 'The most economical form of access to high flats is the normal balcony type access serving the maximum number of flats from any one lift point.'[13] Lifts pushed up costs in multistorey housing. At Park Hill, they could be spaced out and reduced in number, thanks to the continuous system of circulation within the interconnected slabs.

Deck access had been the groundbreaking feature of Alison and Peter Smithson's entry to the competition to design the Golden Lane Estate in central London, in 1952. While the competition was won by Geoffry Powell (later of Chamberlin, Powell, and Bon, who also designed the Barbican Estate next door), the Smithsons attracted much attention for their reimagining of Le Corbusier's *rue intérieure* as an elevated, open-air street many metres above the ground. The appeal of pedestrianised walkways in the sky spoke to both post-war concerns about the erosion of community life and the challenge of traffic posed by expanded car ownership. Here was an effort to recreate the historic sociability of the terraced street within the multistorey slab block template.

Jack Lynn was a miner's son who trained as an architect at King's College, Durham (the Smithsons' alma mater), and had worked briefly at Coventry City Council. Ivor Smith trained at the Bartlett (while it was evacuated to Cambridge), then the Architectural Association. Deck access had been a feature of earlier unrealised designs by Lynn and Smith for different projects. Lynn and the Newcastle architect Gordon Ryder incorporated deck access into their own entry to the Golden Lane competition. Straight after, Lynn worked with Smith on a proposal for a multi-storey redevelopment along the south bank of the River Thames in Rotherhithe which also incorporated street decks, a study that Lynn described as 'instrumental' to their recruitment by Womersley in 1953.[14] 'Such was our confidence (or our arrogance),' Smith recalled in 2008, 'that at our interview we made a condition: that we should work together.'[15] The Smithsons' ideas were significant for them. Lynn acknowledged that their Golden Lane proposal for street access had 'made the first moves towards their continuity by creating street corner junctions where refuse chutes would be located, which they likened to the modern equivalent of the village pump'.[16]

The historian Joe Moran has situated the currency of streets in the sky within a broader cultural preoccupation emerging from the late 1950s.[17] The charming appeal of the street, especially in use by children, was celebrated in the photography of Nigel Henderson (1949–54) and Roger Mayne in London (1956–61), and Shirley Baker in Manchester (1961–81). This sense of romance informed the understanding of community promoted by the sociologists Michael Young, Peter Townsend, and Peter Willmott at the Institute of Community Studies, founded in Bethnal Green in 1953. Young and Willmott's influential book *Family and Kinship in East London* (1957), based on interviews with people in inner-city Bethnal Green and the new overspill estate of Debden in Essex, contended that the squalor-ridden but tight-knit conditions in the slums of Bethnal Green had contributed towards the shaping of a uniquely communitarian and neighbourly way of life for its working-class residents – a kinship model in danger of extinction in the course of slum clearance and dispersal to new suburbs.

'Movement of street and kinship groupings as a whole, members being transferred together to a new setting, would enable the city to be rebuilt without squandering the fruits of social cohesion,' insisted Young and Willmott.[18] Similar advice had been given by central government. In 1956, the Ministry of Housing and Local Government recommended that 'the strongest efforts' should be made to resettle households from slum areas with their original neighbours.[19] This concern was mirrored in contemporary debates about 'suburban neurosis', a term first coined by Stephen Taylor in 1938. A syndrome typically associated with women moving to new estates in the inter-war period, it was attributed to the feelings of isolation, loneliness, and anxiety that could arise after moving away from the communities of their former neighbourhoods. In the 1950s and 1960s, in the context of a post-war housing drive producing a wave of new estates both inside and outside city centres, the concept was revisited in the sociological work of David Riesman, H. E. Bracey, and Josephine Klein.

These anxieties were reflected in architectural culture. In a retrospective lecture in 2008, Smith recalled how *Family and Kinship* fed into 'the sense of social purpose and the vision' of his contemporaries: this was a moment at which 'geographers, economists, sociologists and planners as well as architects . . . exalted the virtues of living in cities, and subscribed to the ideas of husbanding the land and saving the countryside'.[20] He and his co-designer were drawn to the concept of the street as a site for community cohesion. Lynn noted the conviviality that he saw in the old Park area (on the site of the estate) in the early 1950s, praising 'the essential gregariousness of the people'. He observed that 'the way this depended on the open air spaces around the front doors was made even more clear during the Coronation celebrations of that year [1953] when the unit of collective participation was everywhere in the street'.[21]

Park Hill was promoted as a project that would recreate the traditional virtues of slum communities without their squalid conditions. In his 1955 report, Womersley described it as 'a modern redevelopment of an outworn area which will provide for all the various ancillary activities which grew up naturally in the old area'.[22] With reference to the former Park area, Smith later observed:

The houses were so close together that the sun could hardly pene-
trate. Yet for all the hardships (and perhaps because of them) there
was great neighbourliness; despite the dirt and closeness, people
took a certain pride in their houses, and most of them wished to go
on living in the same locality.[23]

Lynn drew a similar conclusion: 'It was obvious that despite the
evils arising out of a lack of proper water supply, sanitation and
ventilation, here was a structure of friendliness and mutual aid
which had somehow to be salvaged from the demolition.'[24]

When Park Hill was completed, promotional material produced by Sheffield City Council placed great emphasis on the role
of the street decks in fostering community spirit and offered proof
of success through evocative photographs taken by Roger Mayne
(on commission). These images had much the same visual tenor as
Mayne's celebrated shots eulogising the informal slum sociability
of Southam Street in North Kensington.

The sociological virtues of the decks were widely applauded in
the architectural press. The *Architects' Journal*, praising the
estate's 'fresh approach', highlighted the deck-access system as 'its
biggest success': 'the virtues of social contact, which existed in the
old streets of back-to-back houses, have been retained.'[25] Reyner
Banham, an ally of the Smithsons, admired the decks upon the
estate's opening in the *Architectural Review*: 'Functionally and
sociologically they are streets without the menace of through
vehicular traffic.'[26] In 1961, Park Hill looked to Banham like 'a
piece of architectural community-building that is going to work
out'.[27]

In the autumn of 1963, Park Hill received a visit from two
members of the Institute of Community Studies, Peter and Phyllis
Willmott – and won their approval. The Willmotts stopped off
during a journey through the industrial North of England, travelling from Scotland back to their home in London. Phyllis had not
been enthusiastic about the route, as she recorded in her diary:
'Petie wanted to do it to show it me. I was not too keen to see

anything except perhaps the Sheffield flats.' In the event, the old cities of the urban north left her mind feeling 'littered like an untidied room', and reaching Park Hill was a relief:

> Leeds was the shock . . . Black, soot black. Dramatic clear-cut black against bright shower-clouds of yellow and patches of blue sky . . . 'The buildings are black'; 'It really is black and grimy.' Such things I've heard people say of the north. And I've listened and yet not realised. It sounded from those kind of words, horrible really, repulsive. But the sight I actually saw was dramatic almost to the point of a discordant beauty. Still, outside these towns I did 'see as others see' the dreadful despoliation of the countryside. Mucky air, grey chimneys, neither town nor country . . . The Sheffield flats turned out being the things I was *wanting* to see – interesting, stark and drafty. The 'decks' looking as if they work, as they were meant to, like pavements outside terrace housing. With a little more of the slumminess of such places.[28]

The street decks in use, photographed by Roger Mayne for Park Hill's opening brochure.

FORGING A NEW CONSTITUENCY

In the autumn of 1959, Sheffield's local media was abuzz with coverage about the opening of the first part of Park Hill. The two largest local papers, the *Star* and the *Sheffield Telegraph*, showed particular interest in the estate's very first tenants, Fred and Helen Jackson. They had been residents of a house on nearby Duke Street, which was due to be demolished under a compulsory purchase order.[29] Fred Jackson told the *Star* that 'it will just be a question of moving across the road from their old home to the new one'.[30]

The implication was that the Park Hill project was committed to community reconstruction through direct residential transfer. This notion has had considerable discursive currency in popular and critical narratives about Park Hill. When the architect and academic Patrick Nuttgens was interviewed by the BBC in 1986, he emphasised such efforts as indicative of Park Hill's capacity to foster a community ethos:

> When Park Hill was built, they took the people from the old streets, on the hillside there, renamed the walkways, they're huge, fourteen feet wide, sort of roads in the air – renamed them as the names of the old streets and put people back in the streets where they'd come, so to speak. Except now they were in the air, instead of on the ground. Now, people still argue as to whether that actually in practice happened, but if it did, then that was a major thing because there was already a semi-existing community, and that is certainly something people picked up right from the very beginning.[31]

This news report hints at the slippery relationship that existed between representation and reality in discussions of Park Hill. The transfers of tenure during the opening of the estate were more complicated than Nuttgens described. The story of Fred and Helen

Jackson may have been attractive to the local media, but it was not representative of the experiences of most Park Hill tenants. During the 1963 appraisal of Park Hill at the RIBA, an architect working for the Ministry of Housing and Local Government's research section, John Bartlett, asked whether the tenants were people from the original area or new occupants entirely. Park Hill's estate manager, Joan Demers, replied:

> Something like 40 per cent were already living on the site in clearance property; another 45 or 50 per cent came from another clearance area in another part of the city, quite close also to the city centre; and the remaining small percentage – 10 or 15 per cent – were off the housing list, or what were called pre-tenancy exchanges.[32]

These figures seem to have been an exaggeration. According to a survey that Demers herself had conducted the previous year, only 22 per cent of a sample comprising 197 households had originally lived in the Park area.[33] A later investigation, by Chris Bacon of the University of Sheffield's Town and Regional Planning Department, indicates that the figures Demers quoted to the RIBA were not accurate. Based on an examination of slum clearance records from the housing department, Bacon judged any effort to preserve existing communities from the neighbourhood 'an outright failure'.

Bacon found that 512 households were moved from Sheffield's slum-clearance areas to Park Hill, occupying only 52 per cent of the available dwellings on the new estate. He also discovered that these slum clearance households were allocated primarily to 'the least popular parts' of the estate – the least accessible decks. Bacon's report indicates that no more than a quarter of Park Hill's first residents came from the original area. The proportion could have been as low as 12 per cent. He concludes that 'there was no concentration of slum clearance residents from the Park in the new Park Hill'. Overall, 922 households were moved during the Park site's slum clearance; they were relocated to at least 21 different estates all over the city. In total, 16 streets and 12 courts were demolished in the Park area, and their occupants were dispersed across up to 229 streets around Sheffield.[34] Across England and Wales, 1.48 million houses were demolished or shut up during slum clearance from 1955 to 1985, displacing 3.66 million people.[35]

In 1965, a few years after Park Hill's opening, Jack Lynn wrote:

[Park Hill's] initial scheme was carefully programmed for the simultaneous development of both parts so that the least number of people would need to be moved out of the area to enable a start to be made and the great majority of the local residents could be housed without leaving the district at all.[36]

But these initial commitments to community transfer did not withstand later discussions. By the time the scheme was submitted to the council, the proposal to rehouse local residents directly into the estate had been set aside. The majority of the existing properties were flattened and their occupants rehoused before building commenced.

Although the Park Hill project drew inspiration from some aspects of the Park area's slum spirit, its development team also had their reservations about its social constituency. Nicknamed Little Chicago, the Park area was perceived as an insalubrious district of Sheffield. Henry Foster maintained that the 'undesirable features' of Sheffield's slum living conditions were mainly 'the result of the activities of its inhabitants'.[37] While the Ministry of Housing and Local Government had recommended that families be moved with their neighbours as a general rule, its 1956 guidelines made an exception for 'unsatisfactory families'. 'It is a mistake to rehouse too many problem families in one street,' they warned. 'They generally have a bad effect upon each other and they will almost inevitably cause discomfort and resentment amongst their neighbours.'[38]

Reyner Banham, an early proponent of the Park Hill project, later looked back on the community element of the scheme with a more critical eye. In his article 'Park Hill Revisited' for the American magazine *Architecture Plus* in 1974, he remembered:

> I used to go up to Sheffield quite a bit in the mid-Fifties on teaching assignments, and used to get my ears pinned back pretty forcefully about Park Hill by the Young Turks in the City Architect's office who were designing it.

Drawing on his memories from this experience in Sheffield, he wrote:

> The use of the word *community* touches a monster irony about Park Hill. It is no secret that one of the City's main motives for building Park Hill was to destroy – I mean that, *destroy* – the local community. There was a well-known and well-studied body of persons living on the lower Park Hill slopes whose outstanding characteristic was the highest rate of criminality in Britain, and the City simply decided to extirpate them, and destroy their lairs.[39]

A REAL TRANSPOSITION?

'The pattern of the neighbourhood has been almost completely transferred,' declared Park Hill's estate manager, Joan Demers, in 1960.[40] Was this true? Putting streets in the sky was no easy task: the planning process saw hiccups and hand-wringing. Lynn and Smith's first 1953 design for the estate proposed to replicate the site's old residential pattern by overlaying orthogonal multistorey complexes on the footprints of the original buildings.[41] This plan used right angles – 'borrowed from the Ville Radieuse', as Smith put it.[42]

The first plan was discarded. It had to be revised to fan out more flexibly at the joining points. Smith explained: 'We struggled to design a right-angled corner that would avoid overlooking, not involve a fire hazard across the corner, and not give very large corner dwellings.' The final scheme had corners of 112.5 degrees and 135 degrees, akin to the Smithsons' Golden Lane proposal. The building, in Smith's words, 'meanders down the hill' in a more organic undulation.[43]

Choosing address names for the new streets in the sky proved difficult. The matter caused friction between Lewis Womersley as city architect and Henry Foster as city engineer, which is clear from a series of terse exchanges over several months in their correspondence records. In one letter from the spring of 1959, Foster referred to a point of stalemate: 'You will, no doubt, remember that I said I do not like the name "Decks" and since then we have not made any progress.'[44] They eventually managed to agree on 'Rows'.

That summer, Sheffield's Housing Management Committee proposed reusing the names from the area's original streets. But this caused more disagreement. Foster chastised Womersley for his suggestion of 'Stafford Row', inspired by the former Stafford Street.

The name 'Stafford Row' is so phonetically similar to Stafford Road as to be likely to lead to one being confused with the other. Perhaps in the event of similar circumstances arising in the future affecting the allocation of postal addresses to buildings, it would be best to let me see your proposals unofficially first so that I could point out any difficulties of this kind. Street naming is full of snags.[45]

Other options were 'Rhodes Row' or 'Lord Row', but neither Womersley nor Foster was enthusiastic about these – Foster gave them a flat 'NO!'[46] Ultimately, the estate recycled three former names for Gilbert Row, Hague Row, and Long Henry Row, and devised one brand-new address, Norwich Row.

Though they were similar in nomenclature, Chris Bacon highlighted salient material differences between the old streets and the new estate in his 1985 study for the University of Sheffield. He

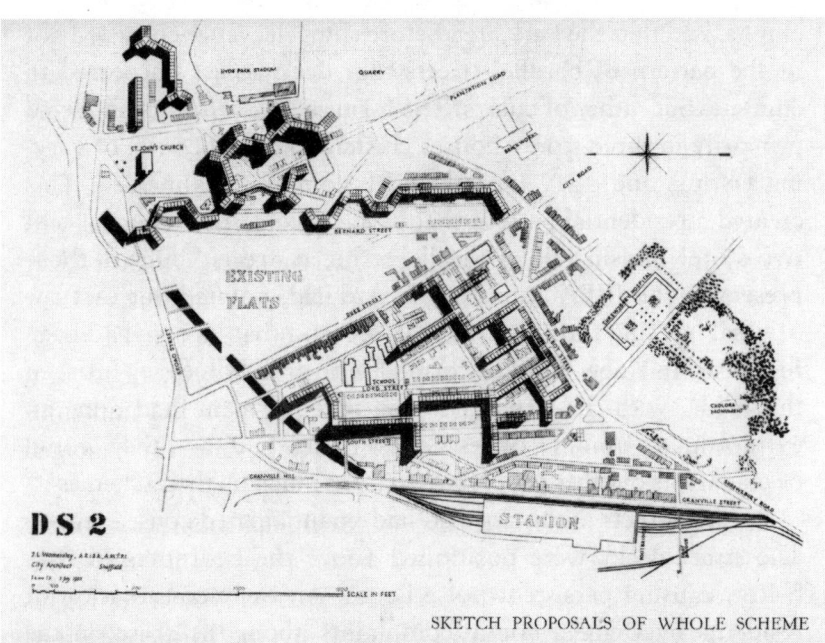

SKETCH PROPOSALS OF WHOLE SCHEME

The first site layout plan, which went unrealised.

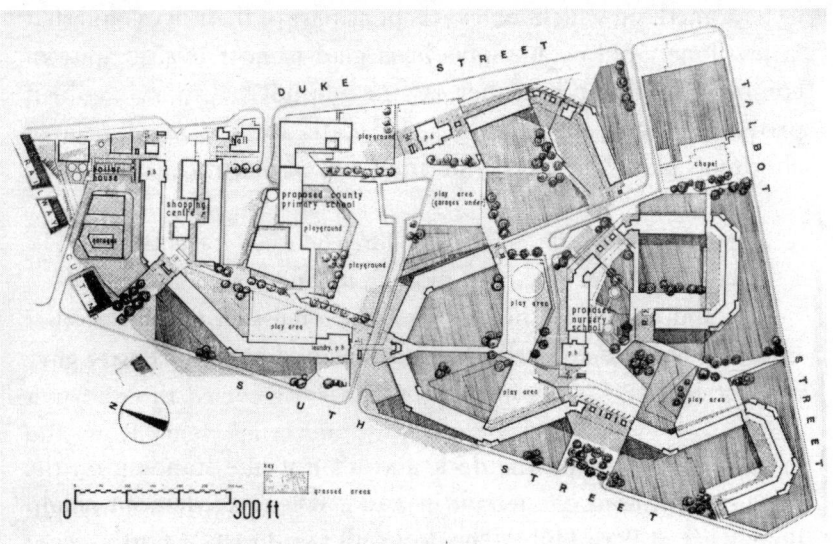

Park Hill's final site layout.

emphasised that the Park area before slum clearance consisted not of the pattern of parallel streets that deck access purported to emulate, but rather of courts. The former Park residents had lived primarily in three-storey houses clustered around courts of varying layouts and sizes around which communities melded. This created a residential pattern that was less consistent than rows of two-storey housing along parallel terraced streets.[47] One of those present at the RIBA appraisal, T. A. Field, pointed out that the original housing form had been 'upset' and that 'people had been re-housed in a new building form'. Smith and Womersley brushed this aside, with the latter retorting that his team 'had done an extraordinary amount of research on Park Hill, and they would be glad if lots of other people would do as much on their schemes'.[48]

Putting streets in the sky also had unanticipated consequences. The street decks were positioned above the bedrooms of flats below, causing persistent noise issues. An early consultation of residents by Demers noted 'complaints about the noise on the decks over bedrooms' as a result of people walking above. While Demers played down the problem – insisting that such noise 'seems to be something which many accept as part of their lives' and that 'a few lonely old people have been glad to hear this, in spite of complaining about it, as they say they do not feel so isolated' – it provoked recurrent grumbles and calls for the regulation of children's play.[49] One resident, interviewed in 1973, explained:

> There is [sic] no facilities for the children here in – at night-time . . . and hence you get the, um, running up and down on the landings and things like this and it's quite a nuisance to the elderly people here. And myself, I'm quite annoyed about this noise at night, I mean it's really awful the noise, here.[50]

'You've to go out on the deck and it's not like standing on the door-step,' mused one tenant in 1966, when asked about neighbourly life at Park Hill.[51] The decks all faced east or north so did not get sun for most of the day. In his 2008 lecture, Smith acknowledged a 'major shortcoming' of Park Hill's streets compared to the ground-level originals. The flats lacked windows overlooking the decks, which would have served to 'enrich both the dwelling and the street; from the house one could see passersby, keep an eye on the kids and watch out for any vandalism'. This element was incorporated more successfully, Smith conceded, in the Byker Wall project in Newcastle designed by Ralph Erskine.[52] It bears mentioning that Erskine's design process incorporated tenant consultation.

Upon Park Hill's opening, a solitary note of disapproval was struck by the Town and Country Planning Association, who sniffed at its designers' subscription to a 'bogus sociology': 'Huddle people closer together, arrange their front doors and accesses so that their paths must frequently cross, and they will quickly become more sociable and community conscious. This is a naïve and unwarranted assumption.'[53] Their position was a defensive one against the high-density crusade. Young and Willmott's thesis had been a direct attack on their decentralising approach to residential planning. Yet as time went by, more people came to agree. The amateurish methodologies of the Institute of Community Studies came under increased scrutiny in the 1970s, notably in Jennifer Platt's highly critical 1971 study.[54] In the same year, the architectural critic Martin Pawley wrote in *New Society* (a magazine established to review discussions in social science) that Park Hill's streets in the sky were based on pure 'sociological balloney [*sic*]'.[55]

Historians have since reanalysed the institute's original interview transcripts. Jon Lawrence found that the use of interview data was highly selective for *Family and Kinship in East London*, over-egging suburban malaise and painting a simplified and romanticised representation of slum living. Lawrence wrote: 'If *Family and Kinship in East London* was powerful politics, it was poor sociology.' Michael Young himself later conceded that their depictions of working-class cohesion in the slums of Bethnal Green were exaggerated: 'We probably did overdo it.'[56] This book was invested in a flattened image of working-class life – a vision that was already, as Joe Moran has noted, an anachronism at the point of its conjecture.[57]

In the early 1970s, Reyner Banham looked back with some cynicism on the 1950s conviction that

[Park Hill's] decks would promote those patterns of healthy community relationships that my generation was happy to impute to traditional working-class streets, after a hurried reading of Young and Willmott's *Family and Kinship in East London* . . . a book from which neither architecture nor sociology has fully recovered in Britain, twenty years later.[58]

He reflected that he might have benefited from being more critical of the sociological vogue that 'I, like the rest of my generation, had swallowed whole from those great myth-makers of our time, Willmott and Young.'[59]

MANAGING A COMMUNITY

The year after the Second World War ended, the RIBA held a conference during which it was affirmed that 'the Science of Social Studies provides the information needed to plan a community, whether a town, village or housing scheme'.[60] Park Hill was a consciously sociological project. Womersley attested to the RIBA during its 1963 appraisal that one of 'the most significant aspects of Park Hill' was the architects' foregrounding of concerns which were 'Environmental and Sociological', citing the 'inter-relationship of physical layout and community sense'. Smith backed him up, emphasising that the estate's development team had approached decisions as self-styled 'amateur sociologists'.[61]

These commitments to sociology were, however, conditional. Sheffield City Council took a stern view of sociological surveys conducted by external figures. The minutes of the Housing

Development and Housing Management Committees for 1963 reveal an altercation between the Council and Paul Ritter, an Australian academic based at the Nottingham School of Architecture. In June 1963, the Housing Development Committee received a request from Ritter to conduct a survey of tenants at Park Hill and the nearby Woodside Estate but refused to give him permission, with no reason recorded.[62] Ritter was not a nobody: the following year, he was appointed chief planner for the city of Perth.

In September, the chair of the Housing Management Committee reported that Ritter's employees had been intercepted undertaking research without permission, after which Ritter approached the town clerk and 'questioned the legality of the committee's decision and had suggested that he might take action for libel and for damages arising from the interference with the work of his employees'. The committee decided that 'investigations involving personal interviews with the tenants at Park Hill should now be restricted so far as possible'.[63] At Park Hill, sociology was not appreciated as a neutral method for the surveying of residential opinion; it was valued as a management tool.

Park Hill's first estate manager, Joan Demers, was crucial to the in-house sociological mission. Prominent in estate life, she was invited to the lunch attended by a select group of guests for the formal opening celebrations in 1961, alongside prominent city councillors and the leader of the opposition, Hugh Gaitskell.[64] She was present to answer questions from senior members of the RIBA at the 1963 appraisal, and photographs show her taking foreign dignitaries on tours around Park Hill.

Demers had been attracted to Park Hill because she was 'struck by the tremendous promise which the whole scheme appeared to hold in terms of the rebuilding of a city centre; where a real community could be developed as a conscious policy supported by a Local Authority'.[65] She stressed that residents 'need all possible support to help them achieve a high standard of community prride [sic] as possible. The Estate on its side must foresee and avert dangerous and socially disintegrating trends.'[66]

Demers first appears in a 1959 report to the Housing Management Committee, which recommended that she should be made assistant superintendent. This proposal was reconsidered. 'Superintendent' was crossed out on the typed report and 'Estate Manager' substituted in ink.[67] Smith described her as a 'skilled and sympathetic housing manager', the figure who 'sorted out [residents'] problems and made them feel at home'.[68] Demers's frequent use of the language of conscious community-building, however, suggests that her purview went further than this.

One attendee of Park Hill's RIBA appraisal of 1963, George Richmond, remarked that he thought 'the scheme tended to be alive because there was always someone there who represented the authority. Their presence also served to keep down damage by undesirables.'[69] The approach taken by Demers combined paternalism and self-help. In her 'Sociological Report' of 1960, she stated that 'there is much which can be done yet to help these people to "help themselves" . . . making them aware of their responsibilities and of how they can help to foster a good spirit among themselves'.[70]

This attitude had roots in the nineteenth-century operation of voluntary associations and private philanthropy, and particularly in Octavia Hill's moralistic style of housing management. Hill highlighted female housing managers as especially effective conduits for the application of moralising codes. The deployment of female housing managers facilitated more intimate intrusions in the lives of tenants. Women often occupied roles as public health visitors during the inter-war period and onwards to the 1960s, when the woes of 'problem families' were often attributed to the deficiencies of mothers.[71]

The assessments of tenants' behaviours in social spaces by Park Hill's management resound with the language of respectability. The city's Housing Department praised the moderation and responsibility displayed by tenants at the new purpose-built bars in 1961: 'Mention . . . must be made of the pubs, which are restful, tastefully furnished and being so well conducted are an asset to

Teenage boys 'larking about' at Park Hill, photographed by Roger Mayne in 1963.

the Estate.'[72] Park Hill in fact lacked the same range of pubs as had featured in the previous neighbourhood. The former Park area had eight pubs, whereas the new estate had just four.

Younger people proved difficult to control. Demers was irked by teenagers hanging around the estate's café:

A coffee bar on the site is responsible for gathering together a good many of the less desirable types of adolescents, from a wide area, who create unnecessary noise and disturbance and generally finish their evening loitering on the decks or in the lifts. Something more interesting and yet more educative is needed to counteract this type of hooliganism.

She chastised younger children for playing on the decks, where they were 'a danger and a nuisance to themselves and everyone

A quick bout of forbidden football on Long Henry Row in 1969.

else'. 'Play activities "provided" by the children themselves may be divided into the socially acceptable and unacceptable,' Demers wrote in 1960. 'Anti-social play includes the riding of (adult) cycles on the decks, and on the slopes on the Pavement, and across from West Block.' She found the boys aged between ten and fifteen unacceptably boisterous. 'These lads require the use of an isolated room, where under supervision their activities can be channelled in the right direction.' Demers suggested the employment of a youth worker to help channel behaviour into 'socially acceptable patterns'.[73]

Ball games were strictly prohibited on Park Hill's decks. The former raucous street football matches photographed by Roger Mayne – which emblazoned the cover of Peter Willmott's Institute of Community Studies production *Adolescent Boys of East London* (1966) – were not sanctioned on Sheffield's streets in the sky. Mayne's photographs are often used to illustrate accounts of Park Hill, but he was not wholly convinced by the scheme. 'They were essentially the same as my street pictures,' he recalled, 'only against a much less romantic background.'[74] Despite the regulations, Mick

Jones, a Park Hill resident and student at Sheffield College of Art, managed to sneak a picture of an illicit football session a few years later. The foreground is out of focus in his quick-fire shot, snatched before neighbours came out to reprimand them.

Of course, children are rarely fulfilled by structured play in railed-off play-pens. The son of one of the estate's caretakers, who moved to Park Hill aged eleven in 1959, reminisced:

> We used to like – underneath the flats, if you can imagine the width of them, it's about ten foot wide, underneath and under there is every pipe you can mention, where the sink stuff goes, the toilets, electrics, gas. And they all run under there, it's like, it's like an underground system. And, of course, my dad had all the keys to everything, and when he went out, I got with my mates and we used to borrow the keys and get under there and that was like an adventure. And every four houses, every four flats, there was an inspection ladder and you could go up the inspection ladders right to the roof and everywhere. You could hear people on the toilet talking. You had a whale of a time . . . If my dad had known what I did on there, he would have killed me![75]

As for the adults, Joan Demers was anxious about their ability to manage their finances in the face of new temptations in the form of consumer goods. 'Canvassers of varying kinds have been a nuisance all the time,' she complained. They plied washing machines, electric razors, and photography equipment to Park Hill's residents. 'It is not possible to say yet if many housewives have been cajoled into buying articles which they can ill afford, and which a family financial crisis might make an impossible burden.'[76] Similarly, Womersley told the Parker Morris Committee in 1961 that he was worried about council tenants' capacity 'to ward off the temptations of leisure', such as television, which 'we can easily imagine . . . destroying family life'. His preferred pursuits for tenants included opera, drama, literature, and nature study.[77]

Womersley was one of a number of architects and planners across Britain who by the 1960s were becoming concerned by the burgeoning challenges posed by 'affluence' for designing new urban forms. In this, they were echoing concerns being aired contemporaneously by a range of figures on the political left. The historian Selina Todd has emphasised the limits of affluence in 1950s and 1960s Britain: poverty and precarity continued to shape working-class experiences.[78] Yet new consumer durables did percolate into working-class homes, including those on council estates, thanks in great part to hire-purchase deals. Womersley insisted,

> The challenge today is not to remain sufficiently healthy to earn a living and keep out of the poor house but to learn to develop one's talents so that ever-increasing leisure hours may be used profitably and not frittered away in idleness and mischief. The present-day challenge may well prove to be the more difficult of the two.[79]

Park Hill was a remarkable architectural composition, dreamed up by two young men just out of their school training. It was a bold riposte to urban dispersal and suburban decentralisation, on a challenging site, achieving a high density while also providing an infrastructure for sociability. The estate had proper community facilities and plenty of open space, reminding us of the virtues gained by building upwards. Unlike the visions of towers in parkland hailed in the 1930s and realised at Roehampton in the 1950s, Park Hill's spaces were encircled and shielded from the biting Yorkshire winds by the long arms of its buildings. The high-rise block amid a sea of grass was a sublime image, but it had a somewhat agoraphobic effect. Park Hill created a sense of enclosure.

However, we need to think more critically about some of the estate's central claims, primarily the idea that Park Hill salvaged a form of working-class community from the slums razed during the rebuilding of Britain's cities. In fact, the design of the estate did not recreate the pattern of nineteenth-century housing that formerly stood on the site, nor did it recreate the working-class community that had existed there. Park Hill did not strengthen the site's original constituency. Through continuous social management, it sought to build a more respectable community in its place. Park Hill may have been a radical feat of modernist architecture, but it was not a site of radically progressive politics; we cannot read the former as a cipher for the latter.

Although Park Hill's streets in the sky differed in many ways from their predecessors, their system of deck access nevertheless represented an important step forward in the design of socially conceived high-rise housing. When the government's Sociological Research Station surveyed tenants at Park Hill in 1967, they found only 10 per cent were unhappy living off the ground. Just 11 per cent were dissatisfied with their flats, and 17 per cent with the estate as a whole. Nor was density a point of discontent: a mere 12 per cent thought there were too many people living on the estate. Tenants fed back favourably on the light in their homes, the safety of their children from traffic, and the social provisions at Park Hill.

However, 49 per cent reported that the provision for children's play was inadequate. Given the estate management's constant obstruction of children's spontaneous games, it seems little wonder that 55 per cent of respondents complained about vandalism. The unreliable lifts drew complaints from 59 per cent, and 52 per cent thought the rent was too high. Opinions were split on the estate's appearance – 22 per cent thought it was attractive, 30 per cent reported it 'all right', and 48 per cent found it unattractive – citing insufficient colour and the atmosphere of a 'barracks'.[80]

In the late 1970s, Park Hill came to be classed as an 'area of worst deprivation'. This deprivation was the result, in large part, of high unemployment when the closure of Sheffield's steelworks was torpedoing local manufacturing jobs.[81] Throughout Park Hill's rise and fall, characterisations of the progressive idealism of its inception have persisted as part of the estate's essential mythology. If anything, these characterisations have been strengthened by the melancholy contrast with its ultimate decline. This makes for a rhetorically compelling story, but one balanced precariously on a more complicated history.

In his study of British architect-planners in the post-war period, Otto Saumarez Smith notes that beneath 'an outward veneer of radical futurism, [their] plans often reveal a surprising degree of uneasy conservatism'.[82] Britain's post-war welfare state was not forged in the mould of a revolutionary socialist universalism. It was an extension of an older, inherited, liberal-paternalist model of social security, based on concepts of the deserving and undeserving poor. This seems eminently clear at Park Hill. 'Paternalism was written into the fabric of the new welfare state,' wrote Jon Lawrence in his assessment of modern Britain, and this should be remembered as 'a corrective to accounts of Britain's embrace of modernity'.[83] Such paternalism would prove insupportable as the post-war decades unfolded.

3

The Ronan Point Disaster

Newham, 1968–73

On 11 March 1968, the London borough of Newham opened a brand-new, twenty-two-storey tower block on the Freemasons Estate in Canning Town. It was named Ronan Point. This was the second of nine identical point blocks to be built on the estate, all named after members of the Housing Committee in the former borough of West Ham. Tenants moved in on the same day, leaving Victorian housing in nearby slum clearance areas to settle into their first homes in the sky. These flats were equipped with modern comforts: indoor bathrooms, up-to-date kitchens, underfloor heating, and spin dryers. They were designed according to the guidance of the Parker Morris report. In fact, their space standards exceeded the report's generous recommendations.

Just two months later, an unprecedented disaster struck. At around 5:45 a.m. on 16 May, the building's entire south-east column collapsed. This was triggered by an explosion after Ivy Hodge, a resident on the eighteenth floor, lit a match to boil water for a cup of tea. She had not realised that her new stove had suffered a gas leak overnight. The explosion initiated the progressive collapse of the entire corner section of the block above and beneath her flat.

James Chambers, a resident on the seventh floor, woke up with a shock:

The whole place shook. Suddenly our bedroom wall fell away with a terrible ripping sound. We found ourselves staring out over

London. Our heads were only a matter of 2ft. from the 80ft. drop. The room filled with dust and showers of debris and furniture were plunging past us.[1]

He said, 'I heard dreadful screams, I think they were from people falling past our room.' 'After the explosion,' recounted his wife, Lillian Chambers, 'there was a deathly silence and then we heard shouts and cries.'[2] Tumbling panels of concrete had crushed victims in their path.

Four people died in the collapse and seventeen were injured. The fatalities were Edith Bridgstock, Thomas McCluskey, Pauline Murrell, and Thomas Murrell. Ann Carter, an elderly resident in

The collapsed corner of Ronan Point.

The Salvation Army handing out tea to survivors at the foot of Ronan Point.

her eighties, died later in hospital.[3] The death toll could have been much higher had the explosion happened at a different moment in the day – around dinner-time, say. The collapse tore through the living rooms that were positioned in the block's corner, while most of the inhabitants were still asleep in their bedrooms closer to the centre.

The Ronan Point disaster caused a national scandal. The safety of the many tower blocks erected since the Second World War was thrown dramatically into doubt. 'WHY? WHY? WHY?' asked the *Evening Standard*.[4] The ensuing Griffiths Inquiry found that the explosion in Hodge's kitchen was in fact quite small, so small that she was mostly uninjured, aside from some minor burns.[5] The inquiry concluded that the collapse occurred because of the outrageously poor quality of the building rather than an explosion of exceptional force. Ronan Point was constructed using a new large-panel-system building method, without an internal frame, in which all walls were load-bearing. If a wall was knocked out, the

WHY? WHY? WHY?

22-storey flats collapse

3 DEAD, 12 INJURED

AN entire wing of a 22-storey block of flats in Butchers Road, Canning Town, collapsed at 6 a.m. today after what appeared to be a gas explosion.

Flats in the 200-foot Ronan Point block fell "like a pack of cards"—but all but four of the 260 residents escaped.

The bodies of two men and a woman were found in the debris. The wife of one of the men is missing, feared dead. A dozen people were taken to hospital.

One man living on the 15th floor had a miraculous escape—sliding all the way down to the ground on a concrete slab.

The flats were completed last November and the 80 families moved in between three and six weeks ago.

A full-scale inquiry—possibly in the form of a public tribunal—will be held into the disaster. The Government arranged to make a preliminary statement in the Commons later today.

Fuller report—Page 22.
Theory of the gas blast—Page 23.
The boy who was there—Page 16.
Anne Sharpley Reports—Page Seven

PICTURE BY EVENING STANDARD CAMERAMAN VICTOR DREES

This aerial view of the flats shows the full extent of the collapse. The entire corner dropped away "like a stack of cards" taking with it people and furniture. More pictures Pages 16, 17, 22, 23 and 44.

The front page of the *Evening Standard* on the day of the Ronan Point disaster.

structural integrity of the entire building was compromised. Eye-witnesses reported that it collapsed like a 'house of cards'.[6]

Ronan Point appears as a passing reference in book after book. The disaster has become a major hinge moment in commonly received arcs of urban change. It has been characterised as the death knell for high rise in Britain: the moment at which, 'in an irresistible wave of unanimity, the nation decided that high flats should cease to be built'.[7] In many narratives, Ronan Point is portrayed as the gravestone not only for high rise but also for architectural modernism as a whole: 'a spectacular indictment of the utopian modernism that had inspired British city planning since the Second World War'.[8] The former Prince Charles bran-dished Ronan Point as a central case in his personal treatise on the superiority of traditional architecture (although he recorded the death count incorrectly).[9] Ronan Point looms large as a symbol. Yet its full history remains underexplored. By digging into its archives, an even murkier story of wrong-doing and eva-sion emerges. This scandal would extend long after 1968, for decades to come.

HOUSING FROM THE FACTORY

The London borough of Newham (established in 1965, merging West and East Ham) was under huge strain in the 1960s. This was 'the front line' of housing need.[10] During the Second World War, the Luftwaffe had targeted the nearby Royal Victoria Docks to devastating effect. Over 2,000 bombs were dropped here during the Blitz, with more landing in West Ham than in any other bor-ough (inner or outer) in London.[11] The ageing housing stock that remained was notoriously slummy, especially in West Ham, which had 5,808 households on its waiting list by 1963.[12] The local Labour council was also concerned about housing overspill, which threatened to haemorrhage core voters to Essex, thus eroding their electoral power basis. It was in this context that Thomas North, the borough architect for West Ham and then Newham, resolved to build up. Of the new units built in their housing programme during the 1960s, 70 per cent were in tower blocks.[13]

Local authorities across Britain were juggling the priorities of design versus production.[14] In areas with major urgent housing demand – such as Newham, Glasgow, Liverpool, and Salford – the imperative of production usually won out. System building offered an appealing route forward: using mass-produced, prefabricated building components which could be assembled on-site by unskilled labourers. This was 'housing from the factory'.[15] It had a brief heyday in Britain during the mid-1960s. System building accounted for 28 per cent of public housing tender approvals in 1965, climbing to 42 per cent in 1967. After the shock at Ronan Point, this figure dropped to 19 per cent in 1970, then dwindled to just 5 per cent in 1977.[16]

In Newham, Thomas North had been attracted to system building for the advantages of speedy construction it afforded to his overstretched department, which was also grappling with a skilled-labour shortage. In 1964 they approved the use of the Danish Larsen-Nielsen industrialised system. This was the favoured system of Taylor Woodrow-Anglian, the construction giant that secured the contract for the Freemasons Estate. Their marketing material promised that system building offered an 'improved quality of workmanship'. 'This results,' they expounded, 'from increased mechanisation, and from labour operating under better conditions.' The company's own system was patented in Denmark, where it had a 'well-proved' record of success.[17] The publicity material failed to mention that in Scandinavia the Larsen-Nielsen system was only permitted for use up to six storeys. Taller buildings required an internal frame.

'Housing from the factory' was not a bad idea in principle. The Bauhaus had been lit aflame by the prospects of standardisation and prefabrication in architecture; these advances could offer consistency *and* flexibility, economy *and* quality. 'The net result should be a happy architectonic combination of maximum standardization and maximum variety,' explained Walter Gropius. 'Were mechanization an end in itself,' he clarified, 'it would be an unmitigated calamity, robbing life of half its fulness and variety by stunting men and women into subhuman, robot-like automatons.' The Bauhaus objective was 'to abolish the individual's physical toil of providing himself with the necessities of existence in order that hand and brain may be set free'.[18]

Nor was this impulse confined to modernist circles. Some of Britain's earliest 'houses from the factory' were in the neo-Georgian village of Dormanstown in Redcar, constructed between 1917 and 1920 to house employees of the Dorman Long iron and steel works. Behind sash windows, pediments, and moulded cornices hid concrete and steel-framed cores, which Dorman Long patented as the Dorlonco system. For large housing schemes, the advantages offered by prefabrication were manifold. Repetitive components, such as plumbing and wall units, could be made more efficiently off-site. Plastering and window-fitting could be done in advance. The dry process of assembly made it possible to overcome the traditionally short building season necessitated by the wet trades. Most importantly, it could considerably accelerate the rate of production.

There was heated debate over system building within the Ministry of Housing and Local Government during the early 1960s. Architects within the Ministry's Housing Research and Development Group, headed by Cleeve Barr, favoured the use of tailored open systems in which architectural design and flexibility remained pre-eminent, employing prefabricated parts where appropriate. Barr had spent his early career in Hertfordshire County Council's acclaimed schools programme, where a talented team of designers produced a tremendously varied stream of modern schools, making creative use of prefabricated components around light steel frames. The Research and Development Group was suspicious of the cruder, repetitive closed systems being pumped out by private contractors, especially for high blocks.

Senior ministers in both the Conservative and Labour administrations of the mid-1960s were not so choosy. Keith Joseph,
Conservative minister for housing and local government from
1962 to 1964, described himself as 'passionate' about industrialised building.[19] His family headed the enormous Bovis construction
firm, which had developed its own Intergrid system. Richard
Crossman, his successor in the Labour government of 1964 to
1966, was also an advocate. His department issued a circular in
1965 in which the use of system building was not just endorsed
but encouraged for local building programmes. Ultimately, the
more complicated and experimental open systems failed to rival
the appeal of the closed systems, which granted local authorities
a more straightforward route for the rapid delivery of mass housing at high densities. These were the systems which took off in the
1960s drive – buttressed by the rise of the package deal, in which
contractors took charge of engineering, design, and construction.

Many within the architectural profession were affronted by this
ascendancy. These buildings were 'not architects' architecture'.[20]
In the aftermath of the Ronan Point disaster, the president of the
RIBA, Hugh Wilson, contrasted the building with the much-
lauded Alton Estate, which showcased his ideals in its solid
construction and incorporation of high- and low-rise dwellings
within a schema of mixed development surrounded by nature:

> Instead, very much taller blocks (some over 30 storeys high) often
> now rise from a sea of concrete and asphalt, are inserted on pocket
> handkerchief sites in areas of semi-industrial squalor, or in gaps in
> low density inter-war or post-war development, where the open
> space that brings the overall density down to acceptable standards
> is often in private gardens inaccessible to the flat-dweller . . . In this
> situation the architect has been pushed very much to the periphery.
> His central planning and coordinating role has been eroded to the
> extent that he has often been able to do little more than vet the
> scheme of a package-dealer or system builder bought 'off the peg'
> by his local authority.

Wilson blamed the disaster on Britain's 'failure to make use of its architects'.[21] Other sections of the architectural press took a different view. 'The architects *have failed* Britain,' retorted the *Architects' Journal*, by deserting their responsibility for oversight.[22] Professionals had allowed themselves 'to be forced too often into a situation where they no longer fully control the design', reported the *RIBA Journal*.[23]

Nevertheless, to consider Ronan Point as straightforwardly representative of architectural modernism is injudicious. Sam Webb – an architect who would dedicate his life to exposing the faults of high-rise system building, first shown at Ronan Point, in the years to come – maintained that 'blaming Le Corbusier for this is like blaming Mozart for Muzak'.[24] Many of Britain's foremost modernist architects resolutely rejected the second-rate high-rise products of contractor-led system building as anathema to their principles. J. M. Richards, the long-standing editor of the *Architectural Review* from 1937 to 1971, felt that the propositions of the modern movement had been hijacked 'to sanction the rape of many English cities at the behest of ambitious local authorities abetted by property speculators'.[25] The communist-sympathising architectural journalist Malcolm MacEwen pointed out, however, that once 'shorn' of their initial idealism, the strands of modernist thought that fetishised the machine and rejected organic growth were 'tailormade for the bureaucratic or speculative developer' to capitalise upon.[26]

The turn away from high-rise building in Britain was also more convoluted than the cause-and-effect narrative which has developed around Ronan Point. It began before the disaster, when the Housing Subsidies Act of 1967 reined back the progressive height subsidy. Heavily subsidising high-rise construction had proved eye-wateringly expensive for central government. Fiscal support for local authority housing was cut in an attempt to prevent devaluation. High-rise construction went into general decline, but this process was regionally varied. Output remained resilient in many outer London boroughs and in Scotland, until the mid-1970s.

WHY? WHY? WHY?

On the day of the disaster, various figures involved in the construction of Ronan Point denied culpability. 'The building,' Thomas North told the press, 'stood up to [the explosion] surprisingly well – there is no sign of any structural weakness whatsoever.'[27] The managing director of Taylor Woodrow-Anglian insisted that there was 'not the slightest indication that there is any structural failure'.[28] Another of the company's representatives claimed it had averted a larger disaster: 'These buildings are made of reinforced concrete – materials similar to that which were used for bomb-proof shelters during the war. If the block had been built by ordinary methods I shudder to think what might have happened.'[29] North even proposed that 'the undamaged flats could be occupied tonight if we could persuade the people to go back in'.[30]

This bluster was met with suspicion. One newsreel summarised, 'We're told it's no less safe . . . this fact can do little to restore the peace of mind of those who live in these teeming towers.'[31] Newham Council was met with 'solid resistance' from the eighty evacuated families against moving back into Ronan Point. The *Guardian* reported that they had 'a crisis of confidence on their hands'.[32]

Memorandums from inside the Ministry of Housing and Local Government betray more anxiety. The government immediately called an inquiry to investigate the collapse, led by Hugh Griffiths QC. The minister for housing, Anthony Greenwood, directed aides the day after the collapse that the inquiry's 'terms of reference should be carefully considered to ensure that they implied no blame on the part of the local authority'.[33] The ministry continued approving precast panel schemes so as to prevent any 'unnecessary alarm among people occupying flats built in this way', while accepting that they would incur 'the risk of another similar accident'.[34] Their barrister advised that they should expect questioning over encouraging the use of the Larsen-Nielsen system, which 'the

Ministry knew or ought to have known' was 'substantially less safe' than framed building.[35]

Jitters travelled all the way up to 10 Downing Street. Richard Crossman (the previous minister for housing, now lord president) told Prime Minister Harold Wilson confidentially of his nerves about the likely revelation of 'embarrassing issues' that could make the inquiry's report 'unpleasant' for the government. Crossman noted that the Ministry of Housing and Local Government had not employed a single constructional engineer for its recent revision of building regulations – the very regulations which had certified that flats built in the Ronan Point style were safe.[36]

The proceedings of the Griffiths Inquiry rattled the government. After the trribunal's questioning of officials, one advisor fed back that he expected the report would 'fairly severely criticise the Ministry'.[37] Hugh Griffiths sent them a pre-emptive warning that 30,000 dwellings in system-built, high-rise blocks nationwide might be at risk of progressive collapse.[38] The ministry decided to take 'precautionary action' by instructing local councils to assess, strengthen, and remove gas from their own blocks.[39]

The inquiry's report found that the gas explosion in Ivy Hodge's flat was not one of exceptional force. The reason for the extent of the ensuing collapse was in fact 'inherent in the design of the building', and the design of many others across the country. The report was most critical of the National Building Agency for issuing certificates of appraisal to industrialised building schemes without adequately investigating their unique risks of collapse, as well as the Building Research Station for insufficient research into structural issues within system building. It pronounced Newham's borough architect and borough engineer as 'too casual' in their approach, 'appearing to treat compliance with byelaws as a tiresome formality rather than as an important safeguard'. They also found the consultant engineer too young and insufficiently experienced.[40]

Beyond this, the report was remarkably tepid. Ministry staff privately considered its criticisms to be 'very mild'.[41] In the final days of the inquiry, Newham Borough Council's representative had argued 'that the Tribunal should not be too extreme and perfectionist, but should balance reasonable safety with the housing needs in Newham'.[42] The tribunal ultimately concluded that 'it would be wrong to place the blame' on Ronan Point's designers or anyone directly involved in constructing the building. Their report contended that the designers 'fell victim, along with others, to the belief that if a building complied with the existing building regulations and Codes of Practice it must be deemed safe'. It adjudged that although its building Codes of Practice were insufficient, the ministry had not received any advice to suggest new ones were needed. The Griffiths Inquiry advised that Ronan Point need not be demolished, but should instead be 'strengthened' and its collapsed corner rebuilt. It recommended that all blocks over six storeys across Britain should undergo assessment to determine if they were at risk of collapse: if so, they should be structurally reinforced and their gas supplies cut off until this was completed.[43]

Central government forwarded the inquiry's recommendations to local councils. The Ministry of Housing and Local Government held a press conference that included a 'personal message' to tenants in tower blocks: 'Leave the worrying to us and to the local authority . . . most of you are living in high buildings which from every point of view are perfectly safe.'[44]

LETTERS TO THE INQUIRY

The week after the collapse at Ronan Point, the inquiry posted a notice in the major national newspapers. It invited the public to submit evidence concerning the collapse. 'Anyone who wished to make representations,' it read, 'may do so by attending or being represented at the inquiry or by sending written representations. All such representations will be made public at the inquiry.'[45] The notice was circulated in several of London's local papers and posters were pasted around Newham. The inquiry's tribunal received 140 letters in response.

Some of these letters came from credentialled architects and engineers, many of whom highlighted the significant risks of using industrialised system building in high-rise projects. 'The precast method of building such flats has encouraged bad work,' explained the head of a London-based firm of civil engineers.

> This firm has said many times that sooner or later these kind of buildings will collapse . . . The concrete units on Ronan Point Flats have distinctly bad joints and the corners are decidedly weak, the reinforcement is also insufficient . . . The incentives to the men [are] also partly wrong, encourages men to be slipshod.[46]

Identical warnings were submitted by a pair of architects, George Fairweather and Sam Webb.[47] Fairweather told the tribunal: 'It is my considered professional opinion that no architect could advise a client to use a design of that kind for a building of that height and number of storeys without risk.'[48]

For such high buildings, an internal frame was essential – as the director of the British Constructional Steelwork Association was (naturally) quick to point out. 'The Association wishes to state quite categorically,' he wrote, 'that had the building been of traditional framed construction, either of steelwork or reinforced concrete, the damage would have been localised in the zone of the initial incident.'[49] On the opposite side of the ring, the System Builders Section of the National Federation of Building Trades Employers was hasty to dismiss 'unfounded critical comments or generalisations' about their favoured construction technique.[50]

Further down the hierarchy, labourers with hands-on experience of system building were more sceptical. Letters flew in from construction workers who had witnessed alarming faults on building sites across the country. Testimonies from those with experience in the building trades reiterated the same concerns: precast panels needed proper reinforcement, through either an internal frame or steel rods.[51] The technical problems of system building were manifold, as one builder from Gateshead explained with great accuracy:

> This structure was passed by the County Architect also Local Officials and Councillors. I shudder to think that we have allowed such words and ideas like Jerry Built, Budging, Peacemeal [*sic*], creep into the Building Industry. What is it Ignorance, Stupidity, Barefaced arrogance, dishonesty, coupled with a total disregard for the safety of human life. Faults as I see them. There is no tie through system . . . Each unit has several sides a top and bottom which should be strongly coupled, locked or joined to its fellows. <u>Now</u>. Even if all these ideas were carried out and according to plan, as a man who has spent a lifetime in all kinds of Building Construction say without fear the whole idea is nasty, cheap, and a disgrace to British architecture . . . This kind of construction is not safe or

A wall panel being swung into place for flats at Morris Walk, under construction by Taylor Woodrow-Anglian using the Larsen-Nielsen system, 1964.

satisfactory over six storeys. Why. Because there are hundreds &
hundreds of joinings which is not only a weakness but a danger
which must not be ignored under any circumstances whatsoever . . .
I want to tell the British people how far we are behind in this form
of Building Construction.[52]

Another labourer employed at the Samuda Estate on the Isle of
Dogs reported that far too few reinforced ties had been fixed
between floor panels during its construction.[53] Indeed, cracks
began to appear at this estate by the early 1970s.[54] 'Workmen on
Blocks see these defects,' he complained, 'but know it is useless to
point them out as no one in authority takes notice of a common
worker.' Although he had raised these concerns before, they had
fallen on deaf ears: 'The Ministry of Housing Planning Dept needs
examining and overhauling. I bet they adopted the same attitude
to Ronan as they did to my complaint.'[55]

The inquiry also received letters from high-rise dwellers in dis-
tress. The Ronan Point disaster posed a terrible fright to those still
settling into newly built tower blocks. A couple of days before the
disaster, a resident on the top floor of Ronan Point had filed a
complaint that water was already leaking through the roof of the
building.[56] After seeing the news, a man penned a letter to the tribunal from the top floor of a twenty-one-storey block on the
Trowbridge Estate in Hackney:

On taking up residence in a tower block of flats, one assumes that
the authorities concerned have consulted proffessional [sic] people
fully experienced with this type of construction. However, since the
Ronan Point disaster, I have heard eminent architects state that
there are many faults to be found with this type of construction,
and putting forward their reasons. It is a little late to voice these
opinions as I, and thousands of other people are now resident in
these type of flats, and find it most disconcerting to say the least to
hear these opinions . . . what has been sacrificed for speed and
cheapness in the construction of these flats feel a possible

catastrophe could ensure. This makes me feel very apprehensive about the safety of my family.[57]

Just up the road from the Freemasons Estate, in Plaistow, those who had been 'a bit afraid to live in such flats in the first instance' were now justifiably nervous. 'Most people [are] shocked [by] the way the floors collapsed like a pack of cards,' wrote in one local witness. 'I myself would have expected the floors to have been linked, welded, or bonded into some sort of superstructure which could have flexed and taken the strain of the explosion.'[58] These worries were not unfounded: many other system-built high-rise blocks would soon begin cracking up, quite literally, as panels pulled apart.[59]

Some letter-writers felt that it was altogether safer to keep people in houses on the ground than to install them in 'sky homes' – or, as one person described them, 'Rabbit Hutches 200 foot off the ground'.[60] Others retained faith in the possibilities of high rise. 'Can you tell me why sky-scrapers are built so shoddy at Custom House & Canning Town,' asked one woman. 'As I have seen beautiful[ly] built flats of entirely different design & structure.'[61] A number of correspondents imagined alternative ways to design improved high-rise blocks. 'We could have real multis,' said one,

> ones which could kick present day horrible efforts into a cocked hat so to speak . . . I'm not a Taylor Woodrow. Nor a Wimpy. Nor have I any letters behind my name. But I have half a dozen Multi ideas that will knock the bottom out of these supposed experts.

He proposed providing spaces for table tennis, coffee mornings, mothers' meetings, and play-areas on every storey.[62]

Another person suggested investigating possible uses for fibreglass, a promising modern material, in high-rise buildings.[63] Perhaps tower blocks could be built with wider bases to prevent top-heavy collapse.[64] A fourteen-year-old boy sent in pencil diagrams of suggested joint fixtures, learned on a secondary-school building course, to forge stronger intersections between wall panels in flats.[65] He received a personal reply with thanks for his 'very neat diagrams'.[66]

Pulsating throughout all these letters is a burning sense of betrayal. Council housing was supposed to provide protection against the ills associated with rapacious speculative house-building. The post-war reconstruction of Britain's cities had been enabled by partnerships between local authorities and private con-tractors, forged in a public-sector context of acute housing demand and limited capital resources. At Ronan Point, it became clear that the state had failed to shield the public from the worst excesses of private-sector profiteering; worse, it was complicit. This felt like a perverse subversion of post-war hopes, as one writer explained:

> I would not live in one over 6 stories for all the tea in India. My main concern is these people are human beings not cattle . . . Mr Marlow would you like to take a family of children to a flat 22 stories above the ground. And pay a little over a third of your income for the privilage [sic]. While this is not problem of Inquiry I'm deeply concerned that with green fields acres of them 60 miles from London owned by a certain Duke cannot have factories built in heart of country that people human beings should be packed in concrete coffins miles high till day they die because greedy business men insist they stay where the Stock Exchange & Banks of Com-merce are all crammed into the areas their wealthy master built them I'm not a Communist just a man who has been around long enough to remember the miseries of the 30s and the war.[67]

This wound would sting afresh a few years later, when the Poulson scandal of the early 1970s revealed the corruption and bribery underpinning many package-deal contracts between construction firms and government officials.

Letter after letter expressed horror and dismay about the cost-cutting measures taken at Ronan Point. Jerry-building, rushed construction, low-quality materials, and height subsidies were recurrent flash points. The dangling of cash incentives to labourers for quick progress was a particular point of outrage: 'These places are built on Bonus Schemes and Incentive Schemes any men on Bonuses plus are going to rush the job to feather their pockets.'[68] The use of bonus systems in post-war reconstruction was linked to a broader casualisation within the building sector through labour-only subcontracting and piece-rate pay. This period saw building workers' pay falling behind that of other industrial workers and bonuses offered a much-needed top-up to wage packets. Predictably, standards of work slipped.

The state seemed distant, impervious, and unsympathetic. Many of the people who wrote in expected that their concerns would be disregarded: 'Oh no you don't want to know, you, I think are saying Mr Coyte is a crank'; 'I know civil servants wont [sic] let this get to the Home Secretary himself'; 'you may ignor [sic] this letter but the governments [sic] days are numbered . . . the next election you will hear the bells toll for you & the parties acting against [the public's] wishes'.[69] As it transpired, these written representations were not 'made public at the inquiry', as had been promised.[70] The secretary of the inquiry at the Ministry of Housing and Local Government responded to the majority with an identical blueprint letter of acknowledgement to confirm that their points would be 'considered'.[71] Only selected professionals were cross-examined.

These letters were discarded – but to us, they are valuable. Here we have a rich 'archive of feelings' about Ronan Point.[72] These testimonies leave behind a reflexive fingerprint, through which we gain insight into their authors' opinions and self-actualisations. This was a public who knew it deserved something better; a groundswell of feeling bolstered by the memory and sacrifices of the Second World War. These writers expressed themselves in explicitly emotional terms: they felt 'angry', 'so insulted', 'distressed', 'apprehensive', 'afraid', 'very anxious', 'worried', 'very saddened', 'most disconcert[ed]', and 'so ashamed'.[73] In this bank of letters, we see experiential testimony being positioned as equally legitimate as technical expertise. Emotions can serve as a political framework by which to stake claims to human rights; they are proof of our humanity.[74]

WE WILL FLATLY REFUSE

The day after the Ronan Point disaster, the *Guardian* reported a shocking revelation. Thomas and Pauline Murrell, a young couple who died in the collapse, had attempted to refuse their allocated top-floor flat at Ronan Point at least seven times. They eventually 'gave in' when their old house was condemned by slum clearance order.[75] The housing programme in Newham was certainly top-down in its administration. Thomas North's team was focused on delivering housing swiftly, so public consultation held little appeal.

This became clear to the local Beckton Ward Residents' Committee. Two thousand residents of the nearby Beckton Ward in Canning Town were scheduled to be decanted into the Freemasons Estate after slum clearance. Ronan Point collapsed in the early morning of 16 May. By lunchtime the same day, five Beckton residents began knocking door to door with a petition objecting to being moved, ultimately forming a committee.[76] They submitted their petition of 639 signatures to Newham Council before a week had elapsed.[77] One of the organisers, lorry driver Stanley Hart, told the *East London Advertiser*: 'We will not move from here unless we can get an assurance from the council that we will be given a house. We will barricade ourselves in if necessary ... They seem to forget that they are our servants not our masters.'[78]

The borough's existing housing stock was in a horrendous state. In 1968, the pages of the *Newham Recorder* flitted between reports of strident protest from those resisting relocation to tower blocks, and grim accounts of unsound and crumbling old terraces whose inhabitants were desperate for a new home. The local authority pushed on. 'There has been no panic,' Newham's housing manager insisted to *The Times*. 'Most people have got full confidence that the public inquiry will establish the true cause, and will be entirely guided in their views with regard to that.'[79]

The Beckton Ward Residents' Committee soon garnered even more support. By June, it had submitted an updated petition of 1,080 signatures to Elwyn Jones, the Labour MP for West Ham South, to pass on to the Griffiths Inquiry.[80] 'Most of us here,' Stanley Hart told the press, 'are waiting to be rehoused but we certainly do not want to go into these skyscraper flats. We would prefer to stay where we are.'[81] In a covering letter the residents explained:

> We, the tenants of Custom House area, wish to express our fears and dissatisfaction of the flat building programme of this Council, our reasons being:- (a) The blocks of flats are built in too close proximity, and we feel that in the future they will be nothing but slums. (b) Due to the recent tragedy at Ronan Point our wives and children are more aware of the dangers of being incarcerated in this type of building. We therefore wish to state that under the present conditions outlined above, we will flatly refuse to leave our present slums to enter modern slums.[82]

Newham Council maintained that it would not consider any petitions while the inquiry was ongoing.[83] When the committee held a public meeting of 200 residents to demand a halt on the construction of high flats in Newham, it was boycotted by all but one of the borough's councillors, Labour representative Bert Taylor, who arrived with an unfriendly attitude. When told that the Beckton residents opposed being moved to 'new slums', he replied: 'If the flat blocks become slums it depends on the people living in them.'[84] Unbeknown to the committee, Elwyn Jones was also dismissive, despite being their MP. Jones forwarded their petition and letter to the inquiry with a disqualification in his covering note: 'Frankly, I do not think that they are at all helpful in relation to the Inquiry.'[85]

The committee was not given legal representation at the inquiry. Beckton's residents were aggrieved by the 'high-handed behaviour of the planners'.[86] They also felt 'cold-shouldered' by the local Labour Party.[87] The inquiry's report confirmed their fears that other blocks were also liable to progressive collapse. In their next meeting after its publication, the Beckton Ward Residents' Committee asked attendees if they would prefer to go to prison over a tower block: 'The show of hands was almost 100 per cent.'[88] Despite its continued objections, the committee's campaign was unsuccessful. Almost a thousand Beckton residents were rehoused into three identical blocks beside Ronan Point by the spring of 1971.[89]

FALLOUT

After forwarding Griffiths's recommendations to local authorities, Anthony Greenwood wrote to the prime minister with a note of relieved finality: 'My dear Harold, Touch wood, but I think the tide has turned on Ronan Point.'[90] This assumption proved misplaced. The inquiry and its verdict were accompanied by a flurry of debate across the British media. When Thames and London Weekend Television ran broadcasts questioning the safety of other high-rise blocks nationwide, Anthony Greenwood accused them of spreading unjustified alarm. David Frost responded on live television: 'What spreads alarm is not television programmes but unanswered ministerial questions.'[91]

Terence Bendixson, in the *Guardian*, accused the government of 'stage management' around the report's publication. The report had been ready since 13 October but was published a month later, on the day that Richard Nixon was elected in the US presidential election. Bendixson believed this had been calculated to bury any cause for panic.[92] The press took a cynical view of the cost-cutting incentives for the turn to system building. In *Private Eye*, Paul Foot observed, 'There seems little doubt that the chief advantage of the Larsen-Nielsen system is in cost. Fixing steel joints into the concrete panels is more expensive, clearly, than not doing so.'[93] A cartoon in the *New Statesman* depicted an unstable 'Groanin' Point' – a 'capitalist, system-built, monetary block' – covered in flags of different currencies. Roy Jenkins, the chancellor of the Exchequer, was illustrated cajoling his own nervous mother to move into the building.

The treatment of local people in Newham gave ample cause for outrage. The Beckton petitioners received extensive coverage in the *Newham Recorder*, and their campaign was picked up by the national press. Paul Foot was enraged that the tenants of Ronan Point and its identical neighbouring blocks on the Freemasons Estate, 'unlike every other interested party, were not collectively represented at the public inquiry'.[94] Forty Ronan Point residents

Cartoon by Arthur Horner in the *New Statesman*, 1968.

88

were called to give eyewitness reports and be cross-examined, but only two received any legal representation (Ivy Hodge and a Mr Pike, who fitted her cooker). Internal government files reveal that Hodge was only granted legal representation after her brother complained that she was subjected to 'malicious and unfounded remarks' about her 'mental health, moral behaviour, and her reasons for remaining single' during police questioning.[95]

At the *Evening Standard*, former Islington Labour councillor Harry Brack ran his own investigation alongside the inquiry. Brack had been an outspoken critic of his borough's demolition of Victorian housing to make way for the new Packington Estate, for which he was expelled from his party in 1965. He was just as enraged by the Ronan Point scandal. 'The Victorian corridors of the Ministry in Whitehall need a spring clean,' he declared upon the publication of the Griffiths Report.[96] Lower down the ladder, he believed the dominance of the Labour Party in local urban council chambers was creating a crisis of political accountability.

Brack went through 1,200 pages of transcripts from the twenty days of inquiry hearings. He also visited the Freemasons Estate site to examine the controversial H2 joints that were still being fitted at another identical block in progress, finding them inadequate.[97] Harry Brack made the Ministry for Housing and Local Government uneasy. His press clippings were kept on file. During the inquiry, he asked them for an interview. Ministry staff privately considered him 'demanding' and believed 'there was nothing to be gained from our point of view at the moment in such an interview'. The ministry refused to grant his request on the pretext that the matter was '*sub judice*'.[98]

A year on from the report, Brack uncovered that central government had a shaky grasp on whether the tower block appraisals they had advised local councils to perform had been seen to completion: 'I was informed by the Ministry that some 700 blocks had been appraised, but that's all they knew – no progress chart was being kept!' He called for Anthony Greenwood to assume responsibility for his 'appalling record' and resign.[99]

By the middle of 1970, central government had been able to gain a clearer picture of affected blocks, though their appraisal records only covered England. A total of 1,893 blocks had been appraised by 112 local authorities: at least 628 blocks (comprising 42,449 dwellings) required strengthening work, with 61 authorities implicated.[100] This would involve substantial expenditure. The Ministry for Housing and Local Government offered to fund just 40 per cent of the cost of remedial work, to the indignation of associated local authorities. The offer was later upped to 50 per cent.

The Greater London Council (GLC) fed back that their local authority officers still 'felt very strongly that this was inadequate'.[101] The Association of Municipal Corporations similarly complained that this grant 'falls far short' of what their members would accept as 'a reasonable contribution'.[102] The association's members insisted that they had been 'pressurized' and 'intimidated' into building system-built, high-rise blocks – a charge Anthony Greenwood denied. 'The responsibility should be shared,' responded the ministry. Regardless, Alderman C. S. Franks of Salford warned that 'if the amount left for authorities to pay was great, they might decide, at their peril, to maintain the *status quo*'.[103]

The Association of Municipal Corporations also called for the assessment of system-built blocks of six storeys and below.[104] The ministry (now under Conservative control following the election of 1970) deemed this unnecessary. Strengthening blocks of five and six storeys would cost an estimated extra £2 million in grant payment.[105] The ministry internally concluded:

> One might expect an explosion in our present stock of 4–6 storey blocks only once in 30 years, even with gas connected. If this explosion resulted in progressive collapse, it could mean the death of 15 or 20 people. But each year over 4,000 people die in accidents in the home, and over 6,000 are killed on the roads.[106]

Meanwhile, in East London, grievances smouldered on. The play-wright Joan Littlewood, who was based locally at Stratford East's Theatre Royal, visited Ronan Point on the day of the disaster and attended the hearings of the Griffiths Inquiry. She was disgusted by the condescension shown towards tenants at the inquiry, describing it as 'a taste of what I call the horrifying theatre'.[107] Littlewood felt that this was lost in the official transcript. Her friend Peter Rankin recalled:

> On looking through it, she noted that she could no longer hear the superior tone of the barristers or sense their tricks. 'I'm sorry, the sound system doesn't seem to be working very well. Could you repeat that?' This was one of them. Rarely did the witness repeat what they said, not exactly. They were too cowed. In the transcript, proceedings were smooth. In the hall, they were not.[108]

Littlewood had a record of producing agitprop work with her local Theatre Workshop and decided to stage a production about the scandal. She initially hoped to put on a 'morality play' about Ronan Point at St Paul's Cathedral using verbatim testimonies from the transcripts. The audience would process around the stage like the Stations of the Cross to consider the disaster from the different perspectives of the tenants, workmen, architects, contractors, and politicians. This way, 'the mirages and monstrosities made by politicians and commercial developers could be shown'. Littlewood intended to foreground 'the life of people in the flats' in their quotidian settings – pubs and music halls, for example. The 'audience themselves' would be invited to build a block in the centre of the stage.[109]

However, Littlewood risked being sued by the government for libellous use of the transcript material. She launched an alternative production: *The Projector*, staged in 1970. It was a thinly veiled critique of the corruption and negligence involved in Ronan Point's construction, in the guise of a Georgian Restoration play about eighteenth-century jerry-building. Publicity posters and pro-grammes highlighted its contemporary inspiration. Sam Webb, the architect who had tried to submit evidence to the inquiry with George Fairweather, helped to design the scenery. Littlewood's canny stunt was admired in the press; for any onlooker, the parallels between Ronan Point's constructors and the play's dodgy-dealing tenement developer were crystal clear.[110]

Ronan Point was more than a crisis for high rise; this was a crisis for British democracy. The political culture of post-war recon-struction had been fatally high-handed. Local authorities had resorted, moreover, to the very same cost-cutting measures for which old slum landlords were so resented. The scandal repre-sented a tragic inversion of the promises of the welfare state. In response, the state was met with powerful public demands for improved housing provision – divorced from private enterprise and responsive to the user voice. The early Fabian paternalism of

A poster for Joan Littlewood's play *The Projector*, 1970.

British council housing had reached breaking point; the post-war settlement needed to become more participatory, more egalitarian, and more accountable.

Complicated psychological currents emerged in British society during the post-war years. On the one hand, the new entitlements proffered by the welfare state helped to enshrine a popular belief among working people that they were truly 'worth something'.[111] At the same time, the limited percolation of post-war affluence into many working-class lives produced justified resentments, as did the shortcomings of the welfare state in living up to the hopes with which it had been invested. Out of this emerged a 'dual sense of grievance and optimism', in the words of the historian Alistair Cartwright.[112] This was a powerful, if complex, structure of feeling. Through it, we can understand how the deficiencies of the post-war settlement became a locus for both disappointment and reimagination.

Ronan Point became an enduring symbol in national discourse. What happened to the building itself? On the day of the disaster, the

Thomas and Selina McCambridge, the only people to return to Ronan Point, look out across the Freemasons Estate in 1973.

93

Ministry of Housing's representative at the scene of the wreckage returned to his office with a stern recommendation: 'It is not to be contemplated that these families should be made to go back to the damaged block.'[113] That summer, around a dozen households from Ronan Point consented to be moved to the top of Merritt Point, a neighbouring block of identical design. The Lane family, with two young children, was one of them. They had been evacuated from their former flat in Ronan Point to a temporary house on Tarling Road, before moving to Merritt Point. Kenneth Lane, a thirty-year-old labourer, explained: 'Before moving to Ronan Point we were in a slum dwelling. And even this house on Tarling Road – for which we were grateful at the time – has seen better days. The flats were like Buckingham Palace by comparison.'[114]

Ronan Point itself was patched up and re-opened in 1973, at which point a new crop of tenants were moved in. Newham Council promised residents on the Freemasons Estate that their blocks had been strengthened with steel girders and would no longer be supplied with gas. This gave some reassurance, although only one former household agreed to move back to Ronan Point. Interestingly, however, one in five of the households which moved into the refurbished Ronan Point had chosen to transfer from other council accommodation. A correspondent from *New Society* pointed out that, in certain ways, the Freemasons Estate was 'actually rather a nice place to live': 'It is set in abundant and well-laid-out open space, near a good shopping centre and a fast road to the coast.'[115]

The following year, however, another *New Society* journalist ventured into the block to find that mistrust was still in the air: 'The most striking reaction to living in Ronan Point, is the extraordinarily live and persistent rumour that the *real* reason it collapsed has never been made public.'[116] These worries would linger on.

4

The Stephen and Matilda Tenants' Co-operative

Wapping, 1975–88

In September 1978, the *East London Advertiser* ran a full-page spread on the opening ceremony of an exciting new venture in London's Docklands. On this bright autumn day, the yard of an old inter-war housing estate in Wapping came to life. It was packed with a throng of locals full of 'high spirits, high hopes, and high jinks'. They were joined by guests from local government and even from Whitehall. All these people were gathered to celebrate the inauguration of a novel initiative: the Stephen and Matilda Tenants' Co-operative. 'Home-made beer and wine flowed' as a local teenagers' rock band put on a performance.[1]

The Stephen and Matilda Tenants' Co-operative was a daring experiment in tenant control for council housing. It was born out of negotiations between Tower Hamlets residents, the Greater London Council, and the Department of the Environment between 1975 and 1979. It was based at the St Katharine's Estate in Wapping, a block of brick, 'walk-up' flats built by the London County Council in the 1930s. Stephen and Matilda was the first local authority tenants' management co-operative in England and Wales: in which tenants were granted management control of a property while it remained under the legal ownership of the local council.[2]

Central and local government hailed Stephen and Matilda as an achievement of great importance and a precedent for British housing. Upon its official opening in 1978, the GLC issued a press release announcing 'England's First Council Tenants' Co-operative'.[3] The Department of the Environment described it as 'a pioneering exercise'.[4] It was hoped that this would be the first of many such co-operative ventures across Britain. When the mechanisms for establishing such housing co-operatives had first been incorporated into British statute in 1975, the Labour MP Bruce Douglas-Mann predicted to the House of Commons: 'In 25 years' time we shall probably be looking back at this proposal and regarding it as an historic amendment introducing a substantially new element into the housing sector.'[5] This would not transpire. Local authority co-operatives had a brief wind at the end of the 1970s. They faded from view after the Conservative victory of 1979 ushered in a transformed landscape of housing priorities from central government.

Brevity notwithstanding, this episode affords us important insight. The late 1970s have conventionally been characterised as a period during which a decaying post-war settlement nose-dived into irresolvable crisis, especially in inner-city areas. The 1970s were indeed a period of crisis, but not of stagnation; the decade's problems generated new ideas in response. This was certainly the case for housing, for which the urban historian Guy Ortolano sees this period as 'a fertile moment offering a range of possibilities'.[6] The story of the Stephen and Matilda Tenants' Co-operative shows that fresh visions were germinating which moved beyond the conventional binary frontiers of private and municipal control. The political landscape of the late 1970s was animated by the discussion of more variegated ideas about how housing tenure might be reconfigured. Both in government and on the street, alternative pathways were developing beyond owner-occupation by which freedom, choice, and self-determination might be achieved.

Local authority co-operative housing was mooted as a third way between private ownership and municipal tenure, granting council tenants greater control while their estates remained in public ownership. Such thinking should encourage us to understand Right to Buy as a moment of historical contingency rather than inevitability. Even upon the eve of Margaret Thatcher's election, important alternatives were in emergence. Investments in public housing remained resilient. However, these investments had sharply expressed conditions: traditional council housing management needed to change, to evolve. Above all, it needed to devolve.

ESTABLISHING A CO-OPERATIVE

Britain saw a flowering of co-operative housing initiatives in the 1970s. The first significant examples sprang up in Islington and Liverpool in partnership with local housing associations. These associations typically bought up private housing on sale, renovated it, and passed it on to tenants' co-operatives for occupation by local people in need of housing – although the dwellings remained within the freehold of the housing association to whom residents paid rent. This movement emerged in response to a triple-bind faced by many thousands of people across the country: vertiginous house prices; inadequate, poorly regulated private rented accommodation; and lengthy council waiting lists. At the St Katharine's Estate, a different approach to co-operative housing emerged, involving council partnership.

Since the mid-1960s, the GLC had been spearheading urban renewal work in so-called 'twilight areas' of housing stress in London. These areas were defined on the basis of unsatisfactory levels of overcrowding, multiple occupation, and insanitary conditions. This approach was incentivised by the Milner Holland Report (1965), which laid bare the deterioration and neglect of much of Greater London's older housing stock. J. P. Macey, the GLC's director of housing, recommended in 1966 that 'immense financial and rehousing burdens can be avoided by early action to arrest the process of decay' in many of the city's older homes. The requisite 'heavy financial burdens' were deterring local authorities from pursuing 'wholesale redevelopment' – 'nor is this immediately necessary over the whole area', the GLC noted. Macey explained:

> Action under Slum Clearance powers tends gradually to replace the small groups of unfit properties by new blocks of flats but these only emphasize the greyness of the rest of the area. These new developments produce a 'pepper-pot' effect which does little or nothing to improve the area as a whole.

The answer, he insisted, was an approach based on 'the three "R"s': redevelopment, reconditioning, and rehabilitation.[7] The GLC's stance was bolstered by the release of the Ministry of Housing and Local Government's White Paper *Old Houses into New Homes* in 1968. This rehabilitative thrust continued into the early 1970s, during which the GLC pursued a modernisation programme for existing council housing, especially flatted estates from the inter-war period.

The St Katharine's Estate was a prime candidate for modernisation, now almost four decades old. It had been built in 1937, to the design of architect Victor Wilkins, on the former site of the Red Lion Brewery. The estate was built in brick with concrete floor slabs. It is a typical example of the early wave of multistorey council housing constructed by the LCC in the inter-war years. It comprised two blocks of five and six storeys: Stephen House and Matilda House, named after the twelfth-century English monarchs. Matilda House was the larger, housing 133 flats. Stephen House had 35.

The estate had been a popular address in the inter-war period. It was located a stone's throw from the docks, where men could go in the mornings to pick up work. It survived the Blitz, during which London's Docklands had been a target for the Luftwaffe, although shrapnel ricocheted to leave fissures around the brick archway entrance of Matilda House. The closure of the docks from 1968 onwards significantly impoverished the surrounding area. By 1976, local unemployment was double the national average. Shops on Wapping High Street began to close and many people moved away in search of work. The flats themselves were glaringly run down by the early 1970s. Residents interviewed in 1974 (for a documentary sponsored by the BBC's Community Programmes Unit) were dejected and dissatisfied with their living conditions.[8]

A new initiative was floated by the GLC in 1973 to modernise and update the flats in line with Parker Morris standards, in anticipation of which the estate was decanted. However, central government cut-backs following the Housing Act of 1974 posed difficulties for the GLC's modernisation programme, and the plan for the estate ultimately stalled for lack of funds. It was left near-empty. In 1973, 150 households had been living on the estate. By December 1974, the *East London Advertiser* was concerned to discover 'row upon row of empty flats', where just twenty homes remained occupied. The *Advertiser* anticipated that squatters might move into the vacant properties.[9] The borough of Tower Hamlets had an enormous waiting list of 7,000

The St Katharine's Estate in the early 1970s. Matilda House dominated the estate, while the smaller Stephen House is just visible on the left.

names in 1974. Meanwhile, the area was replete with empty properties: a total of 3,200 flats in the same year, many of them in dire condition.[10]

Meanwhile, the spectre of private redevelopment was looming over the Docklands – especially the area around the St Katharine Docks, the first to close in 1968 – as portended by a 1973 London Docklands Report by Travers Morgan consultants, commissioned by the GLC. This prompted *Community Action* (a magazine founded by a cadre of disillusioned young planners in 1972, to circulate information about community-led urban campaigning) to ask pressing questions of the Docklands' future: 'Must they close? Does it have to mean a bonanza for developers? Why must the local communities always suffer?'[11] Local discontent was gathering apace in Tower Hamlets, a borough that had already been a site of militancy during the 1968–70 tenants' strike against GLC rent hikes. The East End Docklands Action Group formed to campaign for the prioritisation of low-income residents' needs over the interests of property speculators. The opening of a luxury hotel by the St Katharine Docks attracted particular ire, as local picketers

The run-down St Katharine's Estate in 1973.

made plain at its opening in late 1973. Anxiety thrummed over the prospect that private developers could take over the St Katharine's Estate.

It was in this context that the option of a housing co-operative was first mooted in 1975. A local action group formed, bringing together 'trade unionists, tenants [sic] leaders, people from the Dockland Action Groups, junior football leagues and squatting groups'.[12] At the forefront of the group were two prime movers. One was Mike Jempson, a Wapping community worker who had built relationships with people in the borough as well as officials at the GLC. The other was Mark Phillips, based at Stepney Green Law Centre, who had valuable experience from setting up Tower Hamlets Community Housing and spearheading the establishment of a co-operative at Sumner House in Poplar. Jempson and Phillips had met squatting in a shared house in Tower Hamlets.

This group approached the GLC's Housing Management Committee and its Labour chair, Tony Judge, to propose a plan for a grassroots renewal of the St Katharine's Estate. Still reeling from the financial restrictions on their planned modernisation work, the GLC was interested in exploring alternative 'means of dealing with emptied properties which rapidly become vandalized'. Tenant co-management offered a solution.[13]

A series of preliminary meetings followed between the GLC and the local action group, which culminated in an agreement on 23 May 1975 that arrangements for a housing co-operative should be put in motion. An advance party of four people were given permission to move onto the estate in a caretaking role, soon swelling to twenty. From this, the Stephen and Matilda Tenants' Co-operative was formed. The co-operative opened up applications for membership: to be eligible, applicants needed to have previously lived in Tower Hamlets, or have a family or work-related connection to the borough. Former tenants who were yet to be rehoused were invited to join the co-operative's meetings in 1975. A handful plumped to remain, but most declined the offer. Many were fed up with living on an estate that had been left to decay. But other local people were attracted by the new possibilities the co-operative promised.

Tony Judge's intention was for the co-operative to 'assume responsibility for virtually all management and maintenance responsibilities'.[14] In the mid-1970s, the Labour-run GLC committed itself to tackling 'County Hall's reputation for being a vast, bureaucratic and impersonal landlord'.[15] 'Tenant participation,' Judge insisted, 'has been the keystone of our management policy. Our initiatives have included more active District Committees, encouragement of tenants' associations, co-option on to the Housing Management Committee of tenants' representatives.' He stressed that the GLC's 'pioneer work' on tenants' co-operatives was particularly significant: 'This Council was the first in Britain to embark on such co-operatives.'[16] GLC officials were even sent to Sweden to attend seminars held by the Swedish Housing Ministry and relevant co-operatives in 1975.

The creation of Stephen and Matilda required a lengthy process of negotiations and constitution drafting with the GLC. This proved immensely labour-intensive for the local steering group, with much of the work shouldered by Mark Phillips, who had secured some funding from the Department of the Environment for research into co-operative action. Meanwhile, Stephen House was demolished in 1976, without the consultation of co-op members, to make way for the construction of the South Quay Estate. They decided to keep the name: Phillips described this as 'a little sign of resistance'.[17]

Finally, a date was set for the co-operative's formal establishment in 1978. 'At long last,' the co-operative informed its members, 'the signing of our agreement with the GLC is in sight. The date is fixed for March, with the actual handover on April 1st. (a reflection of what the GLC think of us?)'[18] The official Housing Co-operative Agreement with the GLC was signed on the boot of a derelict car in the estate's courtyard.[19] This agreement put 'the principles of tenant management and control' front and centre.[20] After receiving ratification from the Department of the Environment, the co-operative's Management Committee told its fellow members:

> We cannot rest on our laurels, the fight is now to prove that council tenants can manage their own estates . . . a great responsibility falls on all our shoulders . . . In fifteen months [*sic*] time, the agreement comes up for review, it is up to every member to search their consciences to see what help they can give to the Co-Op.[21]

A NEW FORM OF TENURE

The events at the St Katharine's Estate reflected a mushrooming demand for grassroots empowerment emerging in British urban politics during the 1970s. The value of community-led urban redevelopment was being endorsed by practising architects, such as Ralph Erskine, Walter Segal, Brian Anson, and Rod Hackney. The anarchist writer Colin Ward was an influential contributor to this sphere of debate. During the 1970s, Ward wrote prolifically to advocate for handing the reins of power over the built environment to the public. He hammered out a case for 'dweller-control' within both the private and public sectors.[22] Council tenants, he noted, were especially disempowered: they 'are the victim of a thousand small humiliations unknown to the owner-occupier, and foreign even to the private tenant, who is never expected to feel that the Landlord is doing him a favour'. In his book *Tenants Take Over* (1974), Ward demanded that municipal housing be transferred from council to tenant control, to 'take one third of Britain's households out of the humiliations of municipal tutelage into self-determining citizenship' without selling off public stock.[23]

These problems had long been clear on flatted estates from the inter-war period. In 1936, the housing consultant and early champion of user-sensitive design Elizabeth Denby surveyed many such estates for the RIBA. Residents raised various objections. The blocks felt 'barrack-like' and the rooms were too small. The lack of lifts left small children cooped up in their flats, because their mothers gave up 'dragging them up and down the stairs'. Poor sound insulation meant that older children 'must be kept unnaturally quiet' in their homes, nor could 'a big adolescent family behave in a jolly way, or entertain friends in the evening'. The rigid restrictions imposed on tenants were 'deeply resented'. They wanted to keep pets, to put up window boxes, and to plan their own uses for the yards. 'There is absolutely nothing for anyone to do in these tenement estates,' Denby concluded, 'and leisure is apt to be unwisely spent.' The same frustrations about over-control and poor planning were shared on cottage estates, where residents also missed being centrally located.[24] At Stephen and Matilda, tenant control offered a route for tackling precisely the issues Denby identified.

When the Stephen and Matilda Tenants' Co-operative was formally established in 1978, Ben Birnbaum (chairman of its Management Committee) affirmed the project's core principles in a GLC press release:

> This is the day we have been working for. For years council tenants have been demanding a greater say in the running of housing estates without being saddled with ownership. At Stephen and Matilda we are putting the devolution of control over housing management into practice. We are not saying this will provide more homes, but it will make council housing a more attractive proposition. The lease will be reviewed in about a year from now which we believe will give us the chance to confirm our experiences over the last few years – that working people have the capacity to take complete charge of their environment and living conditions to the benefit of everyone.[25]

Importantly, the St Katharine's Estate remained council housing owned by the GLC, but it was to be managed by its tenants. Rents were sent to the council, which in turn contributed financial

A sign to hail Wapping's new co-operative.

support for maintenance and management costs. In 1971, nearly 80 per cent of housing in Tower Hamlets was council-owned; this was a borough with high demand for public housing, given the low incomes of the majority of its residents.[26]

The Stephen and Matilda Tenants' Co-operative did not spring up in isolation. Enthusiasm for this new form of housing tenure was bubbling up contemporaneously within central government. The figure at the heart of this was Reg Freeson, the Labour minister for housing from 1974 to 1979. Freeson had been a founding member of the Campaign for Nuclear Disarmament in 1957, an opponent of the Vietnam War, and a critic of apartheid in South Africa. In the 1960s, he edited the anti-fascist magazine *Searchlight*, and was a fierce opponent of the first Wilson government's 1965 plan to place a cap on Commonwealth immigration. As minister for housing in the 1970s, Freeson became a champion for co-operative possibilities. His 'tireless advocacy of the co-op cause' was recognised warmly by the Society for Co-operative Dwellings in 1978.[27]

Freeson's Department of the Environment issued a circular in 1974 that tentatively encouraged local authorities to consider sponsoring housing co-operatives. Later that year, he set up a working party led by Harold Campbell to report to government on the option of housing co-operatives, which came back in the strong affirmative. A Housing Rents and Subsidies Bill began its passage through the House of Commons in 1975. Freeson spoke to the House about a growing sense of frustration among council tenants around the lack of consultation about the management of their homes. He affirmed his intention to provide a solution:

> There is the old-established local authority estate, inhabited by families who have lived there for many years, who intend to go on living there, and for whom it is fully their home as much as any owner-occupier's house is his. Yet they have no say as to how the houses shall be managed, not even about the colour of the paintwork. I allow at once that many local authorities have a good practice of consulting their tenants' associations on such points, but a courteous habit is not the same as a legal right and responsibility. This lack of rights and responsibilities strikes very deeply at the attitude people hold towards the houses and neighbourhoods in which they live – the level of identity they have with home and community. There can be something cold and impersonal about even very good, well-run estates.[28]

The resultant Housing Rents and Subsidies Act 1975 gave democratic associations of council tenants the statutory right to participate in how their estates were run and influence how funds would be spent in maintaining their homes. It also introduced a significant new statutory permission for the establishment of housing co-operatives that could manage or lease estates owned by local authorities, thus creating a 'new kind of housing tenure' in Britain. Housing co-operatives had sprung up before as ad hoc projects, but this was the first time that a legislative framework had been set out for the establishment of co-operatives in council-owned property. It became possible for 'tenants of a co-operative scheme to enjoy the benefits of collective ownership of that scheme together with the rent levels of local authorities'.[29] 'I hope,' Freeson told Parliament, 'that local authorities will use their new powers vigorously.'[30]

Co-operatives were not framed as a minority option, nor the preserve of countercultural activists. They were set out as a central aspect of the Labour government's approach to housing: 'The Government believes that the development of co-operative housing is essential to a sound social and housing policy.'[31] Reg Freeson cited his political commitments to democratic socialism as crucial to his support for housing co-operatives. 'I see this initiative,' he explained, 'as an essential part of a Socialist housing policy for the future.' Freeson envisaged housing co-operatives as 'a means of offering a new form of home ownership as an alternative to conventional owner-occupation or renting – not just a half-way house or cut-price owner-occupation but one with its own possibilities, its own individual and community values'.[32] The Department of the Environment wanted co-operatives to remain 'firmly rooted in the public sector'.[33] Department staff reassured the Treasury that they were not 'envisaging disposal of public assets without their agreement'.[34] Freeson even went as far as to encourage the purchase of private-sector housing by local authorities to convert into council-owned co-operatives for its existing residents.[35]

Anthony Crosland, as secretary of state for the environment, shared Freeson's enthusiasm. In 1972, he had written in the *Guardian* about the benefits of 'readjusting traditional concepts of rented property, both physical and social', via a 'third arm' of housing provision in the form of co-operatives and housing associations. Municipal housing should remain, Crosland believed, 'the main provider of housing for all those who wish to rent'. However, the existing system of council housing demanded improvement: tenants should have 'more choice', 'more variety', 'more security', and 'more democracy'. The 'traditional landlord' relationship between council and tenant needed to be rethought to allow for democratisation within the public housing sector. Housing co-operatives, particularly for 'large blocks of flats', offered a prime opportunity for re-edification via 'a diversity of experiment'.[36]

The department received numerous proposals for co-operatives from across the country. All were answered with enthusiasm. Reg Freeson announced to the House of Commons in early 1978 that within three years of the act, around 150 co-operatives had 'come into the pipeline' across Britain.[37] The progress of local authority co-operatives was still slow; around two dozen were known to be in operation by 1979.[38] Prospective early adopters were faced with laborious negotiations in the absence of a standardised framework. The department envisaged that the constitution being drawn up at Stephen and Matilda would serve as a model, allowing for accelerated, and less daunting, negotiations in the years to come.[39]

LIFE AT STEPHEN AND MATILDA

Stephen and Matilda was both a political idea and a place where people lived. We can glean an insight into life at Matilda House via the co-operative's semi-regular, in-house newsletter. Copies were collected and saved by one of the co-op's founding members, Mike Jempson. It went through various formats, reflecting its rotating editorship as each issue was produced by different members. The earliest bulletin in Jempson's collection is from October 1976. It was titled *(vacant lot)* – an official name had not yet been decided. *(vacant lot)* featured a cheeky diagram to illustrate the co-operative's working structure, overlaid onto human anatomy. Different committees made up its vital organs. The glasses were labelled: 'The spectacle of tenants' control (looking for a socialist perspective)'. Also marked was a 'scar left from umbilical chord [*sic*] to GLC'. The co-op figure had 'hands for taking the bull by the horns', fingers 'on the pulse of things', and a 'comradely smile for other tenants'. Its scrotum was a 'bisexual centre for power and regeneration'. The shoulders were 'for bearing the weight of co-op problems (not as square as might be hoped?).'⁴⁰

Members were called upon to submit possible titles for the future newsletter, collated in the Christmas 1976 edition, for popular vote. The suggested titles show that the first residents were having fun: 'SMAT – Stephen & Matilda and all that'; 'SMUT – Stephen & Matilda united tenants'; 'ORGASM – organ of Stephen & Matilda'; 'THE CO-OPTIMIST'; 'ENTRE NOUS'; 'STEPHEN WHO?'⁴¹ They ultimately settled on something altogether tamer: *SoMeTIMES*.

SoMeTIMES provides colourful texture about the rhythms of everyday life at Stephen and Matilda. Everyone was encouraged to contribute; letters from members formed the backbone of these publications. 'We would like to hear from you,' the newsletter declared, in a voice of mock-threat. 'WE HAFF VAYS OF MAKINK YOU WRITE! If you hear a knock on the door at three o'clock in the morning you can bet it's not the milkman.'⁴² It was full of humour, energy, and excitement, but it also reveals some chronic points of conflict. There was regular bickering over the issue of car parking on the estate, primarily between nervous mothers and members struggling to find a parking space in the vicinity. Co-operative life had its challenges. Some members were told off for dominating meetings. Others resented picking up the slack for neighbours who were less proactive. While these grievances could be flammable, the newsletter was designed as a forum for frustrations to be aired and disagreements to be hashed out in order to defuse tension. Life at Stephen and Matilda could be intense. Indeed, this was a defining aspect of collective living.

The project was underpinned by a real commitment to collective endeavour and mutual support. The estate needed extensive rehabilitation work. The co-operative's agreement with the GLC and Department of the Environment confirmed that tenants would collectively undertake caretaking functions, for which they were provided with a GLC allowance of £18,000 for redecoration.[43] The co-operative wanted to restore 'the old pride' of the St Katharine's Estate.[44] When the estate was reoccupied in 1975 it was 'already derelict and badly vandalised'.[45] While it was empty, windows had been smashed and lead had been removed from the roofs. Without grassroots action, the co-operative insisted that the estate 'would have deteriorated beyond repair'. Indeed, the Department of the Environment had refused to grant the GLC a loan to improve the estate in 1975, just before the co-operative formed.[46]

The co-operative was handed 133 run-down homes to refurbish. Its members' tenacity in the face of this enormous practical challenge is striking. John Easterbrook, one of the advance party of residents, coined a founding motto: 'WDFA – We Don't Fuck About!'[47] The co-operative divided themselves up into different teams: decoration, gas, plumbing, glazing, carpentry, electrical, and plastering. The flats needed new linoleum flooring, replastered ceilings, repainted windows, better door frames, mended piping, and refitted kitchen units. To achieve this, co-operative members were required to contribute eight hours of work each week – a significant tally alongside a full-time occupation or a family (though it later halved to four). Importantly, members had to spend these hours helping with the refurbishment of flats other than their own. Prospective members had to demonstrate their commitment to the enterprise by mucking in with work and meetings on the estate before their arrival.

The burden of the repair work was sizeable. Early issues of *SoMeTIMES* were crammed with DIY tips. The co-operative submitted an application to ask for support from the recently established Manpower Services Commission in 1977, but their bid was unsuccessful. They were, however, able to secure some much-appreciated supplementary labour from Community Industry (an initiative providing work for young unemployed people). It was hard graft, but members hugely appreciated the opportunity to remodel their flats, knock through internal walls, put up window boxes, and keep pets. Hitches did crop up. The estate's

The *East London Advertiser* reports on the co-operative's teams getting down to work, 1978.

new feline residents had a cavalier attitude to the co-operative's community spirit; their penchant for using window boxes as litter trays proved bothersome.

There were further tasks beyond refurbishment. Other members were assigned to administration, stock management, the newsletter, gardening, and typing. Book-keeping was an essential responsibility, taken on by Peter Gotham, who arrived at Stephen and Matilda as a trainee accountant and was soon keeping co-operative accounts running to many thousands of pounds. Another was rent collection, handled by a team led by Julie Bevan. Members took turns staffing the co-op shop, which took orders for groceries and maintained a stock list of dry and tinned non-perishables. A co-op minibus was acquired for shared use. An extensive roster of activities was coordinated by the social committee: discos, cinema outings, camping holidays, seaside trips, Guy Fawkes fireworks, and days out for children. A football team and a chess club were established. A pool team was formed 'as both a social event, but principally as a flag showing, particularly around Wapping & the immediate environs. We have a peculiar reputation, it's about time we put ourselves about.'[48]

The commitment required from co-operative members was significant. For a project established out of a critique of the bureaucracy of local authority estate management, life inside Stephen and Matilda was (ironically) somewhat bureaucratic. Members realised that the GLC would need to see evidence of structures to self-manage and maintain the property. This generated a packed roster of meetings, tasks, and decision-making. Co-opoly, a tongue-in-cheek board game of snakes and ladders based on Stephen and Matilda, illustrated the labyrinthine stages and responsibilities of securing membership and a fully refurbished flat: wading through countless committee meetings, work rota shifts, and maintenance problems. Sitting in endless committee meetings could still be stultifying. Attendance occasionally flagged, meaning that some meetings ended up inquorate.

One newsletter joked, 'Please note S & M stands for Stephen and Matilda, *not* Sado Masochism (Same thing isn't it? – Ed.).'[49] It was suggested, however, that sharing around administrative responsibilities created a more egalitarian and accountable model: 'Where everyone takes turns at being a bureaucrat, no-one is a bureaucrat.'[50] Management Committee officers, for instance, could stay in position for no more than eighteen months.

The co-operative was wary about being mistaken for 'a load of hippies' by its neighbours.[51] They were keen to distance themselves from squatting, which had a poor reputation in the East End (although many former squats would later become co-operatives). The co-operative was proactive about attracting families to live on the estate, and stressed the importance of supplying housing to 'young, newly formed households' in an area with a 'seriously declining economically active population'.[52] One early poster advertising the initiative to local people proclaimed: 'East-Enders!

Members relaxing in the yard, photographed by co-op member Paul Barbara.

Why leave the area to obtain decent housing?'[53] As the co-operative explained:

> These dwellings will be made available to young, homeless families in Tower Hamlets, whose housing need does not receive priority from the Borough Council. (Current waiting list for Council Housing is over 7,000) . . . The majority of the present and future families are young couples with or without young children. This sort of family is likely to move on comparatively quickly as their families grow and therefore a great many people will benefit over the life of the buildings.[54]

Families soon came. The first baby to be born on the co-operative was Eddie Armer, in 1976 – 'but did you know,' teased the newsletter, 'that Baby White was the first to be conceived?'[55] *SoMeTIMES* regularly announced new births: 'Babynews, Ga berba derga gaga

On the doorstep at Matilda House, photographed by co-op member Paul Barbara.

lerga blurb . . . SERIOUSLY FOLKS: : : : : : : Announcing the arrival of another Baby on the Estate Steve Micalleff is now the proud Father of a 1978 model 6lb--9oz Boy.'[56]

Stephen and Matilda encourages us to nuance contemporary assertions that families, mothers, and children were repelled by and unsuited to living on multistorey estates. The lack of lifts posed a problem, especially when manoeuvring a pram, but the co-operative's camaraderie around childcare made the estate attractive to families. As one new mother explained:

> We married while at Matilda House and decided that this was a nurturing environment in which we could start a family, surrounded by people we could trust . . . For us, it was an ideal living situation despite having to schlepp my baby, my bike and my groceries up 2 flights of stairs every time I went to the shops.[57]

One ground-floor unit on the St Katharine's Estate was converted to become a popular playflat for under-fives. Members took turns to mind the children. They were keen to develop entertaining outlets for the children's creativity and learning, so trained in education through play using resources offered by the Open University and the Pre-school Playgroups Association. They kitted out the playflat with a Wendy house, a sand area, and a music corner.

The playflat drew in parents from outside the estate, who were dismayed by the dearth of nurseries in the neighbourhood. A playground with new equipment was built for older children in the yard, with the help of a donation from the Wapping Parents' Action Group. The co-operative's Management Committee intended for every child to have their own room, and some flats were expanded by knocking through adjoining drying rooms, creating larger homes for growing families.

When the Stephen and Matilda Co-operative held its official opening ceremony in 1978, a representative attending from the Department of the Environment left with a hopeful attitude:

The ceremony was interesting, and, having chatted fairly freely with the leading members of the Co-operative, I was reassured about their ability and will to make this thing work. They are not, I would say, very typical of the people one would normally find on Tenants' Co-operatives, should we ever get this particular phenomenon off the ground, in that they are very committed and prepared to put a great deal of effort into it, but as an example of what can be done, and despite all the pitfalls and difficulties that have been encountered, I think we can feel reasonable confidence.[58]

The senior assistant director of housing at the GLC reported favourably on the co-operative's progress in another update in 1979. The co-operative's improvements to the fabric and maintenance of the estate were praised. Participation at meetings was high, averaging at about 60 per cent attendance. Vandalism had been kept 'very low'.[59]

The affirmative sense of community and shared responsibility at Matilda House made it stand out. On a rare occasion when vandalism did occur, a member wrote in to the newsletter:

> Presuming that the Graffitti [*sic*] at the bottom of the stairs has not been written by any of the kids on Our Estate, can the kids who live here please STOP their friends or aquaintences [*sic*] from chalking up their fascist and racist ideas on an estate where this crap is unexceptable [*sic*].[60]

A visitor to the estate in 1981 wrote to express admiration for the whole exercise:

> I have lived on many estates in London, and while visiting yours a week ago I saw no evidence of vandalism, little graffitti [*sic*] on the walls, and in the courtyard there were trees and shrubs, children playing, and people *talking* to each other! I was amazed![61]

Outside Stephen and Matilda's playflat, where children wait for a performance to begin, photographed by member Barbara Phillips.

What shines through in residents' accounts is a moving sense of reciprocal care and friendship. Soryl Angel, who lived at the co-operative in the early 1980s, described her time at Matilda House as 'the finest, most life affirming 4 years of my life . . . How could I have been so lucky?'[62]

THE MEANINGS OF SELF-HELP

For all co-operative housing's benefits, *Community Action* nursed suspicions about the government's sudden zeal for this model. In 1976, the magazine characterised housing co-operatives as a poisoned chalice for the tenants' movement: 'This form of control means that tenants or tenants associations have to be prepared to put in an enormous amount of time and effort to get what they want. Often this may be out of all proportion to the real gains.' *Community Action* argued that there were 'real dangers' in the way the government and local authorities were 'pushing their brand of tenant control'.[63]

An editorial of 1977 – titled 'Tenant Co-ops – a Diversion' – asserted that central government was 'pushing tenant Co-ops' to pass the burden of maintenance responsibility onto tenants, and to make savings from doing so. *Community Action* insisted that 'tenant coops enable the government and councils to be seen to be doing something about some aspects of tenant control for a few tenants while avoiding doing anything substantial on the same issues for all tenants'. They argued that co-operative initiatives were an inadequate and distracting olive branch in the context of a broader 'attack on council housing' by central government, which was cutting funding, raising rents, and moving to sell off public housing stock elsewhere.[64]

Community Action's stance was controversial. It split the journal's editorial team and its readership, with plenty penning letters in response. Many came from disgruntled co-operative members who defended their achievements in expanding the frontiers of tenant control and delivering higher living standards. Other readers were dubious. One letter-writer pointed out that on 'the GLC-owned estate of Stephen and Matilda in East London tenants <u>have to</u> work at least 8 hours a week on their slum property. Rather than fulfilling a need this seems to be exploiting it.'[65]

Similar concerns had been raised in a study into tenant participation schemes by the Association of London Housing Estates in 1975.[66] During consultation by Harold Campbell's working party, some members of the association had felt that 'tenant management schemes are being pushed by management so that it can offload a number of onerous tasks which it no longer wants to handle'.[67] Members inside Stephen and Matilda also had qualms. Mark Phillips insisted, in a review of tenant co-operative action in Tower Hamlets, that co-operative housing and tenant participation represented vital steps forward for public policy. He also warned, however, that the co-operative housing method could easily become a smokescreen for 'tenant co-option' – 'letting the council off the hook' while exploiting residents' labour.[68]

Files in the National Archives reveal that these critics were onto something. The Department of the Environment was advised in 1976 that the prime minister, James Callaghan, was keen on tenant participation as a low-cost initiative with popular appeal:

> The Prime Minister said that the constraints on Government action imposed by the public expenditure situation meant that it was important to act positively in ways which did not involve Government money, such as the encouragement of tenant participation in the management of council estates.[69]

The department's Social Research Division fed back some similar 'tentative recommendations' from its fieldwork on the inner cities programme in 1976, in response to the question: 'Difficult to let estates: What can be done cheaply in the short term?' Halfway through examining deteriorating conditions on twenty-five 'unpopular housing estates', the division recommended that an overture of 'consultation' could be a cost-effective solution. Some local authorities were experimenting with different systems of lettings – 'bringing in alternative tenants, using selective letting, more transfers being offered' – but such options were ultimately contingent upon better council housing being available. Tenant participation in management provided a way to 'engage often hidden strengths among residents' and to deal 'cheaply' with existing issues. 'More consultation will mean better guidance for maintenance priorities', presenting the government with an opportunity for an 'offsetting saving'.[70]

Municipal finance had been shrinking for several years. The Housing Subsidies Act 1967 reined back capital grants for local authority housing in the face of devaluation. The Housing Finance Act 1972 curtailed local authority spending and the Housing Act 1974 diverted subsidies to housing associations. Stringent domestic cuts were stipulated as a condition of the International Monetary Fund's loan to Britain in 1976. In other ways, however, municipal responsibilities were being expanded as the decade pushed on, with new statutory obligations to extend security of tenure and to provide accommodation for the homeless. Support for co-operatives from both central government and the GLC was underpinned by the aspiration that they could offer a low-cost policy pathway to decelerate dereliction and social atomisation on housing estates in tandem, by devolving management responsibility and strengthening community feeling among residents. Tony Judge hoped:

> Through on-the-spot management and maintenance by the resident tenants and the utilisation of individual talents which in the conventional context would lie dormant, some financial surpluses may accrue to the housing co-operative at the end of a financial year which the co-operative could then put to a good housing use on their own estate.

Stephen and Matilda was specifically identified as an example to 'keenly watch', with this in mind.[71]

This approach to tenant self-help prefigured how voices on the right sought to invoke the principles of co-operative housing. As leader of the opposition, Margaret Thatcher opened the Tally-Ho Co-operative in her Finchley constituency in 1977. She told its residents: 'Some people in life are spectators and some are doers. You are the doers. It's no good shunting the buck to Government. That's no good for Government and that's no good for the people.'[72] Hugh Rossi, the Conservative spokesperson for housing in the late 1970s, thought that housing co-operatives had 'a great deal to offer'. The Conservative Party proposed that 'housing co-operatives can provide an important stage along the path of full home ownership . . . for that reason alone, the problems and progress of housing co-operatives will receive the next Conservative Government's close attention'.[73]

The Conservative GLC administration of 1977–81 took the same line. George Tremlett, the new leader of the Housing Policy Committee, wanted to reconfigure the council's approach to housing. 'Our country's housing policy these past sixty years has been a total failure,' he proclaimed in his book-cum-manifesto *Living Cities* (1979). The issue at the heart of this failure, for Tremlett, was a dearth of owner-occupation. He argued that the Labour Party's pursuit of 'state ownership of housing for its own sake' (which Tremlett proposed was predicated upon a desire to shore up their electoral base) had created a 'political tragedy' in Britain.[74]

Horace Cutler, the Conservative leader of the GLC, concurred, declaring municipal ownership a 'dictatorship'.[75] Tremlett wanted to 'ease the municipal stranglehold' on London. Housing co-operatives offered a promising route by which – alongside the sale of council houses and homesteading schemes – local government could go about 'reducing the direct involvement of bureaucracy to harness the energies of individual citizens'. He was most interested in equity-sharing schemes and community leasehold developments (forms of co-operative housing in which residents own an equity stake which they can sell) as stepping-stones to owner-occupation. Tremlett supported co-operatives as a short-term option for young people who could not yet afford a mortgage, before becoming owner-occupiers later in life.[76]

Figures on all political sides scrabbled to claim Stephen and Matilda. The new Conservative council was eager to frame the initiative within the lines of its own political stencil. George Tremlett gave the keynote speech at Stephen and Matilda's opening ceremony and presented the co-operative with a framed photograph of Matilda House to mark the occasion. He issued a statement via press release:

> This is a landmark in housing – both in London and the country as a whole. It is a tribute to everyone involved in the project that London has once again pioneered new, exciting possibilities in the housing field . . . The housing co-operative movement has a vital role to play in helping to solve people's housing problems.[77]

The Stephen and Matilda Tenants' Co-operative took pains to distinguish its approach from that of the Conservative GLC, which had made itself especially unpopular on the estate after imposing a rent hike. One newsletter issue of 1980 featured an illustrative one-line 'JOKE': 'Sir Horace Cutler'.[78] 'The GLC,' wrote Mike Jempson after the co-op's opening ceremony, 'favours co-operative housing associations, where tenants buy their estate – though Stephen and Matilda are unique because they refuse to buy theirs. They say that all housing should be in public ownership, but controlled by those who live in them.' It was only after the politicians had left the event that 'the Co-op got down to the serious business of celebrating'.[79]

The co-operative had been unequivocal from its inception:

> We must fight jointly for more housing and better housing in council ownership under tenants [sic] control . . . All council tenants have been treated as second class citizens ever since council housing has been built. They have no rights and no security of tenure; rent always go [sic] up and standards generally go down.

This was to be a 'tenants' takeover' of an area in which redevelopment plans had 'failed to consult local people'. 'We are opposed,' the co-operative affirmed, 'to the sale of council houses, to the expansion of housing associations, to equity sharing scemes [*sic*] and to the speculative redevelopment of Dockland . . . Our constitution has been specially drafted to prevent any future Tory GLC from forcing us to buy the estate.'[80] Mark Phillips summed up internal thinking neatly: the idea that 'ownership is control' was, he argued, 'a false equation'.[81]

During the Thatcher years, the newsletter at Stephen and Matilda became increasingly partisan. 'Under the threat of greater evil even old enemies like the GLC take on a benign aspect . . . Edward Heath suddenly sounds almost socialist.'[82] The co-operative hosted relatives of Irish hunger strikers in 1981. They sent funds to families involved in the 1984–85 Miners' Strike. But Stephen and Matilda was not a hotbed of radicalism. There were strident members, while others, who preferred to 'keep politics out of the Newsletter', were less ideological.[83] In the 1980s, the newsletter reflected these different elements of its membership. Local political film screenings were often advertised, but group trips to watch blockbusters were promoted just as regularly. Some members organised a street party for the 1981 royal wedding of Prince Charles and Diana Spencer. The newsletter advertised this alongside an alternative for others who were 'sick of the wedding': a Rock Against Racism concert in Clissold Park.[84]

An undeniably powerful radicalising impulse came in the form of Right to Buy. This represented the antithesis of the co-operative's founding principles. In 1980, Mark Phillips reported back from a meeting of the Tower Hamlets Federation of Tenants with foreboding: 'The "new" crisis includes the threat to council housing in the "right to buy" given by the 1980 Housing Act, and massive predicted rises in rent and rates while the building programme is completely halted, and maintenance has fallen to an all-time low.'[85] It was vital, another member affirmed, 'to ensure that this pernicious Thatcherite policy does not insinuate itself into this estate'.[86] The co-operative campaigned against the Housing Act of 1986, too. 'The purchase of a flat in Stephen & Matilda would not buy security,' argued member Cyril King: 'It would be buying into a very uncertain future.'[87] But the enormous discounts appealed to some, especially after they reached up to 70 per cent for flats. In 1988 the first handful of flats were sold. By the 1990s, many old members had moved away, and more flats passed into private ownership. Yet the co-operative soldiered on for decades more, until it was finally wound up in 2012.

The 1970s are often narrated as a moment of revival for the traditional terraced house in opposition to the twentieth-century flat. Conservative politician George Tremlett insisted that what the 'ordinary individual citizen' wanted was a 'semi-detached house with a front and back garden' – certainly not a municipal flat.[88] But Stephen and Matilda indicates that the flats-versus-houses conundrum was not necessarily at the forefront of everybody's thinking. Other practical priorities seem more salient, including dereliction, management, and control. Residential judgements on multistorey council housing were not uniform in the 1970s. For the members of this new co-operative, the St Katharine's Estate represented an opportunity for urban renewal and self-government. It was evidently less attractive to former residents who declined the offer to move back. The LCC's inter-war, walk-up estates were more cramped and draughty than post-war housing built to Parker Morris standards. Still, in Tower Hamlets demand for council housing was high. Many people were ready to make do and mend. The borough saw a wave of co-operative activity in this period, testified by the establishment of the Tower Hamlets Housing Co-ops Group, an umbrella organisation for management co-operatives like Stephen and Matilda. They formed in an array of building types, from rows of Victorian houses to multistorey estates.[89]

In 1981, a review of housing management co-operatives by Alison Matthews was published, based on research carried out in early 1979. It had been commissioned by the outgoing Department of the Environment. Matthews concluded that while the take-off of local authority co-operatives had been slow, at this foetal stage with minimal 'hard data' early conclusions could only be 'tentative'. She emphasised the benefits of tenant participation for effective urban regeneration, which the new personnel of the department would do well to instrumentalise in their Priority Estates Project.[90] The Thatcher administration took an interest in tenant co-operatives in a different form, backing the establishment of housing co-operatives that transferred council property completely out of the hands of local authorities. The new department pitched the co-operative model as 'a useful weapon in the armoury of council tenants against a recalcitrant local authority'.[91]

Co-operative housing served a minority of Britain's council tenants. Movement towards tenant participation from the Labour-directed Department of the Environment in the late 1970s was inconsistent across public-sector housing more broadly. By the end of the decade, appeals for tenant control remained fierce and warranted. Widespread dissatisfaction with the poor maintenance of council estates – particularly those with ageing, multistorey blocks – was snowballing. Equally, Stephen and Matilda tells us that the late 1970s were a period in which creative new ideas for improved council housing models were emerging in Britain. A spectrum of housing possibilities created diversification beyond the two-tier system of private-versus-municipal control. On the co-operative's tenth anniversary, *SoMeTIMES* reflected upon what it had achieved:

This weekend sees the first of many celebrations of Stephen and Matilda's Tenth Anniversary . . . So what have we got to celebrate? Well agreed there are several issues . . . The main thing is though, we do have the power to change things. No-where else, as a GLC or Tower Hamlets tenant, does anyone have the opportunity to take part in the running of the estate they live on in the same way we do so don't knock it . . . So maybe we should indulge ourselves a little. Despite all the problems of learning to live in what amounts to a totally different way, the Coop is still going.[92]

The members of Stephen and Matilda proposed a vision of public ownership that was truly public. Power was entrusted at the grassroots, not monopolised by a distant state. It worked, too. A visitor to the much-loved St Katharine's Estate today would never guess that it had once been condemned to dereliction. You are welcomed at its entrance by a blue heritage plaque. It memorialises the Stephen and Matilda Tenants' Co-operative: a pioneering example of 'Homes for People not Profit'.

5

The National Tower Blocks Network

Nationwide, 1981–93

The architect Sam Webb remembered the day of the Ronan Point disaster for the rest of his life. As a young man on the morning of 16 May 1968, he had just arrived at work in the Camden Borough Architects' Department:

> About half past ten it all started to change. An architect, back from a site visit, passed me on the stairs. In his hands, which he held up, were copies of the *Evening Standard* and the *Evening News* . . . At the time, I was reminded of those old Hulton Press pictures of paperboys proclaiming the sinking of the Titanic, the Wall Street Crash or the Outbreak of War. Each carried banner headlines. 'Why? Why? Why?' proclaimed the *Evening Standard*, 'Tower of Terror' screamed the *Evening News*. 'Look at this!' he shouted.[1]

The office was headed by Sydney Cook, Camden's borough architect from 1965 to 1973. After the shock of Ronan Point, Cook himself swooped in with his assistants to assess the plans they had on file. The borough of Camden had only been created three years prior, and the office had inherited buildings from the old metropolitan boroughs of Hampstead, Holborn, and St Pancras, as well as others from the London County Council. They found just one large-panel-system building under their jurisdiction in Kentish Town, passed over from St Pancras.

Sam Webb was born in Finchley, to shopkeeper parents, in 1937. He studied architecture at the Northern Polytechnic in Holloway and after qualifying took up a job at Camden. This was a plum gig; Sydney Cook's team was one of the most respected in the country. They were trailblazing inventive forms of low-rise, high-density housing – an alternative to the prevailing contemporary enthusiasm for tall blocks – which were already being realised in Neave Brown's designs for Fleet Road. System building was anathema to their designer-led approach. It was no small help that Camden was also one of the richest boroughs in London, behind Westminster and the City of London.

The day of the disaster at Ronan Point, Webb remembered being told by Sylvia Bartlett, his first wife, about a construction site visit she had made to a large-panel-system scheme in Greenwich back in 1964, as a student at the Architectural Association. She had seen a load-bearing wall lowered down onto bolts to keep it in place:

> They lower it down and it won't fit on the bolts. So these men come out with these big steel chisels and hammers, and start chipping away. They lift it up, lower it down. It still won't fit. So the foreman beckons to this man, who comes out with a sledgehammer, and he bangs the bolt flat. Quick as a flash one student says, 'Excuse me, should you really be doing that?' And they are all whisked off the site, put on the bus and sent back.[2]

The calamity of 1968 shook Webb irrevocably, and he spent years trying to get to the bottom of the scandal. Immediately after the disaster, he attempted to submit evidence for cross-examination to the Griffiths Inquiry with fellow architect George Fairweather. They were unsuccessful, but Webb remained militant. He even turned up to knock on the door of the Department of the Environment in 1970, demanding to see the backlog of the inquiry's files, which he combed through for weeks.

He went on to team up with another person who had investigated Ronan Point: the journalist Paul Foot, from *Private Eye*.

Together, they contributed to the exposure of the Poulson scandal. In 1974, the architect and property developer John Poulson was found guilty of corruption and bribery of government officials to win building contracts. Edward Heath's home secretary, Reginald Maudling, was forced to resign due to his links with Poulson.

In the mid-1970s, Webb took on a teaching post at Canterbury College of Art and School of Architecture, but in his spare time he made pugnacious contributions to the architectural press. 'Why,' he raged in the *Architects' Journal* in 1975, 'do the houses of the poor always have to be substandard?'[3] He thought the profession needed to look in the mirror:

> Professionalism should have a commitment to society as a whole. Salaried architects are being pushed into the role of mental paraplegics programmed by bureaucrats, to fit like uncomplaining eunuchs into ready-made slots in (rat' [*sic*] race offices. Should architects be penalised for asking why? It seems an awful waste of seven years of education not to.[4]

Webb believed that professional hierarchies were too rigid: 'How many principals or chief officers listen to, or talk to, their staff?' With this in mind, he asked, 'Is it surprising that the gigantic and awful incomprehensive redevelopments of our profession have paid scant regard to the people who use them?'[5] 'The history of the reconstruction of Britain after the neglect of the 30s and the destruction of the war years is a stirring tale,' he argued, 'but it had a dark underside of graft and corruption.'[6]

In 1979, after a lengthy legal battle, the High Court found Taylor Woodrow-Anglian to be in breach of contract at Ronan Point. They were ordered to pay damages to the London borough of Newham to cover the cost of repairing and restrengthening the blocks on the Freemasons Estate. This was reported to be one of the most expensive pieces of High Court litigation of all time.[7]

The Ronan Point scandal refused to dissipate. Sam Webb continued to doubt the block's safety for habitation. In the early 1980s, he met members of a local tenants' group from Newham who shared his trepidations.

THE NEWHAM TOWER BLOCK TENANTS CAMPAIGN

By the early 1980s, Newham was home to over a hundred tower blocks – a proportion higher than in any other area in England.[8] In 1981, a group of high-rise residents came together after the suicide of a young mother. April Merrin took her own life jumping from the twenty-second floor of Dennison Point, at Stratford's Carpenters Estate, after being refused a transfer from a flat she reportedly described as a 'hell hole'.[9] The group was also distressed that Newham Council had announced £40,000 worth of cuts on tower block maintenance.

They decided to form a community group with the object of improving conditions for local tower block tenants, in partnership with a nearby social-action centre called Community Links. It was christened the Newham Tower Block Tenants Campaign (NTBTC). Later that year, the new group went to watch the demolition of the borough's Newtown Point and Stratford Point, which had been declared too expensive to maintain. It was here that they met Sam Webb, who had also come to see them fall.

They stayed in touch. In 1983, two tenants from 26 Ronan Point, Barry and Elaine Meakings, approached Webb to tell him about cracks they had found between the walls of their flat. They and their neighbours had grave concerns about the building's safety. Webb decided to take a term off from his job in Kent to come to Newham and conduct a survey of the building in early 1984. He inspected fifty flats, bringing along a team of students from Canterbury to assist him. Alongside them was Frances Clarke – a former tower block tenant, community worker at Community Links, and key campaigner within the NTBTC. They were joined by supportive councillors from the borough's Housing Committee: Fred Jones, Jean Reeves, and Dick Shepherd.

During the survey, residents reported that winds lifted up their carpets, their fish-tanks' waterlines were lopsided, and they could smell food cooking in flats below. This indicated a liability to wind damage and a lack of fire compartmentation, meaning that flames could spread at speed in the event of a blaze. Webb found that this was caused by structural gaps where panels were cracking, bowing, and inadequately joined.[10] Back in 1968, central government had maintained that the risk of rapid fire spread at Ronan Point was 'remote'.[11] Meanwhile, the official safety advice from Newham Council was that tenants should remain in their flats to wait out a fire, rather than evacuate. Without proper fire compartmentation, this was a disastrous strategy.

Webb presented this information to Newham Council in April 1984, with tenants threatening to march and demonstrate. The findings were damning. The council agreed to evacuate Ronan Point. The decision was met with cheers from over a hundred tenants watching in the chamber and crowded outside. Mandy Hallet, a Ronan Point resident, told the press: 'It is fantastic that we have won. The building is a death trap and I can't wait to get out.'[12] 'It's only the experts who say it's safe,' said Sue McDowell from the NTBTC, 'but they should try living here a while and they'll see just how safe it is . . . every night, if you go into any one of those blocks, you will hear groaning and grinding and sharp cracking noises as the building moves.'[13]

The NTBTC invited George Young, parliamentary under-secretary for the environment, to visit the Freemasons Estate. The Department of the Environment accepted the invitation, but Young was warned that the tenants were 'restive and vociferous'.[14] The NTBTC took him to the top of a block, stressing that living in a high flat was 'both socially and psychologically different from living in a house', listing issues around community cohesion, isolation, depression, and a lack of play facilities. They urged him to replace such flats 'with a more socially acceptable and solidly built form of housing'.[15]

Meanwhile, tenants in the other eight blocks on the Freemasons Estate threatened a rent strike unless they were moved. In October 1984, Newham Council agreed to evacuate them all. This came as a relief to the great majority of people on the estate, but not to all. When Hugh Muir from the *Newham Recorder* asked around the blocks a month after the vote, he found some tenants downcast. Minnie Marshall, a widow in her eighties, had been moved to Dodson Point when her old house in Custom House was demolished thirteen years before. 'The thought of having to leave has been making me depressed,' she said. 'All I want to do is cry. I just hope they will move me near my friends.' Robert Stone from Bauckham Point asked: 'What other places will they be able to give us with rooms as big as ours? If anyone can find a better place to live in I would be surprised.'[16]

The NTBTC claimed a 'massive government cover-up' over the faults at Ronan Point.[17] Webb had found, during his visit to the

Sam Webb on the roof of Ronan Point, after surveying its defects.

131

Department of the Environment to look at the inquiry's files in 1970, that early drafts of the report had included warnings about wind damage, fire, and load-bearing capacity that were excised from the final publication. In autumn 1984, he recounted this to Charles Knevitt, *The Times*'s architecture correspondent, with the intention of pressuring the government to release the documents to the public. The story made the front page.[18]

The minister for housing, Ian Gow, denied Webb's accusations when questioned in Parliament. One letter accessible at the National Archives – from Hugh Griffiths to Anthony Greenwood from October 1968 – does, however, testify that the tribunal had 'deliberately not referred' to the issue of wind loading in the final report 'to avoid undue public anxiety', even though they knew it was a matter of 'general importance' to the building sector.[19] The government eventually conceded to release the files to the public before the thirty-year rule. When it did, over half of the documents Webb reported having seen in 1970 were missing.[20] The NTBTC called for the inquiry to be re-opened. Hugh Griffiths remained indignant: 'The standards of both workmanship and supervision have been painstakingly investigated. It is no exaggeration to say that the building has been put under the microscope.'[21]

Sam Webb's tireless campaign to expose the Ronan Point scandal put his own career on the line. He received rebuffs and personal attacks. When he applied to the RIBA for a research grant to help fund his investigation in early 1984, he was rejected. After he completed his survey, the *Architects' Journal* published an editorial lambasting Webb for endangering 'the reputation of professional competence'.[22] 'History will judge your role in this affair,' he responded.[23] Paul Finch, the editor of *Building Design* (to which Webb had long been a contributor), weighed in:

Over the years, his obsessive quest for the Holy Grail of a unifying explanation for the events surrounding the tower block collapse became sometimes exasperating, sometimes incredible. But who can say that he has been wrong? The triumphant vindication of all those years of investigating, arguing and documenting is only now emerging . . . In the eyes of the building industry, Sam Webb is an embarrassment. He won't go away and he continues to point a finger.[24]

The estimated cost of refurbishing Ronan Point was over £3 million. Newham Council concluded that the 'most economic method in the circumstances' was to demolish the block: 'Officers could not recommend utilising public funds on this scale merely to bring unsatisfactory housing back into use.'[25] Newham's Housing Committee decided to have Ronan Point 'scientifically dismantled' to assess its structure.[26] When this was performed, in 1986, horrifying internal defects were uncovered. Steel bars and tie straps had been incorrectly positioned. The building's joints were packed with old cement bags, newspaper, cigarette packets, and even a tin of corned beef. The weight of the block's panels was loaded precariously on its H2 bolts, rather than the dry-pack mortar that should have been filled around them for support. The exposed bolts had been corroded by rainwater, causing the concrete panels to crack. Scandalously, one of the pieces of newspaper found in the joints was dated 9 September 1972. It had been packed during the council's 'strengthening' measures – *after* the original disaster.[27] Sam Webb saved fragments from the forensic demolition to be deposited at the RIBA, exemplifying the major structural defaults uncovered. At last, years of concern had been vindicated. Webb told the world: 'This has purely confirmed our fears.'[28]

In 1988, Webb gave a lecture at the RIBA on his investigation at Ronan Point, titled 'People in High Places'. Over two hours, to a room packed with architects, he laid out evidence gathered over successive years. The story he recounted was shocking. But, he insisted, council housing could be better than this. Webb compared system-built high-rise with the work of the architect Bill Forrest, his former colleague at Camden, who worked on the final stage of Highgate New Town with co-designer Oscar Palacio. This was Dartmouth Park Hill: a triangular site of postmodern terraces and three-storey flats in polychrome brick, finished in 1981. Though diminutive in scale, they still packed a solid density. Ronan Point represented a missed opportunity. 'Local authority housing doesn't have to be like that,' Webb affirmed.[29]

Sue McDowell, a tenant and leading campaigner in Newham, joined him at the RIBA. At the end of the lecture, Webb invited her to speak. She turned to the professionals in the room and spoke loudly and clearly:

> The thing that's happening to Ronan Point's sister blocks is that Newham Council are considering putting the homeless in them. And they're not considering putting the homeless in them because they want to. Because there are a lot of those members of council that fought like we did, for a whole year, seven days a week, for that complete year. The reason they're thinking about putting them in is because Newham has a large housing homeless list. And there is nowhere for those homeless people to go except bed and breakfast. And the council have to make a decision between putting them in TWA [Taylor Woodrow-Anglian blocks], which they know are structurally unsound, or putting them in bed and breakfasts and using much needed finances. So I'd like people to realise that it isn't because Newham Council want to, it's because Newham Council – like a lot of local authorities, like a lot of public sector housing – it's being starved of finances by central government because the idea is: let's break it up and sell it off.

McDowell urged the room to listen to the inhabitants of these blocks across the country. 'Please do not forget,' she told them, 'there's a hell of a lot more tenants out there, now!'[30]

VICTORY FOR TENANTS?

The Newham Tower Block Tenants Campaign was a crusade for 'fairer social housing solutions'.[31] The NTBTC called for a 'fair transfer system' so that tower block tenants in need could move to safer council housing. 'Reasonable rent and rates' needed to be guaranteed, they insisted, and state funding for housing needed to increase.[32] As *Community Action* noted in a 1982 special feature on the NTBTC: 'In order for everyone who should not be in a tower block to get out Newham needs a lot more council houses. Newham's building has been disastrously affected by cuts in the housing allocation policies of central government.'[33]

Council housing was much needed in Newham, where many people were not in a position to buy a home. In 1983, eighty-six new houses originally built for sale in the council's 'Young Married Couples Save and Buy Scheme' had to be retained as council housing: 'Even before completion it was clear from similar developments around the borough remaining unsold that the people for whom they were intended could no longer afford them,' the council reported. Fred Jones, as the chair of Newham's Housing Committee, explained that local people often 'cannot risk embarking on a 25-year mortgage when many could not be sure of having a job for that many weeks to begin paying it'. He added,

> Not only has the Government removed 2,000 houses from our stock under the Right to Buy scheme but now controls, through the London Dockland Development Corporation, land intended for a large number of houses for rent, but which is now being developed for private housing.[34]

The NTBTC wanted to ensure that '*ALL* tenants of system built and tower block housing are supported'.[35] They lobbied for the improvement of whole blocks on shared issues including rent, repairs, transfer arrangements, communal heating systems, insect infestations, lift breakdowns, soundproofing, and janitor services. They went from estate to estate in an old London bus, which had been revamped by Community Links, kitted out with a mobile Tower Blocks Exhibition. The campaign was pushing for more democratic management. Members set up public meetings,

The Community Links bus on the Brooks Estate, just before the NTBTC was founded.

tenant-elected committees, and open-access community flats for discussion and advice. They ran a bulk-buying food club, bingo, and summer play-schemes.

The NTBTC garnered support from the Greater London Council. The GLC awarded the group several thousand pounds of grant funding to pay the salary of a campaign worker, Mandy Wilson, from 1982 to 1985.[36] Ken Livingstone's left-wing administration (in power from 1981 until the GLC's abolition in 1986) was seeking to move away from the traditionally paternalistic approach to political decision-making of 'Old Labour'. The Livingstone administration came to power on a manifesto promising an 'extension of democratic control', in part via a major grant-giving programme to strengthen the power of community groups.[37]

The plight of mothers and children in tower blocks was a particular point of emphasis in the NTBTC's campaigning. Indeed, the group was dominated by female tenants. They were especially distressed by the death of David Cash, a four-year-old boy who fell from the balcony of Abraham Point in 1983. When George Young, the minister for housing, came to Ronan Point in 1984, he concurred that 'living near the top of a tower block is just no environment for a family'.[38] Although the post-war high-rise boom had been predicated on the understanding that these homes would not be let to families with young children, this often became unworkable for local authorities with long housing waiting lists. The Labour government's Housing (Homeless Persons) Act of 1977 required councils to prioritise rapidly rehousing vulnerable groups to tackle homelessness. With families, pregnant women, and single parents ranked as urgent cases, many were ambulanced to vacant high-rise flats.

A Ronan Point Dismantling Party was organised by the NTBTC in 1986. Invites were sent out to local residents, and television crews attended to broadcast the event as far as Australia. Children were pictured cheering with balloons and hard hats on the front page of the *Newham News*:

> The reasons why didn't matter to these children – all they knew was that Ronan Point was coming down and that was a good reason for a celebration. In the bright sunlight they cheered themselves hoarse! . . . Tower block campaigners passed round the bubbly and tied a ribbon around the block – their last rites on an unmourned edifice.[39]

A celebratory banner was hung across the block, declaring 'VICTORY FOR TENANTS!' Sam Webb interpreted the demolition of Ronan Point as a victory for ordinary people against the right, declaring that the NTBTC had 'defeated the might of Thatcher in the middle of the Miners [sic] Strike'.[40]

But this was a pyrrhic victory. The evacuation of the Freemasons Estate sent 'record numbers' of people into bed-and-breakfast accommodation in Newham.[41] The council – already encumbered with a sizeable waiting list – now had to rehouse the 3,000 people who had previously lived on the estate. Community

Links, partner to the Newham Tower Block Tenants Campaign, set up a No Home Campaign to assist tenants who were stuck on the waiting list and offered advice sessions to people staying in bed and breakfasts.

Newham Council could not afford to demolish the remaining eight blocks until they signed a contract with Barratt in 1991. Barratt announced that they would replace the estate with 388 low-rise houses and apartments, creating a new neighbourhood named Admiral's Reach. But just a hundred homes were slated for rent or shared ownership, to the dismay of the chair of Newham's Housing Committee, Councillor John Isted.[42] The Freemasons Estate was duly demolished. Its concrete remains were crushed to hardcore and used to extend the runway of the nearby London City Airport.

'Residents wanted "proper" houses, with their own gardens and their own front doors,' reported *The Times*. 'They were almost unanimous in wanting the remaining seven glowering tower blocks removed.'[43] Yet when Sarah Boseley from the

Campaigners take down the Ronan Point sign, in advance of its dismantling, on 16 May 1986.

Guardian went to investigate views in the area, many expressed strong reservations about the direction of change. 'Local people,' she reported, 'are less than thrilled at the removal of the eyesores. Yes, they want the blocks to go, but what is there in the redevelopment for *them*?'[44] A residents' group attempted to contest Barratt's bid to the council with their own proposal for the area, with suggestions for an under-fives centre, more streetlights, and a police station. They were unsuccessful. 'These Barratt homes are as unsuitable as the tower blocks they replace,' said Renee Heath, from the residents' group. Campaigners from the National Tower Blocks Network were similarly frustrated:

> Local people are unhappy with several aspects of the Barratt plan and for many history has repeated itself. In the 1960s local people living in the Clearance Area campaigned against the building of the nine 22-story [*sic*] blocks. Their fears, ignored at the time, proved correct.[45]

The housing eventually constructed at Admiral's Reach by 1993 comprised 320 Regency-style homes.[46] These were two-storeyed terraces in brick, with pitched roofs, canopied porches, string courses, and hanging wall lanterns. The end of each terraced row was punctuated by a slightly larger property, faced with plasterwork to create the effect of rusticated stone and a crowning open pediment. The overall effect was fussy and unconvincing, not least on account of the uPVC casement windows. A reasonable effort was made with the detailing, but the proportions were decidedly mean. Many of the new houses were just one and a half bays wide: a cramped fob-off of the Regency mansions they purported to recreate.

One hundred of these homes were marketed for sale and 220 were reserved for housing association rent and shared ownership – a higher proportion than first pledged. Nevertheless, this was a site that had originally housed almost a thousand council units, and rents for the new housing association properties were set above council levels. The *Guardian* responded to the opening of Admiral's Reach with a pertinent question: '25 years on [from Ronan Point] – when homelessness is a national issue – are we any further on with providing a solution to badly needed social housing?'[47]

GOING NATIONAL

The Newham Tower Block Tenants Campaign started small, but it soon resolved to reach a larger constituency. Its members knew that other tower block residents across Britain were facing similar problems. A National Tower Blocks Conference at East Ham's Labour Halls in October 1983 was attended by 170 people, from an array of tenants associations, local councils, universities, and social work services. The director of Shelter, Neil McIntosh, gave a speech. Workshops were led by representatives from the NTBTC, the National Heating Consultancy, the Nottingham Asbestos Campaign, and the Hackney Play Association. Sam Webb gave a session training tenants to spot structural defects in their blocks. He used a homemade wooden model to illustrate the faulty operation of joints in large-panel-system buildings. 'So,' he explained, 'when some pompous engineer or housing officer came and told them how their home was as safe as houses they would innocently ask if he knew how the V3 joint was put together. That took the wind out of his sails.'[48]

Out of this conference the National Tower Blocks Network was formed: an extension operation of the Newham Campaign to build a coalition of high-rise tenants across the country. Frances Clarke was the network's information officer and Sam Webb acted as architectural advisor. 'Through joint work with [nationwide] groups,' hoped Clarke, 'we may be able to exert more pressure.'[49] The network intended to help fellow tower block residents 'tackle the problems of their estate armed with some knowledge about what has and has not worked elsewhere'.[50] By the 1990s, the National Tower Blocks Network employed three workers based between London and Sheffield – Frances Clarke, Mandy Wilson, and Sara Gowen – and encompassed a web of tenant campaigners. They won funding from the Department of the Environment and Shelter.

The network published a regular National Tower Blocks bulletin, titled the *View*, with updates about local campaigning in different cities. It put together National Tower Block Directories, with the contact details of council housing departments, housing associations, architects, tenants associations, youth clubs, social-action groups, legal advice services, and government units. These also included glossaries – explaining the meanings of terms such as 'slip-form', 'no fines', and 'reinforced concrete' – to help tenants navigate the minefield of technical construction language. The directories publicised the many shocking problems tower block tenants were facing nationwide. Some physical issues were structural. Many others were the result of flagging upkeep by struggling, under-funded councils. There were also social complaints about

Sam Webb gives a workshop to tenants at the National Tower Blocks Conference alongside Frances Clarke.

children being isolated in unsuitable high flats, sorely lacking community facilities, and racist harassment.

The picture presented by the network was not uniformly negative, however. It fed back rousing stories of successful tenant action to secure playgrounds, community rooms, art schemes, caretakers, entry phones, and transfers for young families to homes on the ground. One example was the Dragon Garden at the Pepys Estate in Deptford, where the community re-landscaped their central yard into the shape of a three-dimensional sculpted dragon decorated with mosaics, for children's play, with a tunnel, bridges, slides, and seating.

One National Tower Blocks Directory of 1987 reported on the progress made by the Kennishead Tenants' Management Co-operative in Glasgow. This initiative operated much like Stephen and Matilda, in this case on an estate consisting of five twenty-two-storey tower blocks and five blocks of maisonettes. Kennishead's flats had been difficult to let due to poor maintenance and the prevalence of anti-social behaviour from disaffected residents. The co-operative managed to turn things around by taking control of lettings and repairs, setting up an elected management committee, and organising stimulating activities. Hundreds of tenants began attending regular public meetings. The estate's countless void flats filled up, and this formerly unpopular address soon had a waiting list of people hoping to move in.

In the light of the revelations in Newham, structural defects figured as a central concern for the National Tower Blocks Network. 'Heads will roll over this,' warned Sam Webb after Ronan Point's evacuation, 'the tower block campaign is just beginning.'[51] The network was keen to make contact with tenants in other Larsen-Nielsen blocks. Taylor Woodrow-Anglian had used the Larsen-Nielsen system to build 7,951 dwellings in Britain from 1964 to 1979 – comprising thirty-six blocks and roughly 5,000 flats – and several other firms had used similar techniques.[52] The network's ally Charles Knevitt estimated in The Times that 40,000 flats needed surveying.[53]

The network identified unsafe multistorey Larsen-Nielsen blocks on a number of estates: Morris Walk in Woolwich; the Gascoyne Estate in Hackney; the Aintree Estate in Fulham; the St Matthew's Estate in Brixton; the Argyle Estate in Putney; the Jefferson Estate in Bow; the Barkantine Estate and the Barley Mow Estate in Poplar; the Ledbury Estate in Southwark; the Lisson Green Estate in Westminster; and the Ocean Estate in Stepney.[54] The network also found large-panel-system Camus blocks in Hackney and Reema blocks in Glasgow that had not been properly strengthened.[55]

In Nottingham, the Basford Flats Tenants Association was whistleblowing about the shoddy construction of eighteen seven-storey blocks and four twenty-storey towers on their estate, built with the Bison Wall Frame system. They regarded demolition as the 'inevitable conclusion'. The Bison system had been used by dozens of other local authorities. The Basford Flats Tenants Association amassed evidence of insecure wall panels, patchy insulation, leaks, spalling concrete, and gaps compromising heating and fire compartmentation across Bison housing in Manchester, Sedgefield, Hillingdon, Wolverhampton, Rugby, and Kidderminster. The damp, cold, and mould in these buildings posed real health risks, as a local doctor in Nottingham confirmed: 'It is in my opinion that after 7 years practice in the Old Basford area, that we do get a considerably greater number of respiratory problems from patients of all ages in the Basford Flats Complex.'[56]

The Nottingham campaign escalated to form the National Association of Bison Tenants, which in 1983 launched a Bison Charter demanding: first, that 'all Bison flats should be demolished unless all their major problems were dealt with'; and second, that 'central government must provide extra cash for this national scandal and the money to provide new homes'.[57] They were natural allies of the National Tower Blocks Network. A Scottish Association of Bison Tenants was established too, as the system had been used extensively there. In 1984, the groups coordinated a week of protest action during which tenants toured Bison estates across the country in a Bisonmobile bus, setting off in Scotland and ending in London. It carried a travelling exhibition, and distributed posters and leaflets.

'It should not be left to tenants groups to make councils act quickly,' Frances Clarke insisted. 'This is a serious national problem needing a serious national response.'[58] The network demanded that central government disclose the details of historic measures to strengthen and remove gas from other system-built tall blocks after the inquiry's recommendations. By this point, their campaign had a significant national profile – and with it, increased leverage. The Department of the Environment was initially reluctant to respond. Privately, officials commented that 'it would be a misuse of our exceptionally tight staff resources' to go through old files.[59] Moreover, 'there could certainly be embarrassment for the Government and its predecessors if any of the recommendations were not followed up and no creditable reason can be given'.[60] They realised that one recommendation – to review regulations on the storage of explosive fuels and materials in high flats – had been entirely 'overlooked'.[61]

Facing blistering coverage and political pressure in the national press after the Ronan Point revelations, Minister for Housing Ian Gow was ultimately forced to admit that the former Ministry of Housing and Local Government had never required local authorities to feed back on their progress to central government after their initial appraisals, because the 'Ministry did not regard it as its responsibility to see that appropriate action had been taken on each building'.[62] As a result, the department lacked records of specific measures taken. Gow consequently ordered the urgent appraisal of all Taylor Woodrow-Anglian buildings over fourteen storeys across the country in 1985. In 1987, the Building Research Establishment published updated guidance, recommending that local authorities reassess all large-panel-system blocks expected to exceed twenty-five years of service life, subjecting them to a 'full appraisal for structural safety and durability'. They advised that this be repeated at twenty-year intervals in the future.[63]

In the years that followed, the network became increasingly concerned about high-rise fire safety alongside the risk of progressive collapse. It launched a tenant-led spot survey in 1990, assessing seven blocks across Sheffield, Salford, Redbridge, Tower Hamlets, and Wandsworth, and collating reports from more than thirty tenants associations. 'The results,' reported the *View*, 'read like a catalogue of potential disasters.' Each of the buildings surveyed 'failed to meet either the Building Regulations or the British Standards Codes of Practice which refer to tower blocks'.[64] The British Standards Codes of Practice required tower block flats to be capable of containing a fire for an hour, so that it might be more easily extinguished before spreading to other units. The large-panel-system blocks' vulnerability to cracks compromised containment, as demonstrated during a fire test at Ronan Point in 1984, which was aborted within minutes. A host of other fire-related issues were identified: gas leaks, broken fire doors, inadequate escape routes, flammable materials, failing dry risers, and rubbish in stairways. The network feared that over half of Britain's tower blocks could be a fire hazard, and appealed for national action on high-rise fire safety with the backing of the Fire Brigade Union.[65]

At the end of the 1980s, some local authorities started to protect tower blocks from water ingress and heat loss by wrapping them in cladding. This also served a cosmetic purpose, making these stigmatised blocks more aesthetically palatable to passers-by. The network voiced prescient warnings about the dangers of cladding for fire safety.

The *View* reported on a fire at a Merseyside high-rise building in April 1991. Knowsley Heights was the area's showpiece tower block: a recent cladding refurbishment had been completed to minimise its energy consumption. When arsonists started a fire in a bin at its base, the consequences of this renovation proved disastrous. The cladding, assumed to be incombustible, melted quickly – revealing a blunder in industry safety regulations. The local fire brigade testified that the vertical cavity between the cladding and the walls had 'acted like a flue' in a chimney, causing the fire to spread at speed. Hot gas was released as the cladding melted and rose up, uncontained. One firefighter at the scene described it as 'the most frightening thing any of us had ever seen as firefighters. Flames were coming from every window between the ground floor and the roof.'[66]

The new Capex cladding used at Knowsley Heights had been approved by the Department of the Environment and the Building Research Establishment. The department had permitted the omission of vertical fire breaks during refurbishment in order to tackle damp and condensation; more ventilation was expected to make the block more energy efficient. Here was a forewarning of the catastrophic repercussions of poorly regulated over-cladding that became tragically clear at Grenfell Tower in 2017.

BLOW UP

The National Tower Blocks Network demanded that 'structurally unsound and socially unacceptable' blocks be demolished and that substantial spending should be allocated to 'radically improve those that remain'.[67] The 1980s and 1990s saw the demolition of a raft of the country's high-rise housing stock – most notably in Birmingham, Hackney, Glasgow, Liverpool, and Manchester. Tenant demolition parties became a popular weekend event, with careful choreographing for the media's cameras, advertisements in local papers, and chairs set out for spectators. A tenant or child was often invited to press the detonation button. This came as a relief for many people living in system-built blocks, including the Yorkshire Development Tenants Action Group, which had battled against damp and mouldy industrialised schemes across Hull, Leeds, Nottingham, and Sheffield. They used a trademark cartoon to celebrate demolitions in the North East: it proclaimed, 'We've won!' alongside a drawing of a hefty bomb.

However, a portion of the blocks demolished in this wave did not have major structural faults, such as the twenty-seven blocks

The front cover of *High and Dry* (1983), a handbook produced by Yorkshire Development Tenants Action Group.

of the Killingworth Towers complex in North Tyneside, which was razed to the ground in 1987. Demolition ceremonies did not always go according to plan in these circumstances. When North aird Point at the Trowbridge Estate in Hackney was detonated in 1985, the block failed to tumble to the ground. It was not so structurally unsound after all. A study financed by the Rowntree Trust proposed in 1985 that two-thirds of Britain's tower blocks were still 'sound and successful with a long life expectancy'. This study saw demolition as the product of management failure above all.[68]

Ronan Point generated a lengthy and incendiary scandal that took on a range of political meanings. Sam Webb reflected that 'it wasn't just a building. It was like a totem pole or a flagstaff in a mediaeval battle that you fought around.'[69] Ronan Point's demolition – and the others it pre-empted elsewhere – had complex ripples. Although campaigning tenants had hoped to secure better council housing, high-rise demolition ceremonies could easily provide 'ammunition for enemies of state provision', to borrow the words of Daniel Stedman Jones, a historian of the New Right.[70]

This gave credence to the Thatcher administration's mission to convert the British populace into home-owners, an ambition predicated on the annihilation of the council estate. The Right to Buy programme, initiated by the Housing Act of 1980, sold 1.3 million council homes at huge discounts in its first decade.[71] The New Right argued that they were creating a 'property-owning democracy', a mechanism for self-determination that was mooted as a foil to the welfarist state planning that had proved so often to be undemocratic and ineffectual. Yet this policy emerged as one among many contemporary propositions for democratisation for council tenants.

'Privatisation of whole council estates,' warned *Community Action* in 1984, 'is the new threat facing council tenants in some London boroughs in response to their campaigns for repairs, renovation or asbestos removal.'[72] High-rise estates were unlikely to be privatised from the inside, flat by flat. By 1987, flats made up just 5 per cent of sales under Right to Buy; building societies were resistant to lending mortgages on units in large, flatted blocks dominated by council lettings, citing the complications of divvying up maintenance obligations and service charges.[73] But local authorities could hand over estates and the often valuable sites on which they stood to property developers wholesale.

The National Tower Blocks Network called for tower blocks to be replaced with conventional homes, preferably with gardens, to which tenancies could be transferred, but it proved difficult to secure state funding for this pathway. Capital spending for the construction of new council housing was drastically restricted by the Thatcher government from the early 1980s onwards. Campaigns to demolish blocks at the Niddrie House Estate in Edinburgh and the Worsley Mesnes Estate in Wigan, by tenants allied with the National Tower Blocks Network, culminated in outcomes that mirrored the redevelopment of the Freemasons Estate: with bids for public funding rejected, private-sector partners moved in to develop these sites with housing for sale.

THINKING BEYOND DEMOLITION

In 1985, the geographer and housing researcher Alice Coleman, based at King's College London, published a book titled *Utopia on Trial: Vision and Reality in Planned Housing*. In it, she denounced the 'brave new Utopia' of the post-war, high-rise council estate as 'essentially a device for treating people like children, first by denying them the right to choose their own kind of housing and then by choosing for them disastrous designs that create a needless sense of social failure'. The answer, she argued, was to 'return housing initiatives to the free market, with minimum regulation and maximum consumer choice so that architects, builders and developers can become responsive to residents' needs'.[74] Unsurprisingly, Coleman's thesis was much admired by Margaret Thatcher, who appointed her as an advisor to the Department of the Environment.

But consumer choice was not a panacea. For residents grappling with structural issues on the Ocean Estate – a large post-war council estate in Stepney, within the London borough of Tower Hamlets – the free market did not offer an attractive alternative. The National Tower Blocks Network was allied with the Ocean Estate Tenants Association: this was one of the estates the network had identified as at risk of a Ronan Point–style collapse. Tenants at the Ocean Estate were enraged by these structural faults, but they called for their homes to be repaired, rather than demolished.

The Ocean Estate comprised almost 2,000 homes. The estate had a variety of multistorey blocks built at various points between 1948 and 1984, all named after seas and bays. It had three ten-storey and four eight-storey blocks. Other blocks stood at six, five, three, and two storeys. The estate also had around 200 houses, but the great majority of its residents lived in flats.[75]

Concerns first emerged soon after the Ronan Point disaster in 1968. The three ten-storey blocks had been built by Taylor Woodrow-Anglian with the same large-panel system used at Ronan Point: Allonby, Channel, and Studland Houses, completed in 1966. In late 1968, the *Hackney Gazette* reported with alarm that Ocean tenants had noticed problems with their walls:

> On a clear day, you can see Ronan Point from one side of Terence Mahoney's eighth-floor flat in Ocean Estate, Stepney. On the other side of the flat there was . . . a massive crack nearly half an inch wide running right round the floor, walls and ceiling, and between the outside wall and the inside walls.[76]

Workmen were sent in by the GLC to remove the estate's gas supply. They were turned away by 120 residents, on the grounds that more rigorous structural interventions were needed. One person living in Studland House told the *East London Advertiser*: 'These flats are totally substandard, during the hot weather the walls expand and cracks form.'[77] Norman Roffey, a member of the tenants association, said to *The Times*: 'We have been led up the garden path by the G.L.C. . . . there are several things that could make a block like this collapse – a strong wind, stress, any form of explosion, or too much weight in the wrong place.'[78] The estate's tenants wanted the blocks to be properly strengthened.

Between fifty and a hundred Ocean tenants marched to County Hall to pressure Horace Cutler (chairman of the GLC's Housing Committee) into action. Tenants carried banners adorned with the phrase 'We Live in Fear'. Children had slogans stitched on their clothes. One read: 'Mummy is scared of us being under the rubble.' Protesting tenants shouted at Cutler: 'You are sentencing our children to death.'[79] 'We have talked to the tenants and tried to do all that is possible,' he responded, 'but we cannot do the impossible.

The Ocean Estate part-way through construction in 1953. Malacca House on the left, Bothnia House in the middle, Tunis House on the right.

Local children in front of Malacca House, in 1953.

We have been told by the Minister to eliminate gas risk and that is what we are doing.'[80] Cutler refused to carry out structural repair work and the matter was shelved.

Restrengthening finally began at the Ocean Estate after the revelations at Ronan Point in the 1980s. Four hundred tenants were moved out of the three affected blocks for repairs to be carried out in 1985. Cracks were also found in James, Bothnia, Tunis, and Malacca Houses (blocks of six to eight storeys), but their residents were told that there were no plans to tackle these physical problems due to 'a shortage of funds'. Tenants found this 'totally unacceptable'. They regarded the inaction a 'dereliction of [Tower Hamlets Borough Council's] duty as a landlord'.[81] In 1988, tenants put together a petition signed by fifty-four households from James House to pressure Tower Hamlets Council to carry out 'long overdue' repair work.[82] The *Docklands Recorder* printed a picture of the tenants' banner, which read: 'SAVE JAMES HOUSE NOW'. Ocean tenants challenged the leader of Tower Hamlets Council to either insure their lives for £1 million each or try living in the block himself.[83]

The stop-start nature of the estate's construction over many years meant that the Ocean Estate was home to many different building types and construction styles, making unilateral remedial work challenging. In the 1980s, maintenance issues mounted up further due to an insufficient caretakers-to-flats ratio.[84] Residents' homes were plagued by asbestos, which the Tenants Association suspected may have been used 'long after it was known to be dangerous'.[85] Stomach-churning rat infestations were reported in many blocks. Tenants at Pevensey House waited three years for the local authority to repair their leaking windows, during which time some of the frames became so rotten that panes of glass fell out, triggering a rent strike. In 1983, Dick Charlton (chair of the Ocean Estate Tenants Association) declared conditions in some of the Ocean Estate's blocks to be 'appalling' – they had become 'detrimental to the health and happiness of many of the estate's residents'. This was confirmed by a health visitor, who found that the many physical problems at the Ocean Estate had harmful repercussions for its residents. The main health complaints on the estate were respiratory and chest disorders, 'directly related in most cases to inadequate housing conditions', particularly damp and cold. Some flats were severely overcrowded, with injurious consequences for the transmission of illnesses.[86]

In the late 1980s, the Ocean Estate was designated as a concern area by the Department of the Environment's Priority Estates Project. This initiative aimed to 'find ways of tackling the problems of council estates that had become run down and difficult to let', in dialogue with tenants. In 1987, it produced a report based on three months of meetings with Ocean tenants, which covered a staggering scale and range of issues: asbestos; vermin; filth; rot; damp; lift malfunctions; poor lighting; crumbling balconies; paltry play-spaces; and central-heating failures. Tenants demanded urgent repairs to tackle these problems, but demolition was raised as a proposed solution only once across all the meetings. This suggestion was regarded as outlandish: it was recorded with a bracketed exclamation mark. After months of consultations, tenants were told to be conservative in their expectations: 'Please don't expect miracles. Improvements will take time.'[87]

In the early 1980s, Dick Charlton thought that 'in order to achieve substantial improvements to estates it will often be the case that selective demolition is the only complete answer'.[88] But Right to Buy made the Ocean Estate's residents more hesitant as time went on. In 1986, the Tenants Association's newsletter reported on the state of play with plans for four 'problem-ridden blocks' on the estate: Bengal, Bothnia, Malacca, and Tunis. Tower Hamlets Borough Council intended to renovate the first and to demolish the other three to build low-rise housing. While the association was eager to see improvement, residents were not keen on this proposal. They were worried about 'the possibility of selling off some of the new-build housing – we feel the priority should be rehousing tenants from the three affected blocks – and the number of houses to be built – only about 150 are being proposed to replace about 220 flats'.[89]

DEFENDING THE OCEAN ESTATE

The Tenants Association maintained considerable pride in their home, despite its problems. The association's printed materials were decorated with cheerful nautical imagery, drawing affectionately upon the Ocean Estate's name and the sea-themed epithets of its constituent blocks. They used a logo of a ship at sail to represent the Tenants Association, and the newsletter was called *Ocean Breeze*, accompanied by an imitation of Hokusai's nineteenth-century woodblock print *The Great Wave off Kanagawa*. *Ocean Breeze* featured a 'Letter Spray' section, surrounded by water droplets and a doodle of a boat.

'It is ironic,' noted the Tower Hamlets Federation of Tenants, 'that the greatest failing of local government in [Tower Hamlets] in 1983 is its council housing, because it is precisely council housing that is its greatest achievement.'[90] This gives us a pithy mnemonic of the dualistic feelings to which high-rise housing estates – at once a locus of agonising frustrations and dogged investments – could give rise in local communities. The erosion of council housing became a major talking point in the politics of Tower Hamlets during the 1980s.

By 1987, 10,000 households were on the borough's waiting list for housing, and a further 800 were in temporary bed-and-breakfast accommodation. 'Much of the existing housing,' reported the Tower Hamlets Federation of Tenants, 'is in bad condition and many tenants want a transfer or major improvements. However the vast majority of tenants wish to remain as council tenants.'[91] Selling off local authority housing stock in the face of this enormous waiting list seemed 'total madness'.[92]

This was a feeling shared by the Ocean Estate Tenants Association. In alliance with the Tower Hamlets Federation of Tenants, the Ocean Estate became a leading force in local campaigning to reject the imposition of a Housing Action Trust (HAT) in Tower Hamlets during the late 1980s. Housing Action Trusts were first mooted by the Thatcher government in the 1987 election (of which we will hear more in Chapter 6). They were envisaged as quangos that would take over, refurbish, and transfer run-down local authority housing stock to new forms of tenure: into the hands of owner-occupiers, private landlords, and housing associations. The Ocean Estate was identified as a key target site, along with the nearby Berner Estate, the Boundary Estate, the Holland Estate, Shadwell Gardens, and Solander Gardens.

However, the government faced concerted pushback. Surveying indicated significant resistance from residents across the selected estates.[93] The neighbourhood housing manager found 'total opposition' to the proposal of a HAT on the Ocean Estate, based on a popular petition.[94] In the summer of 1988, over a thousand Tower Hamlets tenants staged an opposition rally in Bethnal Green. The Ocean Estate Tenants Association produced a poster which stated its case in no uncertain terms: 'FLATTEN THAT H.A.T.!' The Tenants Association feared a HAT would lead to higher rents, longer waiting lists, homelessness, poorer protections, and a loss of council housing stock. The estate's newsletter set out the stakes:

The Government is considering taking over the Ocean Estate . . . Unless we make our voices heard quickly and loudly, council housing may disappear from the Ocean . . . The Trust would be run by a Board appointed by the Government. There would be several representatives from the Business Community. Even if a tenant were on the Board *there would be no local control.*[95]

The Tenants Association wanted council housing to be protected, but it also resisted big-state intrusion. It demanded 'government funding for necessary improvements'; 'retention of council control'; 'more tenant say'; and '*NO GOVERNMENT INTER-FERENCE!!*'[96] The Ocean Estate Tenants Association wanted to be subject neither to Thatcherite free marketeering nor to the old system of aloof state control, seeking instead a new compact for housing which was both publicly owned and locally controlled.

What especially angered Ocean Estate residents about the HAT proposition was the absence of a ballot or consultation. *Ocean Breeze* reported that a 'secret visit' had been made to the Ocean Estate by John Selwyn Gummer (minister for local government) in the summer of 1988 – with a front-page item titled 'Gummer Sidles Round'. 'Apparently, he was advised by accompanying Special Branch officers not to leave his car. Advice which Mr. Gummer took!'[97] This was felt to be a contradiction of the government's professed mission to extend choice. The Tower Hamlets Tenants Federation believed that central government was using the concept of choice as a 'guise': 'PRIVATISATION MEANS NO CHOICE'.[98] Dick Charlton concurred:

> The Government is also now starting to say that tenant representatives are misleading tenants, and that this is why tenants cannot have a choice. This is, of course, a very strange thing to say, as one of the main reasons why tenants and their representatives are getting angry in the first place, is because *we have no choice.*[99]

Another tenant, Michael Scorer, followed up: 'The message to the minister from tenants is clear. *Yes* we want more money, *yes* we want improvements, *yes* we want better living conditions. But *no* we won't be blackmailed and *no* you cannot intimidate the people of the East End or the Ocean.'[100]

When Minister for Housing David Trippier came to the borough's York Hall at the end of 1988, he was met by a hostile crowd. 'More than a thousand people slow hand-clapped as he defended the Government's scheme,' reported the Tower Hamlets Federation of Tenants. Three informal votes were taken of tenants present: the majority voted in opposition to a HAT. Dick Charlton was in attendance. He told the minister that 80 per cent of residents on the Ocean Estate were opposed to the proposal. Trippier insisted that opposition to the HAT programme in Tower Hamlets had 'been fuelled by irresponsible propaganda' by outspoken local groups. The Labour MP for Stepney, Peter Shore (who was also a previous secretary of state for the environment), lashed back at him: 'What Mr Trippier says about the people of Tower Hamlets not being intelligent enough to decide for themselves is insulting in a way that is truly disgraceful.' The minister was 'hissed and jeered' by tenants in the audience.[101] Afterwards, the press asked Trippier what he had gained from his visit to Tower Hamlets. 'Hopefully the George Cross,' was his reply.[102]

A week later, tenants from the Ocean Estate joined residents from other estates to 'raid' consultants at the Housing Action Trust Study Centre at South Bank House. They stormed right past the security guard into 'the battle zone', as tenant Dave Womersley regaled in *Ocean Breeze*.[103] A song was chanted:

> No we don't want your HAT, we can't afford the rent,
> You'll turn our homes to yuppy flats, we'll end up in a tent.
> Yes we want improvements, we'll take the cash for that,
> But you can stay off our estate 'cos we don't want your HAT.[104]

Within a matter of months, the Ocean Estate Tenants Association hailed 'Victory!'[105] The government officially dropped the HAT proposition for Tower Hamlets in early 1989, in the face of overwhelming opposition. This reflected a broader picture. All the first HATs proposed in Britain were either outvoted by tenants or dropped before a ballot because of prior pushback. Secretary of State for the Environment Nicholas Ridley threw up his hands: 'If they do resist it, don't blame me if they have rotten housing.'[106]

RACISM AND COUNCIL HOUSING

The Ocean Estate was a site of trenchant tenant investments in council housing. Yet these investments also had a darker edge. Residents on the Ocean Estate proclaimed that the state had a responsibility to house its citizens, but the citizenry many imagined was a racially circumscribed one: there were people on the estate who felt that council tenancies should only be offered to white British nationals. Here we have an expression of what the historian Andrew Seaton terms 'welfare nationalism'.[107]

When the Safe Neighbourhoods Unit came to survey Ocean tenants in 1983, it found racist harassment to be 'a very serious problem'. In private consultation sessions with the unit, the estate's small community of Bangladeshi tenants relayed chilling accounts of intimidation and violence from fellow residents and neighbours. 'There is a widespread feeling,' the unit recorded, 'of insecurity and anxiety amongst Bengali residents and the victims have very little confidence in the capability of the police or local authority to act effectively and promptly.' These consultees reported that they had all experienced racist abuse on the estate. They all agreed that it was not safe for their children to play outside: they had been verbally abused, spat at, and chased by dogs. Bangladeshi children were less likely to join the estate's youth clubs, for fear of being beaten up. Blocks where Bangladeshi families lived were daubed with racist slogans and offensive graffiti. Some residents had been shot at with air rifles. One tenant recounted that her father had been stabbed – an incident reported to the police, to little effect. Women spent much of their time isolated, sheltering inside their flats.[108]

During the Safe Neighbourhoods Unit's open consultation hearings with tenants across the Ocean Estate, 'it became evident that some people had a wildly exaggerated idea of the number of tenants whose place of birth had been Bangladesh or Pakistan'. In 1983, over 70 per cent of Ocean Estate residents had been born in England. It also had a proportion of African, Caribbean, Indian, Pakistani, and Bangladeshi residents. Of these ethnic-minority groups at the Ocean, Bangladeshi tenants comprised the largest, but this group still represented less than 10 per cent of the estate's total population.[109]

Tower Hamlets had a rapidly growing population of Bangladeshi residents, predominantly originating from the district of Sylhet. Some had arrived during the 1950s and early 1960s to take up their right to work in the British metropole as Commonwealth citizens (a right that was incrementally restricted in the coming years). This early cohort was almost exclusively male: economic migrants voyaging alone, finding jobs in textiles, furniture manufacturing, and hospitality, and sending remittance money back home. The 1971 War of Independence, a deadly civil conflict during which the Pakistani army and associated militias perpetrated a genocide of Bengali people in its eastern territory, impelled many of their kin to follow, hoping for family reunification and safe resettlement.

Yet Britain was a hostile environment for these migrants in many ways, not least as a place to find physical shelter. Council housing allocation in post-war Britain was plagued by institutional racism. Long-term residency regulations excluded many recent migrants. In the 1970s, applicants to the Tower Hamlets housing waiting list needed proof of five-year residency in the Greater London area and fifty-two weeks of continuous residency in the borough. In her oral history study of Bangladeshi housing justice in Tower Hamlets, the historian Shabna Begum found that residency claims were voided even for short trips back to Bangladesh.[110]

The fates of people of colour who did make it onto local authority housing lists were left to the unfavourable discretion of housing officers. Households of colour were demoted down waiting lists and successful applicants were typically relegated to the oldest and least-desirable council stock. Left to seek accommodation in the equally discriminatory private rental sector, they were condemned to the most dilapidated properties or rejected outright. Pushed out on all sides, many Bangladeshis in East London were compelled to live in squats during the 1970s.

The statutory landscape shifted towards the end of the decade. The Housing (Homeless Persons) Act (1977) placed a legal duty on local authorities to house unintentionally homeless people in priority need, and the Race Relations Act (1976) required that this be done without discrimination. This offered Bangladeshi migrants a brighter horizon. Nevertheless, the 1977 Act left housing departments the scope to shirk their obligations. Bangladeshi applicants in Tower Hamlets were often dismissed as intentionally homeless, on the grounds that they might have alternative residences back in their country of birth. By the late 1980s, Asian people were still greatly over-represented among the homeless population of Tower Hamlets. For those who did make it to the top of the waiting list, the outlook remained grim. Audits performed by the researcher Deborah Phillips in 1986 and the Commission for Racial Equality in 1988 found that Asian and Bangladeshi applicants in Tower Hamlets were being systematically allocated to the poorest-quality council housing and at consistently slower rates than white applicants – amounting, the commission concluded, to a contravention of the Race Relations Act.[111]

In spite of all this hardship, the misconception that Bangladeshis were being offered an easy route into council housing was widespread among white communities in Tower Hamlets, where the National Front had a strong presence. One person on the housing list penned a hateful letter in disgust after a handful of Bangladeshi families were allocated houses on the Ocean Estate:

> Why is it that all the Indians get all the good houses and flats like the new houses in Columbia Road? The whole row is Indians, and what do I get offered – rubbish . . . I waited years and that's what you give me I want a decent flat clean not high rise. Why can't I have a decent place to live in. Why.[112]

In its constitution, the Ocean Estate Tenants Association committed itself to the object of promoting 'a harmonius [sic] multi-racial community and to work towards the elimination of all forms of racism and discrimination within it'.[113] Its newsletters included in-house translations for Bengali readers and often drew attention to the difficulties Bangladeshi people faced over housing and personal security. The Tenants Association helped to fundraise for a local widowed Bangladeshi mother whose five children were being threatened with deportation unless she proved their relation to their deceased father (a British resident for twenty-six years) by shelling out for expensive DNA tests.

In spite of these gestures of solidarity, it was clear that the miserable housing conditions were fracturing the community on the Ocean Estate. Pete Aylmer, a Tower Hamlets councillor and member of the Ocean Estate Tenants Association, explained at a tempestuous anti-racist workshop held in Stepney in 1984: 'There's a crisis in housing. Nineteen sixties system-built dwellings are cracked up now . . . Racism is dividing its victims. Whose fault is it that our flats are falling down on our heads? We shouldn't get diverted. The real issue is bad housing.'[114]

In the same year, six Bangladeshi families were attacked after moving into a new housing complex in Stepney Green. They had been allocated these homes by the GLC, alongside 143 white households. The Ocean Estate Tenants Association newsletter struck back sternly:

THE TENANTS ASSOCIATION TOTALLY CONDEMN THESE ATTACKS AND FEEL SURE THAT WE SPEAK FOR THE VAST MAJORITY OF TENANTS ON THE ESTATE . . . Some Tenants have raised the question of the houses in Stepney Green going to Bengali Tenants. The answer is simple these houses were built for large families in need of re-housing. THE REAL ANSWER IS THAT MANY MORE HOUSES ARE NEEDED. For this and to improve Housing Conditions, we MUST have a united campaign. UNITY IS STRENGTH. Divided we are lost.[115]

But the Ocean Estate's tenants were divided – and so, in fact, was the Tenants Association. A few years later, an ugly battle was waged over school buses. Some Bangladeshi parents at the Ocean Estate began to refuse to send their children to primary school unless transport was provided to protect them against racist attacks, since children as young as five had been assaulted. The Inner London Education Authority agreed that the estate's Bangladeshi community had 'good grounds' for concern about the safety of their children.[116] A bus scheme was approved for dozens of local Asian students in 1989.

However, the treasurer of the Ocean Estate Tenants Association, Bess Haycock, told the press that this expenditure on the bus service was 'disgusting when so many homes on the estate need repairing'. 'White children are being harassed as well,' she added. 'I can't see why Asian parents don't walk their children to school and get them home again afterwards.' Of course, Bangladeshi adults were vulnerable to racial harassment too. 'It is terrible,' said Flordeliza Miah, a resident with a seven-year-old. 'Even when I am with my children they are insulted and kicked.'[117] The bus scheme was soon dropped. And the racist abuse roared on.

In 1990, eight high-rise blocks were blown up simultaneously at Kersal Vale in Salford, providing a gargantuan display for watching crowds. The National Tower Blocks Network was uncomfortable with the optics of this event, sensing that these spectacles were overshadowing the principles at the heart of ground-level tenant campaigning. 'It is just a big publicity stunt and we are being asked to pay the price,' observed one tenant, quoted in the *View*. 'It certainly attracted more media attention than the fight for decent housing by tenants,' the network reported. 'So, has anybody any ideas for media stunts to put tenants [*sic*] views on the front pages of newspapers?'[118] From the first National Tower Blocks Conference of 1983, the network had emphasised its rejection of any 'hollow token gesture'. It demanded real 'consultation' and 'involvement' for tenants to secure progressive change and decent housing.[119]

The National Tower Blocks Network formed in response to a horrifying scandal. Its members lunged for the detonator: they

Students getting off their school bus at the Ocean Estate in 1989.

were frightened and traumatised. Their allies at the Ocean Estate Tenants Association, facing equivalent structural flaws, were more cautious. Campaigning at the Ocean Estate was defensive in the light of a dimming horizon for the construction of public housing. This tenants association considered privatisation an even more menacing threat to residents' security than structural collapse. Disaffection with the dreadful living standards on the Ocean Estate stirred calls for better council housing, but these conditions also stoked a bitter politics of grievance that exploded into violent outbursts of racism against a growing Bangladeshi community who were also in desperate need of proper shelter.

Tenant groups reacted to the problems of high rise in different ways. What comes across clearly through these different strands of tenant campaigning is a demand for democracy. There was an

163

evident lack of accountability at the heart of the British welfare state, and in British governance more broadly. The Thatcherite right's 'property-owning democracy' emerged as one response to this. Another, however, was a grassroots appeal for a reformed model of council housing with community planning, higher investment, and transparent management.

The 1980s were a dark decade for high rise in Britain. The flaws of system building became incontrovertibly clear, while living conditions in many more high-rise blocks were devastated by brutal cuts to public spending. Funding for the Housing Investment Programme (which had been introduced in 1977 to buttress long-term plans for new building, maintenance, and modernisation) was slashed by 70 per cent in the period from 1978–79 to 1986–87. New council house-building fell to an unprecedented peacetime low.[120] Cash-strapped local authorities battled mounting homelessness while the supply of council homes was being depleted beneath their feet by Right to Buy. England was hit badly, whereas Scotland and Wales fared better in maintaining investment in housing. Local authorities in Scotland could reinvest their earnings from council house sales. From 1985, English local authorities were permitted to claw back just a fifth of their capital receipts. Welsh authorities could make use of half. High-rise residents were caught in the eye of a storm – stemming on the one hand from mistakes, shortcuts, and evasions made back in the 1960s, and on the other from wanton neglect by a Thatcher government that deplored council housing and disdained the people who lived in it.

6

The High Rise Tenants Group

Liverpool, 1992–2005

When Michael Heseltine surveyed Liverpool in the late 1980s, he found the city's high-rise blocks utterly repellent. In his eyes, these flats were 'slums that defy description'.[1] Yet Liverpool was no identikit concrete jungle. The city had a long and varied history of multistorey building, stretching back to the early twentieth century.

Liverpool had been a pioneer in flat-building during the 1930s, under public housing evangelist Lancelot Keay. The city was afflicted by severe overcrowding and insanitary slums, but many people in clearance areas needed to remain near the docks where they were employed. The inter-war years saw the construction of a constellation of avant-garde estates in Liverpool that distinguished themselves from the conveyer belt of neo-Georgian flatted developments pumped out by the London County Council.

Liverpool University had a prominent School of Architecture, the first in the country to receive RIBA accreditation for its degrees. Its forward-thinking outlook and emphatic commitment to urbanity fed into the city's distinctive building programme. St Andrew's Gardens (1935) swept around the shape of a bullring with white-ribboned, wrap-around balconies, statement cylindrical staircases, and an air of jazzy self-assurance. The city's new housing was infused with European inspirations, mimicking the curves of Bruno Taut's Horseshoe Estate in Berlin and the archways of Karl Ehn's Karl-Marx-Hof in Vienna.

The City Council remained enthusiastic about building high after the Second World War; overspill onto the surrounding green belt needed to be minimised, so higher densities were necessary. Liverpool's post-war thrust into the sky was announced by its showpiece slab, Coronation Court (1956). Standing at ten storeys, Coronation Court was reminiscent of Tecton's stylish Spa Green Estate. Its long façade, bookended by honeycomb brickwork, was broken up by a jutting rectangular box frame and tessellating window grilles. Liverpool constructed a number of slabs in the late 1950s that made use of a nice schema of projection and recession along their front and back elevations – an effect enhanced by splashes of colour on balconies and wall panels, a lesson learned from the Unité d'Habitation – at the Braddocks, for instance, and Netherfield Brow. Standing even taller was the broad, twenty-two-storey Entwistle Heights (completed in 1964). This block had geometric *brise-soleils* visible from afar, while down on the ground residents were greeted by a large mosaic at its entrance.

By the end of the 1960s, multiple clusters of tall blocks had sprouted along Liverpool's skyline. Roughly one-quarter of the dwellings produced by the Liverpool Corporation from 1956 to 1965 were in blocks of ten storeys or more.[2] This was accelerated by the adoption of industrialised building systems. In 1963, the corporation signed a contract with Camus for a package deal of precast concrete blocks, which fell into disrepair soon after construction wrapped up. The Piggeries stood out as decidedly grim. These were a row of unrelieved, system-built, dark grey slabs – Crosbie, Canterbury, and Haigh Heights in Everton – that soon became a magnet for vandalism, reflecting the mounting city-wide problems of unemployment and crime accompanying the decline of the docks. By the 1980s, the Piggeries had been boarded up, barely two decades into their life.

By the beginning of the 1990s, seventy-eight high-rise council blocks towered over the city.[3] They were becoming visibly tired; local councils across Britain had struggled to firefight maintenance issues and dereliction through ad hoc measures. A more comprehensive approach was needed: holistic regeneration. It was in this context that John Major's government decided to resuscitate Housing Action Trusts during the early 1990s. This time, the Department of the Environment agreed to hold ballots, armed with lessons from the previous mishap in the late 1980s. This consultative overture won tenants round, along with the promise of a significant injection of cash to refurbish the city's housing stock. Six HATs were set up in Britain in the early 1990s, approved by local referendums, in North Hull, Waltham Forest, Tower Hamlets, Castle Vale, Stonebridge, and Liverpool. Seven thousand tenants were balloted in Liverpool in 1992, the vast majority living in high-rise flats.[4] Over 80 per cent voted in favour of establishing a HAT, on a very high turnout, and sixty-seven blocks were transferred into the trust's care with their residents' consent. The Liverpool HAT was deemed unique. It was the largest in the country, taking responsibility for 5,337 properties and encompassing more than thirty sites scattered across the city.[5]

The Liverpool HAT soon discovered that its residents were not seeking escape from high-rise living. There was deep local affection for these homes in the sky. Liverpool had a large and lively High Rise Tenants Group, established in 1991 out of the Liverpool Federation of Council Tenants. The Liverpool HAT was established in close partnership with this group. This partnership committed the trust to an unprecedented degree of tenant participation: this was not just consultation; it was co-direction. This commitment was honoured throughout the HAT's lifetime, from 1993 to 2005, when the project wound up with a celebratory 'HATs Off' party at a Holiday Inn. The High Rise Tenants Group was embedded in the HAT's formal decision-making structure. The group was led by a rotating panel of elected tenant representatives from each block (247 served in total), who also designated tenant members to sit on the HAT's executive board, with a salary. They co-produced a regular newsletter, first titled *A Tall Order* and later *HAT News*.

'Liverpool Leads the Way out of Council Towers of Decay,' splashed the headline in the *Sunday Times* when the decisive HAT ballot carried in 1992. The newspaper interpreted the vote as evidence that tower block tenants in the city had rejected the council housing model. 'Tenants in socialism's once strongest bastion have proved the keenest of all to escape their council landlords,' read their news item.[6] A closer look at the story suggests otherwise. Up in the high-rise flats of Liverpool, perspectives were much more complex.

PROPERTY-OWNING DEMOCRACY

In 1987, after two election victories, the Conservative Party launched its bid for a hattrick. Their punchy new manifesto, *The Next Moves Forward*, hailed the success of their 'capital-owning democracy' achieved through Right to Buy. 'Two out of every three homes,' it read, 'are now owned by the people who live in them. This is a very high proportion, one of the largest in the world. *We are determined to make it larger still.*'[7] Margaret Thatcher believed that the sale of council houses had created 'a real revolution in ownership', but the putsch could not stop there. There remained a dragon to slay: 'The vast, soulless high-rise council estates remained ghettos of deprivation, poor education and unemployment.' In her eyes, these estates were 'the worst source of immobility' in British society, where tenants 'mutually reinforce each other's passivity and undermine each other's initiative'.[8]

Housing Action Trusts were primed as the new foot-soldiers in the Conservatives' battle to end the 'municipal monopoly' on housing in Britain.[9] They were the brainchild of the ultra-dry Nicholas Ridley, secretary of state for the environment from 1986 to 1989. 'Property-owning democracy' was a key tenet within the political philosophy of the Conservative Party in the 1980s. But the New Right's endorsement of democratic culture was tightly conditional; democratisation was conceived as a tactically advantageous conduit for the realisation of more imperative ideological objectives. The New Right regularly invoked its dedication to the idea of choice as evidence for its emancipatory credentials, but this was a fickle commitment.

The Next Moves Forward promised that the Conservatives' commitment to 'capital-owning democracy' would grant 'people the power over their own lives': '*They* would take the important decisions – as tenants, home-owners, parents, employees, and trade unionists – rather than having them taken for them.'[10] Yet the Thatcher and Major governments practised an acrobatic approach to the principle of democracy. The housing specialist Mary Langan has noted that while reforms to dismantle the welfare state after 1979 were 'presented in the rhetoric of user empowerment and consumer choice, it was clear that the government's central concern was to reduce social security spending on institutional care'.[11] The Department of the Environment saw tenant participation as 'a potential vehicle for wider Ministerial objectives' – namely the pursuit of homeownership and de-municipalisation.[12]

After winning the 1987 general election, the Conservative government designated a number of urban areas in which to establish Housing Action Trusts. They were met with public pushback over the proposed transfer of thousands of tenancies from local authority stock to quangos without balloting residents. The House of Lords ruled that a HAT could not be designated unless a majority of eligible tenants within its remit voted in approval. Two ballots were lost, and the government rowed back on the other four.

The HAT programme was resuscitated when Michael Heseltine became secretary of state for the environment in 1990. The Department of the Environment remained resistant to consultation. 'I am very doubtful,' commented one advisor, 'of the evidence that anything more than consulting tenants and taking account of their views is actually necessary, or indeed in many cases desirable.'[13] Another chewed over 'difficult choices' to be made:

Tenants' views must be consulted, and their interests taken fully into account, but given the scope and intensity of the problems they cannot be given a determining role. Where they are so obviously scarred by pessimism and apprehension, and are prey to alarmist voices, the Government must be willing to make decisions in theirs and the wider public interest, whatever the short-term unpopularity.[14]

Ultimately, the department came to accept that the consent of tenants would be critical if they wanted to get HATs off the ground. George Young, minister for housing, inner cities and construction, announced their revived programme with a fresh emphasis on participation:

I believe we have seen the end of tenants as passive dependants watched over – or ignored – by patriarchal landlords. I want tenants to get much more than better consultation. I want them to have more opportunities to make real decisions and to execise [sic] real choice about how their homes are managed. I want them to be more directly involved in managing their estates.[15]

Local authorities – the 'patriarchal landlords' – were framed as obstacles. The Thatcher and Major administrations considered them opponents, rather than partners, in urban regeneration. 'It is local authorities who are succeeding to the title of "slum landlords",' insisted the Department of the Environment in 1990.[16] Central government wanted to 'break down the semi-monopolistic control' of local authorities over housing stock, 'many of whom were out of sympathy with Government objectives'.[17] Demunicipalisation was therefore pursued by way of Trojan horse. In public earshot, the department obfuscated, denying that HATs would attempt to '"demunicipalise" council housing' or 'sell homes off to private developers over the heads of tenants'.[18] Internal government records supply plenty of contradictory evidence. An internal memo summarised their overarching approach:

Two principal objectives underlie housing estate policy: to improve the quality of housing, and social conditions generally, on rundown estates, and at the same time to diversify tenure and reduce the dependence of tenants on local authority provision. These are complementary: estate action experience shows that the chances of selling council property are greater where it has been improved and tenants see some prospect of maintaining and extending the value of the asset they might acquire.[19]

Advisors intended for HATs to offer 'opportunities for demunicipalisation as tenants get used to being away from Council and some exercise RTB [Right to Buy]'.[20] At heart, HATs were to be instruments for achieving 'privatisation objectives'.[21]

The John Major government's democratisation gambit worked; the prospect of regeneration in partnership with tenants was much more attractive than the managerial offer of the late 1980s. However, extending participation had unforeseen consequences for the government. 'Tenants,' the department complained, 'have been given substantial rights by this Government and it is now virtually impossible to make radical changes without their consent.'[22] In Liverpool, local feelings about high-rise estates and council housing would turn out to be quite different to those nursed in Whitehall.

MUCH-LOVED HOMES

Liverpool's high-rise estates housed an overwhelmingly ageing population in the 1990s. A 1993 poll of Liverpool HAT tenants found that 60 per cent of households contained someone over sixty. Only 4 per cent of HAT properties housed families, as Liverpool Council had stopped offering tower block homes to families with small children. Two-thirds contained just one person.[23] Many flats were occupied by elderly, widowed residents who had moved in during the 1960s and raised their families there. The Department of the Environment expected that people who were part of the so-called 'respectable poor' (a category in which they included the elderly) would want to 'escape' from urban housing estates.[24] In Liverpool the case was quite the opposite. The chair of the Liverpool HAT, Paula Ridley, received a 'clear message' from tenants from the very first consultation she attended: 'These tenants were fed up with their environment and poor management, felt themselves to be bottom of the heap when it came to repairs, but were very committed to living up in the air.' She was struck by how these residents confounded typical preconceptions. 'Not for them the often-heard derogatory comments about high-rise living. These towers were their much-loved homes, full of memories and friends.'[25]

Few of these people wanted to escape. The 1993 poll of Liverpool's high-rise residents found that 74 per cent were satisfied with their homes and 73 per cent were satisfied with their estates more broadly. That is not to say they did not want improvements: just one in fourteen respondents reported no problems in their block.[26] The HAT had necessary work to do. Tenant Marjorie Gallimore told *A Tall Order* at its inception: 'I am now looking forward to seeing our homes returned to their former glory.'[27] Three-quarters of the HAT's residents thought they were likely to stay in their homes long-term. Only 18 per cent wanted to move, a high concentration of whom were those with young families.[28]

The Liverpool HAT was first pitched to tenants as 'an efficient, locally-based repair and maintenance service' which would undertake minor repairs and upgrade amenities.[29] But by 1995 the HAT discovered that the majority of the tower blocks in their care would need much more extensive repairs than anticipated. Some, though not all, shared with Ronan Point the faults stemming from large-panel-system construction. Every block was suffering material deterioration with age. Windows regularly blew out and water penetration was a common problem. The expected cost of refurbishment was more than double the figure sketched out by the City Council in an early feasibility study of 1991.

Two options were presented to HAT tenants. The first was to undertake far-reaching refurbishment, during which tenants would

Long-term tower block resident Marjorie Gallimore planting a new tree alongside members of the High Rise Tenants Group in 2001.

be moved into temporary accommodation. The second was to demolish and rebuild low-rise replacement housing – which would ultimately be considerably less expensive, with lower long-term maintenance costs too. Demolition had not been part of the founding agreement signed off by the High Rise Tenants Group. Tenants had been assured that 'blocks would only be demolished in rare circumstances'.[30]

However, the financial picture was plain and persuasive. Moreover, the prospect of being shuttled around temporary accommodation during a lengthy refurbishment distressed many tenants who were physically frail. When the HAT team first suggested at a large public meeting that tenants move out for eighteen months, one resident with a sick husband responded: 'It would kill us.' Another was even more direct: 'Sod off!'[31] The two options were put to a tenant ballot. Rebuilding ultimately won out over refurbishment. Fifty-four of the sixty-seven tower blocks managed by the Liverpool HAT were knocked down. In parallel, the HAT spearheaded an extensive building programme of new low-rise

173

homes across the city, a process that saw a profound reshaping of Liverpool's post-war topography.

The HAT's promotional material tried to summon up an optimistic sense of progress about this arc of urban change. A light-hearted banner was hung on a twenty-two-storey block at Sheil Park before it was detonated: 'Now you see it, soon you won't'.[32] In the HAT's *Half Way* documentary (2000), the closing titles announced the 1,200 new homes the trust had built and the twenty-seven blocks it had dispatched. The credits rolled to the tune of 'Hey Jude' by the Beatles, Liverpool's most famous musical export, which urges the listener to 'take a sad song and make it better'. The HAT's wrap-up documentary, *Liverpool Housing Action Trust: The Story* (2005), showed a tower block being demolished to the sound of Édith Piaf's 'Je ne regrette rien'. Another, *Building Blocks for the Future* (2005), screened a dramatic montage of tower block detonations with a backing track of triumphant classical music.

For tenants, however, the collective decision to demolish was fraught with sadness. After moving into her new-build, Pat Donnelly looked back with mixed emotions:

> It was inevitable they should be demolished – and although we're very disappointed and I personally am still disappointed – although I love the bungalow very much – I'm still disappointed I'm not in my flat. But we did accept the fact that we were going to lose the flats.[33]

The High Rise Tenants Group saw tower blocks as a proud part of Liverpool's civic identity. The high-rise imagery in its publications was warm and chipper, in stark contrast to gloomy depictions saturating the national media. At the HAT's formal launch ceremony in 1993, a cake with tower block icing was baked to celebrate the beginning of regeneration. Residents were keen to learn about the history of the buildings they called home, so the HAT put on a 'Tower Block History' course: 'Why were they

One of a sweep of tower blocks being demolished at Storrington Heys in 2002.

built? Where do the names come from? Where did the tenants come from?'[34] Stefan Muthesius and Miles Glendinning's expensive academic monograph *Tower Block* (1994) was purchased by the Central Library for residents who wanted to read up about the circumstances of their inception.

Affection for Liverpool's high-rise heritage comes through loud and clear across the range of community arts projects steered by the High Rise Tenants Group in the 2000s. The noughties were a vibrant artistic moment for Liverpool: the city hosted the Biennial of Contemporary Art in 2002 and was named European Capital of Culture in 2008. Collaborative workshops between local artists, residents, and schoolchildren produced paintings to go in the foyers of refurbished tower blocks in Sefton Park. These five point blocks on Croxteth Drive happily escaped demolition; they epitomise the early picturesque visions of tall blocks looking out over green parkland.

Tenants moving into new residences at Olive Mount were provided with photography equipment by the Housing Action Trust to document their old housing. A darkroom was set up at the community centre where tenants could develop their own photographs, and edit them with dyes and toners. They created a leaflet in the form of an unfolding tower block, with tenants' photographs embedded into its frame.

At Storrington Heys, the former home to five tower blocks dynamited in 2002, Liverpool Safe Productions ran workshops with local people over two years. Former high-rise dwellers sorely missed the views they had enjoyed up high. On a clear day, a spectator looking out from a post-war tower block in inner-city Liverpool was met with a spectacular panorama out over the River Mersey and across to Snowdonia in the Welsh mountains. A mosaic was made to recapture this outlook on the walls of the Porchfield Community Centre. This mural put the city in context with its surrounding countryside, with shire horses and tower blocks depicted side by side. Here was Liverpool's historic landscape made permanent, helping residents to move into the future. Its high-rise blocks were a valued part of the city's iconography: demolished, missed, but not forgotten.

The Porchfield Community Centre mural.

WE'VE NEVER HAD A VOICE BEFORE

Members of Liverpool's High Rise Tenants Group had deep affection for their homes in the sky, but years of poor maintenance by the City Council had left them feeling deserted and desperate. These buildings were host to a daunting array of physical issues. Council repairs typically took months to get under way. The external wall of one block at Hartsbourne Heights was covered in so much green fungus that it was nicknamed 'the Hanging Gardens of Babylon'.[35] 'The majority of people were absolutely fed up of the slop job done by Liverpool City Council,' explained John Fulham, a representative in the High Rise Tenants Group. They were aware that this was largely a result of financial constraints. 'The main bother was the Council couldn't look after [the blocks] because they couldn't borrow the money,' observed tenant Ken Bray. Representative Jack Sheridan described the ballot for the HAT as 'Hobson's Choice really': 'After nearly thirty years with Liverpool City Council we could have been persuaded to vote for any organisation that promised to listen.' Fellow rep Pat Donnelly elaborated:

> We went for the ballot. There was just no question; you had to go to the HAT because the Council said that every year they could replace the windows in one block of flats and that's all they could do. So 67 years later the last flats would be done. It was just crazy! Even people adamant to remain Council tenants ended up voting to go over to the HAT.[36]

The Liverpool Housing Action Trust made itself immediately popular by taking a rapid-fire approach to maintenance. During the first six months of its operation 19,000 repairs were carried out, over 90 per cent of which were completed within the tight target times promised at its launch.[37] This made a pleasant change. 'Ask the corpy to do a job,' remembered one tenant, 'you were ten weeks to – or maybe never get them. But HAT, there's Bernie. We had Bernie, the housing officer, first and if you rang her up in the morning, your job was done in the afternoon.'[38]

Tenants wanted to speak, and they wanted to be heard. Chief Executive David Green hailed the Liverpool HAT's participatory approach to regeneration as nationally 'unprecedented'.[39] The HAT produced a promotional film about its new template for tenant participation, *Managing the Future* (1993), in which one tenant explained: 'It's the only time in our lives that we've had any influence on what's going to happen to our homes . . . We've never had a voice before.'[40]

Tenants wanted a reformed style of responsive management. This groundswell of feeling differed subtly to the appetite for de-municipalisation within central government. During an early stage of HAT negotiations with the High Rise Tenants Group, one tenant rep wondered aloud how to get residents 'to realise that there's a different branch of the Council starting up, that will do all the things that we should have had done, and why we're in this mess is because of bad management by the City Council'.[41] When tenants were asked, in a 1993 poll, who they would like as their landlord when the HAT programme was completed, Liverpool City Council was still the most popular option. Of the small pro-portion of people who wanted to move out of their original homes, 'nearly all' still wanted to end up in 'another rented property'.[42] After the Liberal Democrats won the leadership of Liverpool City Council in 1998, the council resolved to dispose of all its housing stock to registered social landlords. This caused upset from the High Rise Tenants Group, whose members wanted the choice to return to the council to remain available as a point of principle – as originally promised.[43]

Tenants were nevertheless continuously involved in deciding the future of housing stock within the Housing Action Trust. Resident panels were organised by the High Rise Tenants Group to inter-view potential managing agents who would take on properties after the HAT wrapped up. Their decisions were then ratified by the HAT's executive board. This process had different political meanings for different people. Tenant panellist Eileen Clarke described the experience as one of listening to 'these people trying to sell us their wares, almost like a marketplace but a little bit better'.[44] Another with more socialist leanings, John Fulham, thought: 'It's like a local Soviet where people have an equal input.'[45]

Tenants were also involved in designing their new homes in head-to-head workshops with architects: 'We were fully involved in every way in the design of the estate, design of the properties. We chose the bricks, we chose everything, that was our choice.'[46] Each neighbourhood had its own Community Agreement, drawn up in consultation with its residents, which codified the new landlords' obligations to their tenants and guaranteed avenues for future tenant participation.

With a return to the council off the menu, the 'overwhelming majority' of HAT residents in Liverpool chose to transfer to housing associations. In 1993, there were sixty leaseholders and freeholders living in HAT properties. In the trust's lifetime, forty-eight more residents exercised their Right to Buy and forty more purchased homes using grants offered by the Mobility Incentive Scheme.[47] This was a small proportion of the several thousand residents within the Liverpool HAT. This outcome in Liverpool was mirrored in Britain's other HATs, for instance in North Hull and Castle Vale. Since the 1988 Housing Act, which facilitated the transfer of council units to housing associations, the lion's share of new public housing has been built by these bodies. This ushered in an era in which the label of council housing has steadily given way to that of social housing.

The HAT also launched the country's first Tenant Homefinder scheme. This allowed a tenant to choose a house for sale on the open market that would be purchased (subject to a reasonable price cap) by a housing association, to become social housing. The tenant paid rent at an affordable rate to the housing association as their new social landlord. Homefinder was a popular option. The HAT's 200th Homefinder, former tower block tenant Ellen

Disley, was 'delighted' with her two-bedroom, low-rise home: 'I have been able to choose it for myself, in the area I want to live in and I got to choose who my landlord should be!'[48] Almost 400 tenants found homes through the scheme, but its success tailed off as tenants lost out to wealthier buyers in the more buoyant housing market post-2000.[49]

The Liverpool HAT ultimately oversaw a net loss in social housing stock. In 1993 it had taken possession of 67 blocks and a total of 5,337 homes.[50] By 2005, 13 blocks remained for social rent and shared ownership, after a sweep of demolitions.[51] Overall, 4,564 properties were demolished, and 2,959 new or refurbished homes were left.[52] But Liverpool's population was shrinking; the city was facing a housing surplus. Between 1951 and 2000, the population of Liverpool fell by 39 per cent. Over 600 of the properties taken over by the HAT in 1993 had been vacant.[53]

HIGH-RISE INTERNET TELEVISION

In 1998 the Liverpool Housing Action Trust announced its entry onto 'the information superhighway'. They had just launched a bang-up-to-date new website, and around them millennium fever was kicking off. 'We are slowly moving into the electronic age,' Paula Ridley reported in 1999, 'and have taken as much care as we can to ensure that our technology is not affected by the bug, but only time (midnight on 31st December 1999 to be precise) will tell.'[54]

A flagship initiative stood at the forefront of this leap into the digital age. It was called tenantspin: a community-led internet television channel led by tenants. It sprang out of a pilot experimental project at Coronation Court from 1999. A permanent studio for tenantspin was set up at Sefton Park – one of the few high-rise estates that was not demolished under the Liverpool HAT. Tenantspin was overseen by the High Rise Tenants

Group in partnership with the HAT and the city's Film, Art, and Creative Technology agency (FACT), with extra funding from the Chartered Institute of Housing. Alan Dunn, an experienced community media artist, was employed to facilitate the project between 2001 and 2007. It continued until 2012, in partnership with FACT and Arena Housing.

Tenantspin harnessed technology to give local people a voice within the city's urban regeneration and its 'cultural renaissance', providing a forum for e-democracy while simultaneously creating an online archive.[55] It was conceived as 'a focal point for community identity' during a time of physical displacement when many tenants were moved from their high-rise homes and scattered around new neighbourhoods.[56] The channel was particularly targeted at tackling isolation among elderly people, while making an effort to 'challenge perceptions of tower block living'.[57]

Tenantspin might strike us as surprising. Here we find Liverpudlian senior citizens, plenty of whom were born before the Second World War, at the prow of early digital culture. One of tenantspin's jingles was set to the heavy bass and synths of Joy Division's 'Transmission'. Not only were elderly tenants the subject of recordings; they produced them. Tenants were given free training in digital skills, information technology, studio management, and television production. They broadcast from the top of an old tower block, a long way from Silicon Valley.

Tenantspin produced several hundred webcasts in its lifetime. These were live broadcasts on the World Wide Web that could be streamed by anyone, anywhere. The recordings were hosted on Superchannel, an internet television station created in 1993 by a Danish arts collective called Superflex. From 2000 to 2005, tenantspin worked with around 250 tenants and achieved an average of 30,000 website hits per month.[58] Its purview was to explore the themes of high-rise living, art, new technology, regeneration, and tenant participation. It ultimately went further than this. Tenantspin recorded webcasts 'on every conceivable subject', according to participant Margo Hogg.[59] The tenants chatted about many aspects of their lives, including their memories and hopes for the future. Viewers could contribute from anywhere on a rolling basis through an open-access chatroom, visible to other people tuning in and fed through to tenant presenters live in the studio.

Tenantspin was part television programme, part radio broadcast, part blog, part diary, part oral history, part social space, and part archive. It should be situated in the context of a long lineage of community publishing in Britain, as a digital iteration of a popular historic tradition of autobiographical life-writing. Early internet media were emerging in the 1990s; since then, the digital terrain has become a contiguous plane of urban space, a primary interface at which people interact and social bonds are figured. Tenantspin represents an alternative form of oral history steered by participants, not the academy. For project facilitator Alan Dunn, this was important: 'There were grievances to air, life stories to share, songs to sing, spoons to play and a new approach to saying it all. What was needed was someone quiet to make all the noise happen.'[60]

This channel provided a space for debate. An official from FACT, who came on tenantspin to talk about public art in Liverpool in 2001, was submitted to quite a grilling by chatroom users. For example, eon wrote: 'Don't be so nice, tell us what you really think – maybe some thing about how you consider this as art?' Another user, scouser, complained: 'C'mon mates, lets [sic] take things a bit less seriously, not all this art stuff – I'm working class me.' Someone in the tenantspin studio typed back, 'aren't we all'; scouser responded, 'yes but some more than others'. HAT Chief Executive David Green made an appearance on the channel that same year. He got some challenging questions. One viewer typed: 'The push for owner occupation in 1980s/90's [sic] has created a stigma about social housing how do we overcome this?' Another wrote: 'The Guardian said there would probably be no Council properties by 2014.' During a webcast titled 'Landlords', in 2002, a tenant from the main ChatShop server raised a thorny point: 'Do

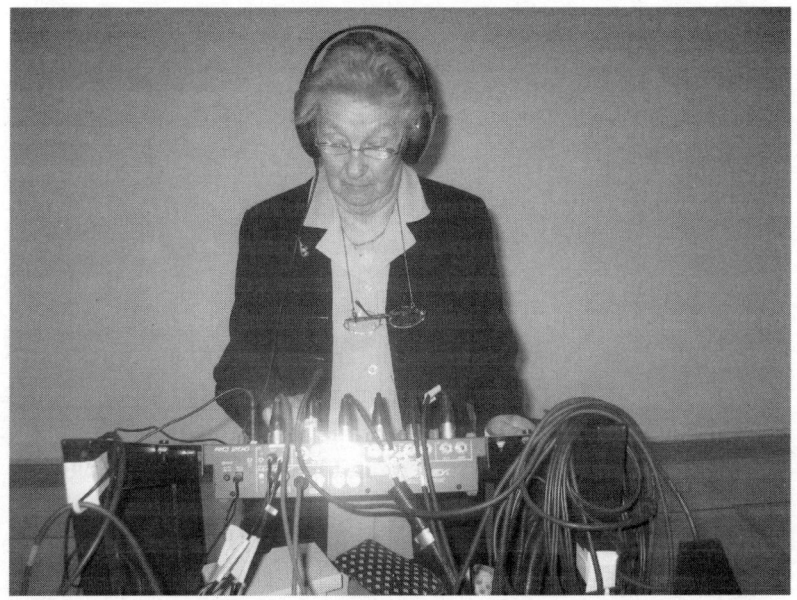

Vera handles the technology for a tenantspin webcast, photographed by Alan Dunn.

we think that RSL's [*sic*; registered social landlords] will give a token gesture of initial interest then gradually become disinterested?' Langholm typed back, 'mmm we are a bit sceptical'. ChatShop asked: 'What makes u sceptical?' apra interjected, 'a lifetime of experience!'[61]

The internet boom of the 1990s had been accompanied by a great deal of breathless speculation about the libertarian potential of cyberspace. Tenantspin was infused with similar starry-eyed aspirations. Superflex's *Supermanual* insisted that tenantspin's use of the 'private webcam reverses Guy Debord's concept of the society of the spectacle'. 'It is in this self-created public domain,' it proposed, 'which is neither market nor state, that true community emerges.'[62] The digital future seemed a tremendously enthralling frontier.

The channel had its fair share of technical glitches. Viewers of one 2002 webcast were faced with a blue menu screen for several minutes, with sounds of presenters scrabbling to fix it in the background. Tuning in was not always easy: 'can't really hear what's being said :-('; 'crikey – visuals have gone strange'; 'Have installed RealPlayer but it made no difference . . . don't know what else to try. I think this computer is cursed.'[63] Technical difficulties threatened to up-end Superchannel's ceremonial thousandth broadcast. Tenantspin's hosts came up against a 'server not available' pane. They finally managed to get back on the air after several frantic phone calls to Copenhagen. 'In the best traditions of show business,' they later recalled, 'we continued with the show while Alan occasionally hurled abuse at the Danes in Copenhagen over his mobile phone. Even though it wasn't their fault it made him feel better.'[64]

Notwithstanding these challenges, tenantspin connected Liverpool's pensioners to a whole different world. The channel's conversations were based around hyper-local issues, with a view to strengthening dispersed former tower block communities. But the material was 'beamed to an outside world' with a global audience

Behind the camera, photographed by Alan Dunn.

in mind too.[65] Tenantspin went on tour to Malmö, Copenhagen, and Wiesbaden to exchange ideas internationally. Members of the group even participated in an exhibition at the New Museum of Contemporary Art in New York City, where they recreated their studio space to record webcasts with American community groups and offer training based on their technical expertise. They fed their broadcasting through to a 'simultaneous plasma screen display' on Broadway.[66] Tenantspin made elderly people in Liverpool feel like they lived in 'a much smaller world'.[67]

REMEMBERING TOWER BLOCK LIFE

Tenantspin co-produced a show called *SuperBlock* for BBC Radio 3 across 2002 and 2003. It was a futuristic drama set in the year 2040, based on ideas from 1,500 questionnaires sent around to tenants. The SuperBlock itself was a fictional 1,470-floor tower block built from the 'salvaged concrete and bricks' of the high-rise buildings demolished under Liverpool's Housing Action Trust.[68] The play's co-writer, Jeff Young, explained the conversations that informed the production:

We spent afternoons drinking tea with people who had lived most of their lives in the sky. Time and again people told us how much they loved living in these buildings. A woman called Josie Crawford talked to me of beauty. When she woke in the morning she could hear the sound of the milkman all those floors below and in the evening she told me she could see the river and it shone like sweet wrappers . . . Some of the residents had political points to make. Jim Jones was a left-leaning firebrand who had issues with the planners and architects who had built these monstrosities in the first place. Even though Jim had an axe to grind about the way tenants had been treated over the years, he was fiercely proud of his home and had declared his intention to barricade himself in when the day of demolition came.[69]

The radio drama opens with the megalomaniacal ramblings of the SuperBlock's architect envisioning 'sixty-seven tower blocks stacked to the moon'.[70] 'There was a space in the sky,' he proclaims, 'and I wanted to fill it.' The architect is the only character in the play with a received-pronunciation accent, in contrast to the tenants' Liverpudlian voices. He deflects any responsibility for the SuperBlock's problems: a typical caricature of the ineffectual modern architect. 'Through the magic of radio drama,' Jeff Young explained, 'we were able to confront this monstrous egotist with some of the questions Jim had never been allowed to ask the architects and planners.'[71] After being physically attacked by residents – crying, 'What the hell are you playing at?' – the architect jumps to his death from the top of the block he designed.

SuperBlock portrayed high rise as a science-fiction nightmare, on one level, but it also dramatised the feelings of loss experienced during demolition. An elegiac sequence follows a young boy watching the demolition of a block in Sheil Park: 'The building bent at the belly and fell over on its knees, and its head hit the floor . . . and then its ghost came out of it . . . We were in the dust, and all alone.' He overhears a woman exclaim: 'The ghosts of all our lives, my god, the ghosts of everything we've lived.' Young wanted to dramatise how the 'ghosts and traumas of those "deceased" tower blocks somehow possessed the fabric of the SuperBlock'.[72]

In the play, a ninety-year-old tenant talks with an interviewer about her life in the block. 'You make it sound terrible!' the questioner says. 'Well yes, it sort of is!' she replies. '[But] I'd grown to know the birds and couldn't bear to leave them.' *SuperBlock* is full of intermingled flavours of sweet and sour. 'Historical memory,' the historian James Hinton reminds us, 'is always in a state of flux, never more so than when dealing with the recent past.'[73]

Heritage was a major concern throughout the High Rise Tenants Group's art initiatives. Heritage work can offer catharsis during periods of shift, providing a therapeutic outlet through which communities can connect with their past, reconcile it with contemporary change, and rebuild for the future. The *tenantspin workbook* framed the initiative as 'neither nostalgic nor a reminiscence project'.[74] 'Crucially,' Alan Dunn explained, 'tenantspin looked forwards rather than backwards. The content is not nostalgic – the channel enables individuals' contributions to tomorrow's situations to be heard.'[75] Tenantspin resisted the perspective of rose-tinted spectacles. It gives us a rounded sense of the pleasures and peccadillos of high-rise living.

The opening introductory sequence for tenantspin's webcasts was a jolly series of clips of tower blocks around the city. It was backed by a jingle trilled by tenants to the upbeat tune of 'Aquarela do Brasil'. 'Enjoy yourself, click onto tenantspin! Enjoy yourself, you're welcome; come on in! Enjoy yourself, there's lots to see and hear! When you log onto tenantspin you'll never shed a tear!'[76] Another webcast had the chirpy title 'Towers of Joy'.

Tenantspin nevertheless explored how people's feelings about high rise could vacillate over time. One webcast was structured as a short documentary about the history of Coronation Court, focusing on a tenant who had moved into the block upon its opening in 1956. She had such affection for the 'brilliant' estate that she showed presenters a framed black-and-white photograph of the building in her hallway. Yet she also accepted that the high cost of refurbishment had made demolition necessary. She was 'looking to the future' with a positive attitude.[77] Mavis Thomas, a tenant from Childwall, expressed her fluctuating feelings on a webcast titled 'Are You Moving?' 'My expectations when – before we moved? Horror, absolute horror, we were looking forward to moving but it was horror coming to live down on the ground after being high-rise tenants all the time but when we actually moved it was [pause] pretty good.'[78]

The experience of moving down to the ground was emotionally complicated. The community history book *The 79 Bus to Childwall* (2002), sponsored by the High Rise Tenants Group, collected testimonies during the regeneration of the Childwall and Netherley areas. Tenants described feeling attached to their high-rise homes. 'Looking back, although it wasn't exactly paradise it was a good bit better than we had had before. In those days council houses were looked on as something special.' It could feel strange to look back after relocating:

I had a lovely view up there, from Runcorn Bridge to Huyton. I do miss it. Now I've been in Dolan Court for two years I wonder, like a lot of others, how on earth we survived, the flats were so cold. But those of us who lived in Childwall Heights enjoyed it – it was our visitors who didn't. I'm sure that if HAT had said that within twelve months of us moving out they'd refurbish the flats and you can move back in, I may well have done so. What's that, high-rise syndrome? The move was very traumatic – it's difficult to explain why. During 35 years you become attached to the four walls even if they're not very good walls. At one point soon after moving someone asked me how I felt and I said, 'I want to go home.' But you get used to new things.[79]

Adjusting to living at ground level was an odd experience. When tenant Pauline Needham was interviewed by the Housing Action Trust about moving into her bungalow, she said: 'The queerest thing I had to cope with was seeing people walk past my window, having just seen birds.'[80] Some found that they were happier than they had anticipated: 'You know, I thought I would miss, you know, the sight of the night, the view. But I don't. I don't miss anything at all. I just like being here.'[81]

For many other people, however, the marvellous views from Liverpool's tower blocks were a deeply felt loss. Art projects endeavoured to preserve them in some form. The video artist Philip Reilly made a simple film titled *Balconies*, which captured a quiet, long-exposure recording out of a flat window across the city. Another photographic reminiscence project called *View from the Window* compiled photos of tenants' views out from their flats in Everton before they were demolished. It was important to tenants that the physical traces of their high-rise history were not obliterated. At the Childwall site, artists from the local verd de gris collective used debris from demolished blocks at Hartsbourne Heights and Childwall Heights to create a memorial of the buildings within the new development.

These acts of remembrance were sometimes partial. From the cheerful mosaics celebrating the city's dockland past, created by Liverpool Safe Productions, one would never guess its darker history of slave trading. This was fairly typical of the city's approach to its past in the noughties. Liverpool's 2003 bid to become European Capital of Culture stressed the city's multicultural credentials in a neutral register:

> Liverpool has deliberately chosen to describe its bid as representing 'The World in One City'. It will draw on its long history as a centre for immigration and emigration and on its more recent experience of waving cultural processes and practices into the task of physical and social regeneration as part of its plans for the year and for the next decade.[82]

The swallowing up of slavery into the vocabulary of voluntary migration is an eyebrow-raising feat of obfuscation. The historian Finn Gleeson has noted that heritage work among white communities reckoning with deindustrialisation and urban change in Britain's docklands has often been predicated on a denial of the thorny imperial past.[83]

The work of Liverpool's High Rise Tenants Group demonstrates a real historical consciousness among the city's high-rise community. These residents were profoundly concerned with civic memory. They wanted their stories to be committed to the archive and preserved for the future as the physical traces of their lives disappeared from Liverpool's cityscape. Digital technology seemed to offer an opportunity for a whole new form of public record. This was a central facet of tenantspin's brief. The 'beauty' of tenantspin, said Alan Dunn, was that 'every single tenantspin show is permanently archived on the website'.[84]

However, most of tenantspin's broadcasts from 2000 to 2005 are now lost. Superchannel, on which the webcasts were hosted, folded in 2005 and its webpage no longer exists. Digital sources can easily fall through the cracks of cyberspace. It is possible to access snapshots of the Superchannel website via WayBack Machine, an open-source project begun by the Internet Archive in 2001 that allows users to browse sample displays of websites at specific frozen points in time. With this tool, we can access earlier versions of web pages before expiry – but clunkily. Way-Back Machine does not have screenshots for every date of the year, and it often fails to reconstitute exact formatting, nor does it capture plug-ins. FACT does not have copies of tenantspin's early webcasts on its internal server. A retrospective exhibition, 'tenantspin the incomplete archive', was held at FACT in 2013. The web page for this exhibition has now expired. Alan Dunn still has around 150 tenantspin files on a hard drive, although many of these recordings are now corrupted or in low resolution.

The Liverpool Housing Action Trust commissioned substantial rolling video record of its activities in the 1990s. The raw footage – comprising 333 tapes – was given to the Liverpool Central Library to be archived. Almost all these tapes are in Betamax format, a form of video cassette in production from 1975 to 2002. Betamax predated VHS but was ultimately wiped out by its competitor: it was more expensive and users could only tape short recordings. Betamax players went out of production two decades ago and the magnetic strips in Betamax cassettes degrade over time. The labour and expense ploughed into this video archive has now become practically valueless.

The story of Liverpool's High Rise Tenants Group should not be forgotten. It turns commonly preconceived notions about high-rise living on their head. These buildings were loved by some people, for whom they were special, the site of treasured memories: home. Residents could harbour warm feelings that elbowed concurrently with frustrations about poor management, delayed repairs, and dereliction. It also stands out as an instructive example of successful regeneration carried out in true partnership with local people. The Liverpool Housing Action Trust's groundbreaking approach to tenant participation was incredibly popular. A before-and-after study into housing and health under the HAT found 'a dramatic improvement in all aspects of management'. Levels of tenant satisfaction were 'exceptionally high'.[85] Some tenants even joked that they felt 'consulted to death'.[86] The demolition of Liverpool's high-rise blocks was accepted because it was a collective decision. The buildings were mourned. But the experience of participatory partnership allowed residents to move forward into the future – with hope.

7

The Heygate and Aylesbury Estates

Southwark, 1997–2015

The year 1992 saw the publication of *A New London* – a book that became a cornerstone of urban policy under New Labour. Co-authored by Mark Fisher, shadow minister for arts and media, in collaboration with the architect Richard Rogers, it declared London to be a city in decline: unequal, depopulated, and traffic-choked. The authors' answer was neither dispersal nor suburbanisation, but instead an affirmation of the virtues of density. They called for investment to fortify the productivity and vibrancy of urban life.

After the Labour Party's landslide general election victory in 1997, the deputy prime minister, John Prescott, promised an 'urban renaissance' for Britain. The new government set up an Urban Task Force, chaired by Rogers, to master-plan its execution. 'Modernism on the cheap', Rogers argued, had involved 'poor construction methods, poor building design and little or no regard for public realm'.[1] But he hoped that the promises of modernity could be reactivated, this time for the better. 'We cannot afford to squander another hectare of land on sprawling, lifeless, car-based housing estates,' he maintained, mirroring the writing of the likes of Thomas Sharp many decades before.[2] Rogers called for substantial redevelopment: dense and vertically directed. The Task Force report, *Towards an Urban Renaissance* (1999), urged urban regeneration through the redevelopment of derelict and brownfield sites, instead of housing overspill.

In 1998, New Labour launched the New Deal for Communities programme. It aimed to regenerate the most deprived areas in Britain in partnership with local communities. The Blair government also committed to a private finance initiative (PFI) model to encourage private–public partnerships in building projects, something which had originally been scoped out by the previous Major administration. Many British architects felt galvanised at the inception of this new national programme. The dismantling of local authority architecture departments under Thatcher had sent most architects into private practice by the end of the 1990s. New Labour's promise of major civic building projects revitalised the prospect of large-scale public commissions. This era could be a *new* New Jerusalem: one of revived, state-led urban redevelopment, equipped with lessons from the first.

Others were less credulous. The critic Will Self thought the Blair government was using design and architecture as 'just two more modes within which to deploy their presentation skills; skills the regime seems intent on substituting entirely for any real substantive policies on the built environment'.[3] Katherine Shonfield, an architect at the all-women practice muf, believed her contemporaries were being naive:

> This represents lemming-like support for a party which, communal head in the sand, we fondly hope will espouse the envisioning building projects of a caring society we associate with the 1945 victory. There is currently absolutely no evidence whatsoever that this is even remotely likely.[4]

A NEW DEAL FOR COMMUNITIES

In June 1997, Tony Blair made his first speech as prime minister at the Aylesbury Estate in the London borough of Southwark:

We've chosen this estate to deliver the first speech that I'm making as Prime Minister, and it's for a very simple reason, and it's a reason that I hope that you will understand and share. I think for the past eighteen years, often the poorest people in our country have been forgotten by government. They've been left out of the great prosperity, told that they were not needed, ignored by the government except very often for the purposes of blaming them. And I want that to change. I don't want there to be any forgotten people in the Britain we want to build . . . There are estates where the biggest employer is the drugs industry, where all that is left of the high hopes of the post-war planners is derelict concrete. Behind the statistics are people who have lost hope, trapped in fatalism.

Blair announced that this 'underclass' of people needed to get off welfare and into work. 'Governments,' Blair said, 'can all too easily institutionalise poverty rather than solve it. They can give money out not because it is the right thing to do but because it is

Tony Blair visits the Aylesbury Estate to make his first speech as prime minister.

the easy thing to do.'[5] New Labour identified council estates as places of social exclusion that needed to be transformed into mixed-income communities.

The adjacent area of Elephant and Castle was designated as a target zone for the New Deal for Communities. Renewal of this area, reported *Building Design* in 2000, was 'universally deemed overdue'.[6] The Pevsner *Buildings of England* guide for London South described Elephant and Castle, in 1983, as 'one of the least loved creations of the London post-war planners', a fate sealed by a roaring traffic junction. The Pevsner guides were generally well disposed towards twentieth-century modernist buildings, but this volume expressed unmitigated dismay in the presence of the long slab block architecture of the Aylesbury (built 1967–77) and Heygate (built 1971–74) Estates, in spite of an instinctive admiration for the projects' ambition. These were 'some of the most notorious products of industrialized building' in the country. A perambulation through the Aylesbury Estate, with blocks ranging from four to fourteen storeys, could be 'recommended only for those who enjoy being stunned by the impersonal megalomaniacal creations of the mid C20'. Down the road, the height of the Heygate's tallest twelve-storey flats made for 'an impressive sight from a distance' – 'but that is all one can say in their favour'.[7]

After the war, overcrowded and poor-quality rental housing had caused many working-age people to trickle away in search of better lives in places such as Bromley and Bexley, leading Southwark Council to press the LCC to raise their density cap from 136 people to the acre to 200 in the 1950s. The Heygate and Aylesbury Estates were designed to resolve these problems. Both were constructed with Laing's 12M Jespersen system, a large-panel system of precast concrete, chosen for its cost-effective and speedy credentials. The initial design for the Aylesbury Estate came from Hans Peter Trenton and Frank Hayes with input from fellow architects within Southwark Council's Department of Architecture and Planning, but it was quickly handed over to the contractors. Neither Trenton nor Hayes was closely involved in its completion, nor were they a regular presence on site. In 1970, the Aylesbury Estate represented the largest single housing project ever undertaken by a London borough, at a density of 175 people to the acre. It was mammoth in scale and repetitive in form.

These elements attracted censure early on – not just from the broadsheets and tabloids, but also from the typically more sympathetic architectural press. *Building Design* ran a 1974 feature on the Aylesbury titled 'Future Slum?', expressing worries about the scale of its slab blocks and the 'desolate' sense of the public space.[8] The *Architects' Journal* was similarly nervous about its 'enormous size and monotony'.[9] The urban historian Ben Campkin judges the later Heygate Estate, designed by Tim Tinker, to be of higher architectural quality.[10] The Aylesbury was disadvantaged by cheaper materials and lift infrastructure. While the Aylesbury reserved the ground level for car circulation and had a tight grid-like arrangement (chosen to allow cranes to move along straight lanes during construction), the Heygate was devised with better public spaces, landscaping, and greenery.

Early in its lifetime, the Aylesbury Estate was unfortunate enough to receive a visit from Oscar Newman, who notoriously disparaged it for lacking 'defensible space' on national television in 1974. Newman diagnosed the design, with its pedways and decks, as a recipe for criminal behaviour and a dissolved sense of ownership. Unlike Newman, the social historian Michael Romyn spent years building up an extensive and thoughtful oral history through contact with residents of the Aylesbury Estate, and the Heygate Estate too.[11]

Romyn found that residents consistently spoke positively about their well-equipped and spacious flats – a huge improvement on previous accommodation – which received good light and were surrounded by plentiful amenities. Many of his interviewees remembered sociable and friendly communities. Yet both estates were beset by serious physical issues – including water penetration, poor insulation, rebounding noise, central-heating failures, and lift breakdowns – from early on. In the 1980s, declining local manufacturing jobs, slashed housing benefit, and urgent need-based allocation policies turned the Heygate and the Aylesbury into areas of concentrated socio-economic disadvantage, with high unemployment and poor educational attainment, at which point crime did rise. Deprivation was compounded by a deteriorating physical environment suffering from stark underinvestment and insufficient maintenance, as a result of cuts to Southwark Council's public spending imposed by central government.

In 1998, the Heygate Estate was surveyed by engineering consultants Allott and Lomax. They found the estate structurally sound but in need of complete refurbishment, citing long-term neglect of the fabric. The Twentieth Century Society classed the Heygate as 'well above average postwar housing' that had 'suffered from a lack of maintenance and good management'.[12] Residents were surveyed about potential redevelopment by MORI in 1999, with 571 households answering the circulated questionnaire. Just under a third said that they were dissatisfied with living on the Heygate Estate: a minority, although not an insignificant one. When presented with choices for the future, 63 per cent

The Heygate Estate from the air in 2012.

ticked the option of living in a council home on a refurbished or redeveloped Heygate Estate.[13]

In 2000, Southwark Council and Southwark Land Regeneration joined forces to launch a £1.5 billion plan for a transformed Elephant and Castle. It proposed demolishing the Heygate Estate to build a transport interchange surrounded by futuristic towers, with Foster and Partners primed to deliver a landmark fifty-storey block for the scheme. This glimmering vision went unrealised. Relations between the council and Southwark Land Regeneration broke down over disputes about land valuation and the division of future profits. The proposal was axed in 2002.

A framework for redevelopment was revived in 2004, when Southwark Council announced that the Heygate Estate was to be demolished and replaced by 4,200 new homes, with 1,200 reserved for social rent. These social housing units were supposed to be delivered on fifteen sites nearby, to which former Heygate tenants could move upon demolition. Southwark Council teamed up with Lend Lease private developers to deliver new housing on the footprint of the old estate. By 2009, just one of the early housing schemes had materialised and several had been scrapped altogether – while the decanting of the estate was already under way. By 2015, ten had been completed, housing just forty-five former Heygate residents. The Heygate Estate was demolished between 2011 and 2014. It was replaced with Elephant Park, a complex of mostly private homes built by Lend Lease in partnership with Southwark Council.

A parallel process took place down the road, at the larger Aylesbury Estate. The New Deal for Communities granted £56.2 million for the renewal of the Aylesbury Estate in 1999. A sum of £36 million was apportioned to physical regeneration and the rest was reserved for social interventions to tackle crime, anti-social behaviour, and educational issues. The Aylesbury's tenants were formally balloted by the council about their future in 2001. They were presented with two options: to remain council tenants without guarantee of refurbishment; or to undergo stock transfer to a

Southwark Land Regeneration's proposed new view from Elephant and Castle's transport interchange, 2000.

housing association for redevelopment. Just over three-quarters of the Aylesbury's tenant body turned out to deliver a resounding result of 73 per cent against transfer.[14] There were fears on the estate about higher rents and displacement.

In 2005, 700 units in the Aylesbury's five-storey and six-storey large-panel-system blocks were found to be at risk of a Ronan Point–style collapse in a report commissioned by Southwark Council. Taller slabs at the Aylesbury had been strengthened after the revelations in Newham in the 1980s, but the rest had not. They were still fitted with gas, too. Sam Webb weighed in: 'The council have confirmed a lot of what I told it for free.'[15] He demanded a 'national plan' for the replacement of these buildings across the country.[16]

A refurbishment of the Aylesbury was estimated to cost between £315 million to £350 million in 2005. Jane Rendell, an architectural professor at University College London's Bartlett School of Architecture, has since questioned the estimated price of refurbishment. She argued in 2015 that the price tag would have been closer to £191 million.[17] In 2005, councillors were presented with the first tally. They voted unanimously to demolish the Aylesbury Estate and vowed to build a denser development that would accommodate all the displaced tenants in social housing. But when the council unveiled its Aylesbury Area Action Plan in 2010, the previously promised social housing quota was drastically reduced. The council partnered with Notting Hill Housing Trust (later rebranded as Notting Hill Genesis) and London & Quadrant Housing Trust for the Aylesbury regeneration, in spite of the earlier vote against stock transfer. Decanting began in 2010, with demolition commencing in 2015 – it is ongoing at the time of writing.

The collective redevelopment of the Heygate and Aylesbury Estates has involved the construction of 6,979 new homes (some of which are still to be built). Although the transformed area is much taller and much denser, it has resulted in a net loss of social housing stock. The sites originally housed 3,435 council-rented units, which will be replaced by 1,897 social-rented homes (27 per cent of the total new-builds). Joe Penny, from University College London's Urban Laboratory, grades none of these new social housing units as 'truly affordable', because their rents have not been pegged to average incomes.[18]

A clutch of campaign groups sprang out of the battle over Southwark's regeneration. These included – to name just a few – the People's Republic of Southwark, the 35% Campaign, Better Elephant, the Elephant Amenity Network, Elephant and Castle Urban Forest, the Heygate Tenants and Residents Association, the Heygate and Aylesbury Leaseholders Action Group, and Heygate Was Home. One stands out as extraordinarily active and prolific: the community collective Southwark Notes. Thanks to Southwark Notes members' prescient commitment to saving every scrap of campaigning material they came across, we now have a substantial archive of housing activism through which to understand the grassroots experience of this turbulent period of urban change.

THEATRE OF STIGMA

In 2005, Southwark Council's regeneration project manager authorised £40,000 worth of funding to the London College of Communication to sponsor a student-led photographic project, titled 'Elephant Vanishes', about the Heygate and Aylesbury Estates. Southwark Notes was incensed by the resulting exhibition of photographs displayed at the local Cuming Museum in 2007. 'These publicity shots are regeneration propaganda at its purest!' they wrote. 'The images in this book do little except reinforce typical regeneration discourses hegemonised by the planning industry and middle-class media students' prejudices towards post-war social housing; i.e. "sink" estates are full of alcoholics, teenage-mums, drug addicts and squatters.'[19] Southwark Notes continued to emphasise this point in 2014: 'The implication that existing residents are the unlovable modern demons of the underclass . . . enables the Council to displace its own brutality onto a supposed demand from a mythical general public to "sort it out."'[20]

The Heygate Estate had 1,033 social housing units and 179 leasehold tenancies in 1998. It was commonly believed that Southwark Council had disinvested in the estates for years to justify compensating leaseholders with shockingly low pay-outs for their spacious Zone 1 flats. One was offered £150,000 for his two-bed flat on the Heygate, while two-bed flats in the replacement development were put on the market for £455,000.[21] The Heygate and Aylesbury Leaseholder Action Group was enraged by these discrepancies, as detailed in a 2011 blog post:

Southwark council is claiming that homes on the Heygate and Aylesbury estates are significantly lower in value than other properties in the area. The council is claiming that this is because the 'properties are unmortgageable on account of construction, social and service charge issues'. This is ridiculous, firstly because there are plenty of leaseholders who have managed to secure mortgages for their homes. Secondly, the 'construction, social and service charge issues' are a result of the council's neglect over the past 12 years since the estates were first earmarked for demolition.[22]

Southwark Council regularly let the two sites to film crews, to serve as gritty backdrops for dramas about poverty, delinquency, and narcotics, such as *Harry Brown*, *Top Boy*, *The Bill*, and *Luther*. Depictions of the Aylesbury and the Heygate as crime-ridden sink estates were considerably exaggerated, although drug use was a genuine issue. Allott and Lomax's 1998 survey of the Heygate Estate reported that crime was minimal.[23] Across 2000–05, crime rates were lower on the Aylesbury Estate than the borough average.[24]

Residents objected to the frequent disturbances caused by filming on their doorsteps and the effect on their reputations. A film crew painted graffiti on the Heygate Estate to create a more threatening environment, then failed to remove it when the production wrapped. The Heygate and Aylesbury Leaseholders Action Group complained to Southwark Council's Film Office about disconnected lighting and hazardous waste (including Molotov cocktails) discarded around the Heygate. Another crew left a burned-out grand piano after recording a music video. Heygate leaseholder Adrian Glasspool sent a letter on behalf of the Action Group demanding that 'the long run of filming on the Heygate involving gangs, crime or violence be halted immediately, and that a stop is put to any future filming that could lead to the further blighting of the Heygate estate'.[25]

Across 2007 to 2010, the council licensed seventy-six films on the Heygate Estate alone, earning £91,000.[26] Labour Councillor Kirsty McNeill argued in an op-ed in *Southwark News*:

The council makes a pretty penny from these filming projects – but all the residents get is a token donation to their tenants' association and yet another chance to see their neighbourhood paraded to the rest of the country as if every flat has a gangster or murderer behind the door. Every single pound of profit made by these filming projects should either be given to the local tenants' and residents' associations to spend as they see fit; or be ring-fenced to be spent on improving the estates themselves.[27]

The last leaseholder at the Heygate, the same Adrian Glasspool, was forcibly evicted by bailiffs from his Heygate home of sixteen years at the end of 2013. With depleted assets and surging neighbouring property prices, leaseholders had to move long distances from their former homes – as far as Cheshunt, Thurrock, Rochester, and Slough.

THE NEW FACE OF HIGH RISE

The noughties offered a curious paradox. At the same time as old, multistorey council estates were denounced as sites of poverty, fecklessness, and vice, New Labour was flaunting lavish, glass-sheathed, high-rise housing as emblematic of prosperous British cities. Richard Rogers professed a passion for density, his essential ingredient for urban vitality. Stacked offices and flats were on the top of the menu. Blair himself was drawn to architectural novelty: alongside Richard Rogers's, he admired the high-tech work of the architects Nigel Coates, Zaha Hadid, and Elsie Owusu. John Prescott, as deputy prime minister, declared that the government wanted architecture with a 'wow factor'.[28]

At the turn of the millennium, London faced an acute shortage of housing, especially affordable housing. Almost 200,000 people were signed up to council waiting lists across the capital.[29] Social housing stock was shrinking, house prices were climbing, and completions of new-builds were stagnating. In 2000, the Blair administration established the Greater London Authority (GLA), with an elected assembly and mayor. The first mayor was Ken Livingstone (former leader of the GLC before its abolition in 1986), who ran as an independent against the New Labour candidate, Frank Dobson. Livingstone's Housing Commission strongly recommended that half of London's new housing stock should be affordable, with at least 35 per cent for social rent.

Livingstone also backed height, even in the form of corporate skyscrapers. He supported the construction of Heron Tower in Bishopsgate and the Shard in London Bridge. 'I intend to extract the most out of London's growth for London's citizens,' he explained in 2001. 'That is why I am using my planning powers to allow higher density in return for more affordable housing and more mixed-use sites.'[30]

High-rise remained a bogeyman in some quarters. John Redwood (Conservative MP for commuter-belt Wokingham) hit back at the Urban Task Force in 2000: 'Do you understand the damage that architects and planners did in the sixties when they tried a high density approach? In my constituency people just don't want to live in this kind of development.'[31] *The Times* journalist Richard Morrison described the noughties skyscraper craze as 'the biggest change to London's skyline since the Blitz'. He characterised it as pure 'mania' – the result of self-important egotism from Livingstone and a coterie of 'millionaire architects', 'hard-nosed City planners', and 'slick property developers'. English Heritage and SAVE Britain's Heritage warned that towers would obstruct important historic views in the city, especially over St Paul's. Reversing a historic conservationist battle cry deployed against modernist comprehensive redevelopment from the 1960s, Livingstone charged them as 'the greatest threat to London's future since the Luftwaffe'.[32]

Housing output in London rose significantly from 2000 to 2008. The production of affordable housing increased, but at a slower rate compared to private stock. The housing specialist Duncan Bowie has noted that as a proportion of net delivery, the output of affordable housing in this period was smaller than before.[33]

The burnished skyscrapers of the noughties seemed symbolic of a hierarchically segregated society, plainly vertically spatialised. Campaigners in Southwark were disgusted by the forty-three-storey Strata SE1 Tower (2010), a building shaped like an electric razor and topped by green-gesturing wind turbines (which never worked). It contained 25 per cent affordable housing units, but they were all for shared ownership rather than social rent. Controversially, there were separate lifts for these two categories of residents. The architecture critic Ellis Woodman found the Strata Tower truly malevolent: 'This is a building that appears to be auditioning for a supporting role in a James Bond title sequence.'[34] It won *Building Design*'s Carbuncle Cup in 2010. Nearby, the thirty-seven-storey One the Elephant tower (2015), built in partnership between Lend Lease and Southwark Council on the site of the old Elephant and Castle leisure centre, attracted similar ire for containing not a single unit of affordable housing.

The computer-generated, swarm-modelled dreamscapes for the taller and denser Elephant Park, advertised on local display boards,

The Strata SE1 Tower next to the Heygate Estate in 2013.

left many unconvinced. Better Elephant predicted that profit-incentivised regeneration in Elephant and Castle would 'result in characterless streets with a bland retail offer, overshadowed by rapidly-aging high-rise blocks'.[35] Southwark Notes found London's regenerated spaces sterile and anonymous:

> If you contrast some of the architectural drawings that you see on the hoardings of development sites with the reality afterwards, you tend to find that these new 'public' spaces are either privatised at night when the development gates are firmly put in place OR despite the concrete benches, lit-up trees and snazzy blue lights in the pavement, no-one feels like hanging out there because they feel like urban morgues policed by zealous security guards with a list of no-no's for the newly privately owned space.[36]

When Tony Blair stepped down in 2007, the *Guardian*'s architecture critic Jonathan Glancey lamented the architectural record of the last nine years: 'The most visible legacy of the past decade has been a glut of crass or sensationalist buildings largely in the service of high finance, while the public realm has been kicked to the side.'[37] In 2009, Rory Olcayto identified the ascendency of 'a new mode of architectural expression' since the millennium, in the *Architects' Journal*. He called it 'Cabe-ism' – in reference to the Commission for Architecture and the Built Environment, established in 1999 to advise the government on design. 'Throw in a bit of old-fashioned modernism, concern around climate change and some mixed-messages about "iconic" design. Finally, sprinkle liberally with branding concepts culled from 80s-style advertising culture.'[38]

Touring around Britain, the writer Owen Hatherley produced a scathing gazette of the buildings of the New Labour era, *A Guide to the New Ruins of Great Britain* (2010). Hatherley described the New Labour approach to architecture as 'pseudo-modernism', 'a Modernism without the politics, without the utopianism, or without any conception of the polis'. Visually, he found little to recommend from this spate of building, abhorring its glass towers and barcode façades. PFI-driven urban renewal, Hatherley argued, had created 'a horrible, unplanned new landscape, the embodiment of New Labour's attempt to transform the Welfare State into a giant business'.[39] The regeneration of Elephant and Castle was one of Hatherley's particular *bêtes noires*, regularly cited in his journalism as the mendacious apogee of Blairite urban policy, where an 'infantile, jolly aesthetic' was being pasted over 'class cleansing'.[40]

Owen Hatherley is the most forceful British architectural writer of his generation. The architectural historian Otto Saumarez Smith has described him as 'a "béton brut" Ruskin for the 21st century', situating Hatherley in a long line of idiosyncratic chroniclers of Britain's built environment, alongside Nikolaus Pevsner, Ian Nairn, and John Betjeman.[41] Remarkably prolific, his writing is both astute and politically uncompromising. He articulated a widespread contemporary vexation with the perverse dissonance within Britain's urban landscape, where stunning exorbitance jostled with deindustrialisation and deprivation, and looked back to the mid-century for alternatives.

Hatherley's book *Militant Modernism* (2008) influentially reappraised the architecture of the post-war welfare state as an inspiring political tool with the capacity to reactivate the contemporary left. The book was enthused by the notion of the 'concrete New Jerusalem':

> Concrete walkways and windswept precincts have always seemed to me to have a sharp poignancy. What might be at work here is the common contemporary phenomenon of nostalgia for the future, a longing for the fragments of the half-hearted post-war attempt at building a new society, an attempt that lay in ruins by the time I was born. These remnants of social democracy can, at best, have the effect of critiquing the paucity of ambition and grotesque inequalities of the present.[42]

Yet the disturbing history of system building in council housing – a damning product of public-private-sector partnership that produced defects hushed up for decades – shows up the irrefutable deficiencies and contradictions of post-war social democracy in Britain. The novel disappointments of the present must not distract us from historic injustices. To regenerate the welfare state, we might look beyond the physical legacy of our built environment, to instead draw energy from the social history of residential campaigning, which has proffered new visions for a reformed public housing compact, decade upon decade.

THE CONSULTATION GAME

New Labour's New Deal for Communities pledged to inaugurate an era of citizen empowerment and popular participation in urban renewal. In *The Third Way: New Politics for the New Century* (1998), published by the Fabian Society, Tony Blair insisted on the importance of 'finding new ways to enable citizens to share in decision-making', and of 'making government more open and responsive' to meet the rising 'demand for more democratic self governance'.[43] Southwark Council declared its approach to regeneration to be 'deeply rooted in a continuous sequence of public consultation'.[44] Across the ensuing years, poorly executed consultative overtures from the council and its associated developers left local people feeling marginalised and exploited.

Consultation has long been a thorny word in town planning. The American policymaker Sherry Arnstein devised a seminal theorisation of 'citizen power' in 1969, illustrated by her 'ladder of citizen participation'. Arnstein's diagram depicted gradations in the balance of control, ranging from non-participation (in the form of therapy and manipulation) to tokenism (placation, informing, and consultation), as distinct from real citizen power and partnership at the top of the ladder.[45]

In 2008, Southwark Council distributed flyers to residents on the Heygate Estate, titled 'Coping with Change – Stress Busters!' The council was advertising a series of workshops organised in collaboration with the Happiness Project (a creative consultancy) to teach residents how to deal with the 'change, anxiety and fear' involved in being moved out of their homes. 'Shift Happens', punned the flyers to Heygate readers – they needed to learn 'how to accept and grow with change'.[46] Local community groups were incandescent. Southwark Notes wrote in a blog post:

Yes, it's true, the Council with it's [sic] infinite tact is paying The Happiness Project £2000 to train Heygate tenants 'to be happier and less stressed'. The project's motto is 'Success is a state of mind; happiness is a way of travelling; love is your true power'. We suggest the Council adopts this as the new Borough motto. In this way the non-appearance of flats for the decant tenants can merely be seen as a state of mind and not the shameful scandal it is.[47]

Heygate Was Home described the Stress Buster workshops as 'a blatant attempt to pathologise and therapeuticise discontent'.[48] Ernie Hart, a member of the Heygate Tenants and Residents Association, commented:

All they need to do to stop tenants feeling anxious is to talk to us and give us what we need . . . What we want is very simple: to move into a nice new home that is decorated with no fuss. We just want to be treated properly – we don't need therapists.[49]

He explained: 'If they hadn't come along and said, "Right, we're gonna move you out, force you out", I'd have been happy for the next thirty years hopefully.'[50] Sherry Arnstein's warnings about therapy were still pertinent, four decades on. The 2008 financial crash and ensuing recession were followed by a boom in happiness entrepreneurs emphasising the role of personal choice and attitude in the pursuit of success. In 2011, the critical theorist Mark Fisher lambasted the mass 'privatisation of stress'. Fisher saw the promotion of personalised therapeutic approaches to stress management as a depoliticisation of social malaise. He insisted that depression was a consequence of depressing material realities.[51]

In 2011, Southwark Council hired a consultancy called Soundings to run community 'involvement' sessions at its Consultation Hub, during which participants reported apprehension about the ratio of social and affordable housing units being built. Soundings told residents that the post-consultation plan sent to Lend Lease would require a minimum of 25 per cent affordable housing in the Heygate redevelopment (a constriction of an earlier commitment to 35 per cent).[52] However, Lend Lease subsequently declared that it would only build 'as much affordable housing as is financially viable'.[53] The Elephant Amenity Network – which had called for open master-planning in their Elephant and Castle Regeneration Charter, incorporating neighbourhood forums and community right-to-build orders – sent a public letter to Soundings complaining of 'a serious misrepresentation of the amount of affordable housing to be built'.[54]

Southwark Notes published several detailed blog posts about Soundings. One was titled 'Listening to No End'.[55] They argued that Southwark Council's Consultation Hub exercises were mere 'spectacle':

> The 'inclusive' aesthetics of the Hub and of the various consultation events meant post-it notes and colourful display boards with a minimum of numbers or technical details. In most cases, the 'participatory' approaches consisted in using infantilising techniques: encouraging single word comments, post-it notes, squiggles marking regular through routes, scoring issues by preference etc. . . . The constant use of the words 'community', 'participation' and 'invovement' [sic] are essential to this process of group hypnotism.[56]

Soundings' overtures of engagement struck Southwark Notes as disingenuous: a 'shiny happy method where listening really only becomes nodding'. This approach seemed to be 'a new kind of "charm offensive"', 'different from either straight-talking developers or the bureaucratic approach of councillors'. It involved 'mapping out your local knowledge, sharing your organic wisdom about the place where you live [which] then seems to be fed into Place Making mincer and presto – (un)affordable housing and/or luxury flats appear!' Locals gave up many hours to consultation meetings without remuneration. Soundings spoke of celebrating 'people power'. Southwark Notes asked, 'Is this the same as free labour?'[57]

These initiatives had operated to facilitate gentrification rather than resist it, legitimising the process through the pretence of community involvement. Consultation, Southwark Notes concluded, acted 'to diffuse dissent, reframe it in the interest of regeneration and cherry-pick the ideas most suited to the developer and council to be integrated into the plan'.[58] The crucial problem was a fundamental imbalance of power within the process:

> The New Labour-embraced notion of 'the stakeholder' . . . is to pretend that when it comes to 'stakes' a council tenant, an owner of a grocery or electrical store, a playgroup run by mums, an adventure playground and so on has the same voice, time, resources and power as the Council, property developers, large retail chains, local government bodies etc. Such Third Way politics tries to seek a politics where any necessary social tensions and antagonism between different people, groups and communities are erased in favour of a mythical consensus.[59]

The fallacy of choice offered to the Heygate and the Aylesbury Estates' residents has led scholars – influenced by the thinking of Jacques Rancière and Chantal Mouffe – to interpret the regeneration as a 'post-political' process, in which 'neoliberal' New Labour governance prioritised economic growth over democratic decision-making. In 2014, the geographer Loretta Lees argued that in Southwark 'contestation and conflict have been supplanted by consensus-based politics which smother (but do not replace) conflict/dissent through carefully choreographed processes of participation. In so doing they have depoliticised the political.'[60]

Loretta Lees, the London Tenants Federation, Just Space, and Southwark Notes Archives Group were jointly awarded a Scholar-Activist Project Award for community-partnered research in radical geography by the Antipode Foundation in 2012. Drawing on their experience in Southwark, these actors co-produced a guide titled *Staying Put: An Anti-Gentrification Handbook for Council Estates in London* (2014). As a warning to other readers in similar circumstances, *Staying Put* denounced 'the consultation con' and 'the consultation game', ironically captioning a cartoon of a builder's digger with the label 'consultation mechanism'.[61]

At the Siege of the Elephant in 2013 – a day-long open event 'to share evidence and discuss alternatives' to gentrification in Elephant and Castle – attendees reflected on the importance of 'the pressure and ideas of the Labour movement' in the history of British public housing. 'Why have labour-led councils turned their back to their working-class constituency?' they asked. 'Councils were more or less in collusion with developers to raise their council tax base,' it was suggested. 'New Labour administrations,' it seemed, 'were disconnected from their own history and legacy and were acting against their own constituency.'[62]

New Labour strategy was instrumental to the course of regeneration at the Heygate and Aylesbury Estates, but it was not solely responsible. The London borough of Southwark was under continuous Labour control from the 1960s up to 2002, when the party lost majority control of the council. Power was split with the Liberal Democrats from 2002 to 2010. The council was dominated by the Liberal Democrats when the decision to demolish the Heygate was taken in 2004 and the Aylesbury in 2005. In 2010, the Labour Party regained control in Southwark, yet ceded power in central government. In the same year, the new Conservative–Liberal Democrat coalition government cut the social housing budget by 75 per cent. The new mayor of London, Boris Johnson, rescinded Livingstone's 35 per cent quota for affordable and social housing in redevelopment projects in 2011. Yet for many people active in grassroots campaigning, the sense of treachery by the Labour Party became the overriding logic of complaint. Attacks on social housing were expected from the right; from the left, they constituted a betrayal.

Adrian Glasspool and the investigative journalist Oliver Wainwright discovered in 2015 that the situation in Southwark reflected a broader covert problem. Developers were able to exploit a loophole in Section 106 of the Town and Country Planning Act (1990), which enabled them to wriggle out of minimum affordable housing quotas by presenting financial-viability assessments demonstrating insufficient capital to deliver these units. They could massage the sums by predicting high construction costs and lower-than-likely sales prices.

Glasspool lodged a Freedom of Information request in 2012, asking to see documentation to justify the breach of the affordable housing quota at Elephant Park. This was released after three years of legal wrangling, revealing that Lend Lease's original financial-viability assessment had predicted average sales values of £600 per square foot. By doing so, the company was able to pull down the required affordable housing tally on the grounds of commercial infeasibility. In 2015, however, their apartments were priced at an average of over £1,000 per square foot.[63] In this landscape, local councils lack negotiating power. While developers can simply withdraw from negotiations to find more profitable projects, local authorities are under political pressure to deliver regeneration as smoothly and swiftly as possible. Southwark Council currently stands to make a loss on both the Heygate and the Aylesbury schemes.

STAKING TERRITORY

Gentrification, as the urban scholar and activist Rebecca Amato points out, requires 'the production – and perception – of empty space ready to be filled'.[64] During the decanting of the Heygate Estate across 2007 to 2014, local groups attempted to re-fill the space with community projects, exhibitions, and film screenings. Better Elephant held a 'Transforming the Heygate' exhibition on the emptied estate, showcasing their alternative masterplan for the regeneration, in 2012. The Heygate Pop-Up Cinema showed documentaries charting the experiences of residents forced to move away. Felipe Lanuza, a researcher who visited the Heygate Estate between 2011 and 2014, argued that these uses of the site 'expressed an alternative vision to the "official" vision emphasising failure, stigmatisation, and an intended progress determined by the regeneration'.[65]

Elephant and Castle Urban Forest, a pressure group established in 2011, focused its efforts on spotlighting the Heygate Estate's green legacy. The group pointed out that the new housing to replace the estate would in fact be higher and denser than before, threatening the existing mature natural infrastructure. Members sought to raise awareness about the impressive range of trees and shrubbery on the estate by setting up an Urban Forest School, mapping greenery, and inviting speakers. Mobile Gardeners, a collective established in 2012, took over parts of the Heygate Estate for community-led gardening, planting wildflowers and bulbs.

Southwark Notes, in collaboration with other local groups, led a series of anti-gentrification Walking the Rip-Off tours around Elephant and Castle and its surrounding area from 2011 to 2014, with a strong focus on the Heygate and Aylesbury Estates. The first recorded tour occurred in October 2011, as part of a day-long event followed by a barbecue and film screening, organised by Southwark Notes and 56a Infoshop, a radical, non-profit social centre in Walworth, first founded as a squat in 1991. Its success led to the formation of a regular Gentrification Study Group at 56a Infoshop, and a commitment to organising more walking tours.

By navigating, occupying, and commentating upon gentrified sites, the Southwark walking tours sought to overwrite recently privatised spaces as irrefutably public. This was also an educational exercise to equip local people with more knowledge about the area's history. Attendees were given detailed fact files on the sites and buildings they visited. Campaigners distributed booklets with snarkily annotated maps to allow people to take themselves on self-guided tours: 'You can find the sites of gentrification in the area since the 1990s and then shake your fist at them using the map.'[66] The tours were intended as a spur to action. 'Join the Southwark Notes folks,' one flyer advertised, 'on another ramble around the sites of old & new gentrification in The Elephant area looking at what's going on, who's making decisions and asking what we can do about it!!'[67] The self-guided maps reminded readers on the final page: 'IT AIN'T OVER YET! Confused? Angry? Write to us.'[68]

Importantly, the tours were 'intended as a community conversation rather than just us lot going on about it all'.[69] 'Although we always start the walk and the talk,' Southwark Notes explained, 'the best bits of the event is [sic] always when those who have come begin to take over the chatting, sharing of anecdotes and chipping in all the differing senses of both frustration and sometimes anger over what is going on'.[70] Residents took the reins at the Heygate and Aylesbury Estates. A member of the Soundings team turned up to join a Walking the Rip-Off tour of the Aylesbury Estate in June 2012. 'We told her that she definitely wasn't welcome on the walk,' reported Southwark Notes.[71] The walking tours were fashioned as a public commons, a contrast to the restricted formal channels for consultation offered by Southwark Council. They provided the opportunity for local people to create critical pathways – both literally and intellectually – to reclaim agency within a rapidly changing built environment in which their voices were being effaced.

An extensive and multifaceted micro-blogging ecosystem blossomed in Southwark during the 2000s and 2010s. The interacting community groups that emerged from the struggle for the Heygate and Aylesbury Estates set up their own websites, saturated with hyperlinks cross-referencing allied sites and resources. Many were built with Wordpress, a popular free platform that allowed users to create their own web pages without specialised programming skills.

On a simple level, these sites functioned to publicise campaigning. However, they also served a host of other purposes: as alternative news sources, e-petition hosts, social spaces, archives, printable resource banks, and open-access libraries of scanned literature. Web activism allowed for an enormously expanded reach at much-reduced cost. This was a new public sphere with a new, immaterial print culture. By building a digital architecture and infrastructure, local people fought to maintain a foothold in Southwark's urban politics amid mass displacement. The internet provided a space for present-day action and for preservation of the historical record.

The internet allowed ordinary people to build their own phenomenological archive. Chris Wood recorded two 'soundscapes' of the Heygate and Aylesbury Estates in 2012 and 2013, which he posted on SoundCloud. These recordings do not sound like dangerous sink estates. We can hear South London accents, the clangs of building construction, and Caribbean music. We also hear pockets of peaceful quiet, in spite of their inner-city locations; the estates' fortress-like construction was intentional to shield them from the roar of traffic noise. There are sounds of planes overhead, footsteps on the grass, chickens clucking, and birds singing.[72]

The nearby Michael Faraday Primary School, located just north of Burgess Park, posted its year-six pupils reciting poems about a visit to the decanted Heygate Estate in 2014 on Audioboom. Local children, practising the use of personification, wrote mournful reflections on the site's abandonment. A child described 'a heart-broken garden, never to be harvested again', another 'the dark stairway, lonely, waiting for children to run over him'. One child personified the empty flats: 'Number 76 glared left and right, hoping someone would come, they waited and waited crying out loud, and their hearts broke into pieces.'[73]

The Heygate Was Home website compiled a collection of residents' testimonials between 2013 and 2015, as well as a press and film archive on the estate's demolition. This archive pits a resistant narrative told via inhabitants' voices against mainstream media portrayals of the estate. Heygate Was Home argued that the 'numerous references to sink estates and crime served well to reinforce the council and developer's regeneration agenda, while erasing the real history of the estate'.[74] One resident, Nicola Redpath, explained: 'I am fed up of reading that the estate was a hotbed of crime and deprivation by the media and local politicians.'[75] Another, Doreen Gee, said:

I feel quite angry when people call the estate a slum. It's not a slum and it never has been. It's run down because of the regeneration . . . A lot of people in the flats didn't want to go either – all they wanted was renovation.[76]

'To write in a digital age,' explains the feminist scholar Kate Eichhorn, 'is to write in the archive.'[77] In cyberspace, past and present exist simultaneously. But we cannot rely upon the digital future. Diverging from early celebrations of the internet as a free commons, the web rapidly became beholden to less egalitarian forces. Online space has become privatised, owned, and commercialised. Furthermore, digitally archived material is never static; these sites remain live, mutable, and fragile. The Heygate Was Home website is now defunct. Visitors are redirected, at the time of writing, to a Russian cryptocurrency exchange.

Southwark Notes – acutely conscious of the need to record work for perpetuity – set up its own archive group. Magpie-like, members saved all sorts of campaigning ephemera at 56a Info shop: booklets, flyers, posters, and event write-ups, down to a coffee-stained Costa napkin covered with hastily scribbled meeting notes.

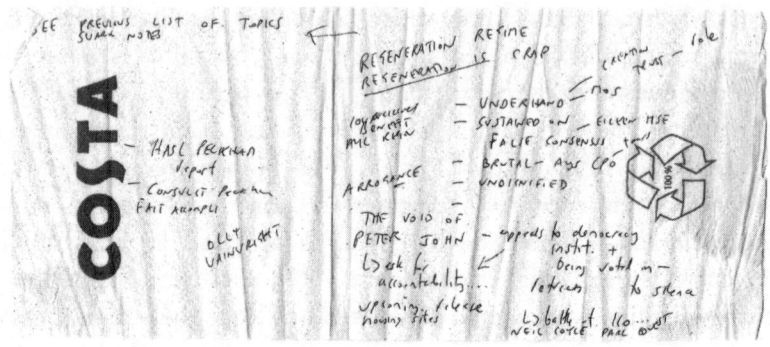

Furious jottings on a Costa napkin, filed away carefully among documents in 56a Infoshop.

The archive group was resourceful in aggregating and preserving documents from other community groups too. While other groups' web pages expired, Southwark Notes made sure to materialise its own digital paper-trails, instead of relying upon the supposed permanency of a web archive. The group printed out blog posts, web-art, email chains, and computer-processed notes. Southwark Notes also collaborated with MayDay Rooms, an archive of social movements, to transfer crucial documents into a more secure and searchable digital collection: the London Housing Struggles Archive.

After the Heygate Estate was demolished in 2014, tensions ran higher. When the Aylesbury Estate was condemned for demolition in 2015, protests escalated to culminate in a full-blown occupation of the site. On 31 January 2015, around 150 people from the Fight for the Aylesbury pressure group occupied Chartridge House on the estate. The dispossession of the Aylesbury, they declared, was 'the same bullshit that we have seen on the nearby Heygate estate, and all across London'. In a blog post the next day, they explained:

> We are tenants, squatters, and other people who care about how our city is being grabbed by the rich, by developers and corrupt politicians, socially cleansed and sold off for profit . . . No demolition of the Aylesbury. No yuppy flats. Homes for all. We are here to fight for the Aylesbury. We are here to fight for our city. We are here to liberate this space and bring it back to life.[78]

The occupiers hosted an array of activities across February and March, including daily open assemblies, demonstrations, teach-ins, barricading workshops, acoustic jams, litter collections, film screenings, and a football tournament. They filled the estate with banners, saturating the space with visible evidence of protest.

Riot police were eventually sent in to evict the squatters using physical force. On 2 April 2015, the occupiers decided to vacate the premises under the threat of arrests. An interim possession order was granted to Southwark Council in court. Yet the occupation had won press coverage and public backing from other groups, including Southwark Notes, Aylesbury Tenants and Leaseholders First, the People's Republic of Southwark, Southwark Defend Council Housing, and Housing Action Southwark and Lambeth. Fight for the Aylesbury declared on its blog: 'Even when we lose in court, we win in the streets. Victory to the Aylesbury!'[79]

DARK LAUGHTER

Southwark Notes circulated flyers and posters around the locality during the 2010s. A favourite stunt was the production of parody versions of the official marketing materials produced by

Southwark Council to promote the regeneration of the Heygate Estate, complete with council and Lend Lease logos. These materials poked fun at platitudinal jargon, rewriting their content in plain terms to highlight the emptiness of the promises touted to residents. 'Please help us to chuck you out the area!' appealed one flyer, titled 'The Final Rip-Off!'[80] They also impersonated Soundings, renamed 'Schmoozings': 'you tell the story! we listen! we package it up! the developers come in! you get displaced!'[81] Another poster jokingly invited passers-by to 'Take the Heygate safari'. It called out to 'Artists! Photographers! Journalists!' and promised 'Wild estates! Poetic ruins! Zero tenants!' 'Visit the place where people used to live! Make art, take photos and add to the myths. It's a great story but you weren't so into it when we all used to live here.'[82]

Southwark Notes printed a tongue-in-cheek 'regeneration noir' comic series titled *The Affordables* in 2012. It starred two shady characters, dressed as gangsters in dark coats, Council Dude and Developer Dude. These comics were distributed for free but were teasingly priced at £1 million each, reflecting the astronomical inflation of the cost of living in Elephant and Castle. They announced,

> SOUTHWARK NOTES thought it would try it's [*sic*] hand at putting some of the most obvious aspects of the Great Elephant and Castle Regeneration Rip-Off into a supposedly funny comic strip . . . It's also about the human side to both Council workers and developers and how both are weirdly enthusiastic about regeneration but so deeply cynical at the same time!![83]

In one meta issue of *The Affordables*, Council Dude and Developer Dude find out about the cartoons in which they star. 'The moaners are always cheap,' they respond. 'Cheap and nasty . . . Poor folks with nothing better to do.' One exclaims: 'They should get a life, eh?' The other replies: 'Exactly. But somewhere else. Not round here.'[84]

Local people could not arrest the physical process of gentrification at the Heygate and the Aylesbury Estates, but they could leverage moral capital to disrupt public understandings of gentrification as socially acceptable or beneficial. Wealthier new residents would not be allowed to forget that their homes were the products of working-class displacement. Campaigners put up spoof posters. 'COMING SOON,' one joked: 'Waitrose.'[85] 'Seemingly doing well yuppies, welcome to the prison of your own making,' another warned.[86] Southwark Notes produced a mock *Guardian* clipping reporting on the construction of a prison to house young professionals 'locked up for crimes of lifestyle' (in reference to the apartments popping up) next to a South London council estate. It read:

> Unlike the social housing opposite with it's [*sic*] community feel and it's [*sic*] day-to-day neighbourliness, the new development will not allow the new residents to mix freely with those long-established in the area . . . The prisoners will be let out on day release to work jobs in the creative industries and in The City but at night they will be securely locked in behind large heavy stripped pine doors. A press release from the developers said that most of the upwardly mobile will be inside on charges ranging from receiving Prada catalogues, soul murder, coveting of silver cutlery or simple possession of coffee-table books but would only be staying in the prison for a few years before moving on.[87]

Humour is inherently subversive. Southwark Notes wanted 'to make sure that a counter-narrative could be maintained by residents against the spin and soundbites of the Council'.[88] The group used a darkly sardonic voice to author alternative discursive scripts in resistance to the mass licensing of gentrification in twenty-first-century London. Humour operated as both an intellectual and ethical riposte: by mocking the duplicity, elitism, and profiteering which they saw as inherent to the regeneration process, campaigners reframed gentrification as morally reprehensible and politically motivated.

These jokes served as political ammunition. They also provided consolation. During a brainstorming session, Southwark Notes privately summed up on paper: 'Need a sense of humour to deal with the depressing reality.'[89] The gloomy situation was satirised in the group's Gentrification Top Trumps pack, which indexed the buildings appearing in Elephant and Castle. Each was allocated points for market value, ratio of private to social housing units, and an overall gentrification score. Southwark Notes' comic strategy was a means of dissent. At the same time, as the regeneration scheme progressed, it acted as a form of gallows humour – characterised by the social historian Marjolein 't Hart as 'a psychological escape from the unalterable'.[90]

The meanings of high rise multiplied in twenty-first-century Britain. The inner-city populations of London and Manchester rose – part of the push for densification at the heart of Blair's 'urban renaissance'. Yet this was a renaissance from which a huge proportion of society was excluded. Richard Rogers had professed a loathing for 'the appalling market-driven Thatcherite view of society' in the 1990s.[91] His Rogers Stirk Harbour partnership went on to attract censure for designing luxury apartment blocks such as the Montevetro building (2000) in Battersea, One Hyde Park (2009), and the Riverlight development (2016) in Nine Elms.

The buildings replacing the Heygate and the Aylesbury Estates were many times taller than their predecessors. The numerous shifting masterplans dreamed up for the sites during the noughties advertised a clutch of glass-plated towers with glossy façades. By the 2010s, taste was shifting, as these buildings garnered ugly associations with criticism piling up for their weak contextualism and insensitivity.

Elephant Park, which is still in progress, has ultimately taken on the so-called New London Vernacular, originally paraded by Boris Johnson and which planners have been encouraged to use since 2010.

The New London Vernacular took inspiration from the squares and terraces of the eighteenth century. These historic brick elevations were scaled up for dense multistorey blocks, with rationalised, fully glazed portrait windows and protruding metal balconies, in an effort to replicate the refined proportions and warm tones of Georgian housing. The motivations of the New London Vernacular and its material manifestations throughout the capital (and beyond to new-build developments far from London, dislocating the rationale of the vernacular) feel strikingly similar to the interwar period's neo-Georgian flat boom a century prior.

London has a rich built heritage upon which to draw for inventive, historically allusive design, but the latter is not in evidence in Elephant Park. It is also missing its historic community. The copy-and-paste multistorey blocks emerging here lack the vigorous, idiosyncratic flair of Peter Barber's rewardingly higgledy-piggledy brick housing projects going up at the same time in Stratford and Barnet, which pay tribute to Victorian back-to-back court typologies and the parabolic arches of the LCC's 1930s estates. Nor do they pack the geometrically exciting punch of Darbourne and Darke's Lillington Gardens (1971), Kate Macintosh's Dawson's Heights (1972), or Donald Bell's Odhams Walk (1979) – all of which are much more accomplished in their handling of brick elevations and incidental sociability at high densities.

In 2012, the American academic Sarah Schulman first put forward her theory of 'the gentrification of the mind'. Gentrification, she argued, was not just a physical process; it was also a 'spiritual' one. Schulman observed the rise of 'gentrified thinking', in which gentrification is understood as a natural, evolutionary progress.[92] Society thus becomes alienated both from the realities of contemporary dispossession and from the possibility of alternatives.

In Southwark, campaigners seized the chance to shift gentrified thinking. Though disempowered to halt the physical process of demolition and displacement unilaterally, they sought to shape a new moral economy around gentrification. The Marxist historian E. P. Thompson seminally conceptualised the moral economy as a 'popular consensus as to what were legitimate and what were illegitimate practices' within a society's collective matrix of understandings of social norms and obligations.[93] Local campaigners at the Heygate and Aylesbury Estates endeavoured to destabilise arguments that the demolition of post-war, high-rise housing estates was legitimately necessary. Seeking to stretch the Overton window, in alliance with sympathetic academics, they reframed gentrification as a political choice.

The erosion of affordable inner-city housing precipitated a reappraisal of the legacy of the post-war welfare state and council housing in Britain during the 2010s. Many council tenants had called for their high-rise homes to be demolished in the 1980s. By the 2010s, demolition had flipped in meaning; an option once conceived as emancipatory became suffused with violence. The Heygate and Aylesbury Estates were by no means dazzling works of modernist architecture, unlike Ernö Goldfinger's beautifully detailed Alexander Fleming House (1967) or Roger Walters's powerfully articulated Perronet House (1970) nearby. The Aylesbury had serious structural flaws. But in twenty-first-century Southwark, it became clear that these buildings would not be replaced with improved social nor affordable housing. These circumstances gave rise to a necessarily defensive political mode: local campaign groups argued that the Heygate and Aylesbury should be saved. Post-war estates, however imperfect, came to represent a foothold for working people in an expensive city, a last bastion of a fading welfare state.

In the noughties, the architecture critic Amanda Baillieu held up the regeneration of Elephant and Castle's post-war housing as an opportunity for amends to be made for the mistakes of the 1960s and 1970s.[94] Over the coming years, the experience of a whole community of residents on the Heygate and the Aylesbury Estates transpired to be painful, confounding, and degrading. In the 2010s, Southwark's coalition of campaigners came to a dismayed conclusion: 'Decision-making in "urban regeneration" remains as top-down (the council/developer making decisions for council estate residents) as it was during the "slum" clearances after World War II.'[95]

Epilogue

In 2012, a pressure group was established under the name Create Streets. Its founding mission was to promote the planning of traditional streets in urban redevelopment, in opposition to the construction of multistorey estates. The group is closely allied with the right-wing think tank Policy Exchange. Create Streets has secured significant influence in British public policy, acting as consultants for local councils across the country and for the Conservative government's Building Better, Building Beautiful commission of 2020. Its director is the former investment banker and unsuccessful Conservative Party candidate Nicholas Boys Smith, who has made no secret of his revulsion for Britain's 'cloying, maliciously-coddling welfare system'.[1]

Create Streets argues that multistorey housing has been universally loathed in Britain. Its members regard this architecture as incompatible with 'so many essentially private and domestic notions of British life'. Cited key influences include King Charles, Roger Scruton, Oscar Newman, and Alice Coleman, whose arguments the group enthusiastically and uncritically reproduces. Create Streets' analysis is frequently blinkered, flippant, and weakly evidenced. 'Multi-storey housing is more risky and makes people sadder, badder and lonelier,' pronounced its report, *Create Streets: Not Just Multi-Storey Estates* (2013), written in partnership with Policy Exchange. 'Without wishing to be glib, tower blocks don't just make you more depressed,' they remarked, glibly, 'They make it easier to kill yourself – you can jump.'

The group's policy briefings are risibly historically illiterate and littered with errors. 'Ernest Goldfinger, who built Trellick tower, lived in it for just two months before moving back to his house in Hampstead,' read its paper of 2013.[2] Presumably they mean Ernö, who never lived in Trellick, but in Balfron Tower on the other side of the city to gather feedback from residents and to check how its facilities were working. Of all the figures to condemn, the architect of some of the finest and most thoughtfully conceived tower blocks in Britain makes for a cackhanded choice of target.

Up in the Air has attempted to provide an antidote to this cavalier approach to the history of Britain's high-rise council housing (which regrettably reflects much of the discussion in public discourse) to suggest a more nuanced relationship between space and subjectivity. Residential opinion about these homes has been mercurial, fluctuating across time, place, and life-cycle. Over the decades, high rise has signified both modernity and decay; community and exclusivity; privilege and disadvantage; luxury and privation.

High-rise homes summoned forth high hopes and biting critiques. These buildings raised big questions about the operation of Britain's welfare state. They sprung from a moment of optimism for working-class people, yet were also shaped by a paternalism that was deeply rooted within British political culture – mutual currents that danced an intriguing *pas de deux* at Park Hill in Sheffield during the 1950s and early 1960s. In the aftermath of the Ronan Point disaster, the truth of council housing's grubby underbelly of private-sector outsourcing and patchy regulatory oversight became clear. The state failed to protect the people who depended upon it and proceeded to respond disdainfully to a public petitioning for a voice within urban reconstruction. It then failed to correct grievous mistakes built into thousands of flats across the country. Many multistorey blocks, however, had solid structures. Some were architecturally superb. Lots were average but humane, providing commodious dwellings with novel mod-cons and wonderful views.

Scholars have consistently highlighted that Britain's high-rise environments have deteriorated because of inadequate maintenance. This is certainly true and has valuably undermined previous influential contentions by Oscar Newman and Alice Coleman that high-rise design invariably produces malaise and criminal behaviour. All buildings need to be maintained. Even the exalted ashlar stonework of Oxford's colleges has required refacing. We have to update our homes regularly, with upgraded heating, better-glazed windows, re-insulation, re-wiring, and new fixtures.

That said, maintaining high-rise buildings is particularly difficult and particularly costly. Their internal construction is complex and multifaceted. Tall blocks house multiple components, including lifts and cladding. They have more external fabric exposed to weather and wind pressure. The post-war high-rise housing drive did not involve realistic long-term modelling of the costs of these buildings' maintenance in the years to come. Meanwhile, today, many local authorities are still paying off the loans taken out to build their tower blocks in the first place – even for those long since demolished.

High-rise buildings are more than blank, mute canvasses upon which commentators have projected and pontificated. They have been living spaces thronging with conversations, arguments, demands, and propositions. High-rise estates have been battlegrounds: arenas for rethinking how housing should be designed, distributed, and governed. High-rise communities have reacted to their environments in different ways, but the unifying rallying cry across the decades has been for democratisation and devolution of management. What also comes through in the stories we have traced is a persistent demand for public housing: reformed but protected. Right to Buy was a flagship policy which has gone down in history as a critical rupture, resulting in the sale of a sizeable chunk of Britain's public housing stock. In its long shadow, it is easy to forget that millions of other tenants were not involved in the Right to Buy.

At the St Katharine's Estate in Wapping, one cohort of disheartened tenants was haphazardly decanted from two run-down blocks of inter-war flats in the 1970s. They later declined to return. Yet this same estate appealed to a more hopeful constituency of people who were seeking shelter, self-management, and a communitarian way of life. They established the Stephen and Matilda Tenants' Co-operative, which tenaciously refurbished and reconfigured the estate's accommodation and facilities, forging a groundbreaking model for self-government in council housing.

The National Tower Blocks Network, on the other hand, had little faith in multistorey housing. Originating out of a campaign to expose unrectified structural defects at Ronan Point in the 1980s, members of this pressure group were traumatised, angry, and frightened. They desperately wanted to escape their flats and to obliterate future dangers conclusively through mass high-rise demolition. Yet the network's allies at the Ocean Estate Tenants Association in Stepney, who faced dire living conditions and identical design flaws to Ronan Point, were more hesitant. They were doubtful that their flats would be replaced by better council housing, a dimming horizon during the 1980s. This tenants association accordingly lobbied for renovation over demolition. In the process of this reckoning, the flames of racism were fanned in a borough gripped by a housing shortage.

In Liverpool, there was a real sense of affection for the tower block environment within the city's High Rise Tenants Group, persisting well into the 1990s and 2000s. The city's most notorious Piggeries blocks had been swept away in the 1980s, but dozens of other towers remained. Many of their occupants, especially elderly tenants who had lived there for decades, expressed heartfelt love for their flats. These high-rise homes were cherished receptacles of family memories, neighbourly bonds, and experiences unique to sky living. In spite of these deep-seated attachments to the tower blocks, members of the High Rise Tenants Group were able to settle into alternative, low-rise houses – thanks to an admirably sensitive and participatory regeneration process that delivered good-quality social housing to replace high-rise stock too costly to maintain. Looking back today, however, retrofit strikes us as a greener alternative to demolition.

The residents of the Heygate and Aylesbury Estates, in twenty-first-century Southwark, were not so fortunate. Their inhabitants faced major problems with the physical fabric of their homes, on account of poor maintenance and inherent structural issues. Here, residents took a defensive position against an often callous regeneration programme that privileged private developers' profit margins over meaningful social housing provision. A raft of local campaign groups called for these estates to be refurbished to avert the deracination of their communities. We do not seem to have learned from the mistakes of mid-century slum clearance; they have been repeated in contemporary urban regeneration, but this time in the service of wholesale dispossession.

This text is far from definitive. There are thousands of high-rise buildings in Britain, all with their own stories. This clutch of case studies has, nevertheless, offered a flavour of the diversity of residents' feelings about high-rise council housing. Recent research into other high-rise contexts testifies further to this pluralism and variation across different estates and within any single estate. Isabelle Carter has explored how Hulme Crescents (1972) in Manchester, which came to house a distinctly youthful population of single people and students in the late 1970s and 1980s, was alternately interpreted by different residents. Certain people thought of Hulme as a countercultural haven, while others defended its respectability. Some appreciated the solidaristic connections they could make in this multiracial space, but others remembered racist incidents.[3]

Sean Burns has drawn attention to the queer history of Clydesdale and Cleveland Towers (1971) in central Birmingham.[4] Spitting distance from the city's Gay Village and nightlife, the buildings acquired a large gay community in the 1980s and 1990s, as a place of refuge from the unaccepting suburbs and a top spot for late-night intimacy and after-parties. During the HIV/AIDS crisis, they were the site of mutual care and shared grief – but also of stigma in media coverage and vandalism by far-right vigilantes. The buildings were known as 'Dorothy Towers' or 'Fairy Towers'. Other similarly populated blocks in Nottingham, Manchester, and Brixton shared the latter nickname. This label was a slur in the mouths of some; others claimed it as a badge of pride.

Glasgow, a conurbation with its own historic multistorey tenement tradition, became one of the most concentrated areas of post-war high-rise building in Britain. The city does not feature prominently in this book because high-rise Glasgow has recently been the subject of a thorough and wide-ranging oral history by Lynn Abrams, Ade Kearns, Barry Hazley, and Valerie Wright.[5] Glaswegians had long struggled with appalling housing conditions and overcrowding, so the improved living standards and particularly the privacy of new high-rise flats were much appreciated in this locale. The researcher Pearl Jephcott found that 90 per cent of surveyed high-rise residents in this city reported overall satisfaction with their homes in the late 1960s.[6]

Abrams and co-authors stress change over time, citing flagging maintenance and changing patterns of transient occupancy as critical factors degrading residential contentment in Glasgow by the 1980s. They also point to inferior outcomes for high-rise housing located on disconnected urban peripheries and in cities with an intemperate climate. The appeal of the veranda balcony or sun-roof at the Unité d'Habitation in the South of France did not necessarily translate to cold and rainy Glasgow, nor was the radiance of the concrete simple to preserve in these weather conditions.

A key take-away from this book is one of multiplicity. We have taken a tour through a range of multistorey typologies – journeying from the standard 1930s walk-up, to the bolshy brutalist jewel, to the system-built horror; from the point block to the slab block; from façades of brick, to concrete, to glass. Britain's high-rise housing has varied enormously in form. The experiences of its inhabitants have varied further still.

In recent years, we have witnessed a heartening reappraisal of Britain's legacy of public housing and the 'municipal dreams' of decades prior.[7] In 2018, the Architecture Foundation declared Britain's social housing a 'project interrupted' – rather than failed and finished.[8] We need to learn from historic mistakes to forge a new social housing programme. Nostalgia for a historic era of council housing is not a constructive strategy for the future; it can make us blind. In his celebratory account of British brutalism, *Raw Concrete* (2016), Barnabas Calder dismissed Ronan Point as 'a solitary case'.[9] This book has shown that Ronan Point was one example among many. Large-panel-system faults pose risk of collapse and fire spread. They also subject their residents to water ingress, damp, mould, and cold.

In July 2009, a fire broke out at Lakanal House, a fourteen-storey slab block on the Sceaux Gardens Estate in Camberwell, South London. It was initiated by an electric fault in a television, then spread rapidly from flat to flat within twenty minutes, with smoke choking the building's exit route. Six people were killed, including two children and a baby, just three weeks old. The block had no working sprinklers, faulty fire doors, and its firefighters' lift was out of service. Lakanal House, which was built in 1958, had just one staircase. It was designed on the basis that proper fire compartmentation would permit a 'stay put' policy; it was not suitable for mass evacuation.

Sam Webb stepped in as an expert witness to advise the legal team representing the bereaved families. Webb went into the block to assess the evidence:

Nothing in your education can prepare you to go into a room, a tiny room – 2 by 2.5 metres with a bath, a toilet and a sink. Nothing can prepare you to go into that room and see the imprints of all these tiny feet and other feet and realise five people died in there.[10]

He identified combustible panels on the building's exterior, added in 2006 and 2007. The Lakanal House inquest found that a refurbishment of the block, undertaken during the 1980s, had removed fire-stopping materials between units and had fitted windows made of flammable materials. The disaster had been caused by Southwark Council's botched renovation work and insufficient maintenance. A proper review of building regulations was demanded.

In the early hours of the morning on 14 June 2017, Webb was woken up by his phone ringing. 'Get up. Turn the TV on. It's happened,' said Ronnie King, a fire advisor with whom he had worked at the Lakanal House inquest. 'A tower block in West London is on fire, from top to bottom.'[11] It was Grenfell Tower, a twenty-four-storey block in North Kensington. A fire started by a malfunctioning fridge-freezer spread at speed across the building, engulfing people in their flats, where they had been advised to stay put by the fire brigade. Seventy-two people were killed. Their final moments must have been terrifying beyond the bounds of language. The total death count may well be higher, because undocumented people might have been in the building. A disproportionate number of victims and survivors were people of colour.

'We are still wrapping postwar high-rise buildings in highly flammable materials and leaving them without sprinkler systems installed, then being surprised when they burn down,' responded Sam Webb, on the day of the fire. He pronounced Grenfell 'a disaster waiting to happen'.[12] The National Tower Blocks Network had warned about such laxity in the 1980s and 1990s. Grenfell Tower residents had lobbied their landlord, Kensington and Chelsea Tenant Management Organisation, to correct fire safety breaches noticed within the block. They were ignored.

Grenfell Tower's aluminium-composite rainscreen cladding, installed during a renovation of 2015 to 2016 to make it more heat-efficient, was cheap and highly flammable. The cladding, supplied by Arconic, was bonded with polyethylene, made from petroleum. 'It is literally solid petrol and will burn like it,' explains the investigative journalist Peter Apps. 'In fact, in solid form it is denser and even more combustible.'[13] Grenfell Tower's new insulation material, made by Celotex and Kingspan, was also combustible and emitted noxious gas when burned. Several firefighters who served at Grenfell Tower have since been diagnosed with cancer, with many more suffering from respiratory and digestive diseases. The Grenfell Inquiry has confirmed that all these dangers were fully known to Arconic, Celotex, and Kingspan from their product tests.[14]

The installation of these dangerous materials was enabled by a progressive dismantling of building regulations over decades by successive governments, allowing manufacturers to certify their products while deliberately concealing inherent risks for the pursuit of profit. Years of poor management and maintenance meant that Grenfell Tower, like many other blocks across the country, had a malfunctioning smoke-control system, defective fire doors, and no sprinklers. There were no plans in place for the evacuation of disabled residents who could not use the stairs, many of whom were housed on floors too high for their mobility needs. The indictments also go far back to its inception. Grenfell Tower was designed in 1967 and completed in 1974. The bones of the building were structurally sound: it was built around a reinforced concrete frame, a deliberate choice in the aftermath of Ronan Point. However, it only had one exit stairway, as a second staircase was discarded on the drawing board. Since the tragedy in Kensington, flammable cladding has been identified on thousands more blocks across the country. This has not been confined to social housing; leaseholders have also been stuck in homes that they cannot sell. The government has estimated that up to 8,890 high-rise blocks could be affected.[15]

The atrocity at Grenfell Tower spurred other high-rise residents to investigate fire safety issues in their own homes. At the Ledbury Estate in Southwark, tenant Danielle Gregory found large gaps between the wall panels of numerous flats, posing a risk to fire compartmentation. The Ledbury Estate, comprising four thirteen-storey tower blocks, was built by Taylor Woodrow-Anglian from 1968 to 1970 with their Larsen-Nielsen large-panel system, without a frame, like Ronan Point. Sam Webb and a team of experts came to the estate to find that gas was still installed. After lobbying Southwark Council to reassess the Ledbury buildings, in late 2017 Arup engineers found that they were not structurally strong enough to withstand a gas explosion. They declared the buildings to be a collapse risk and could not confirm that they had received proper strengthening measures in the aftermath of the Ronan Point disaster.[16]

The newly formed Ledbury Action Group sent out Freedom of Information requests to several local authorities to investigate other suspected blocks. It quickly became clear that the Ledbury Estate was not a one-off. Numerous blocks had unrectified structural defects of the same nature, including buildings on the Lethbridge Estate in Lewisham, the Aintree Estate in Hammersmith and Fulham, and Broadwater Farm in Haringey.[17] The National Tower Blocks Network had specifically named these blocks as places of concern back in the 1980s. Councils in Leicester, Rugby, and Portsmouth soon found equivalent defects in their own housing stock.[18] Sam Webb, Frances Clarke, and Liz Lowe – former members of the National Tower Blocks Network – re-formed to establish Tower Blocks UK. These people have dedicated decades of their lives to whistleblowing about high-rise safety issues that remain unremediated. Sam Webb fought for justice until the day he died, in September 2022, aged eighty-five.

In 1970, the Ministry of Housing and Local Government recorded that at least 42,449 dwellings in 628 system-built blocks required strengthening work.[19] They had no records for Scotland, where reams more had been constructed. Nor did this figure include buildings of six storeys and under. Sixty-one local authorities were advised to take action, but they were granted limited funding with which to pursue it. At the time, a borough council representative from Salford had cautioned the ministry that 'if the amount left for authorities to pay was great, they might decide, at their peril, to maintain the *status quo*'.[20] It seems that in the case of some local councils, this prophecy proved correct. The evidence of slipshod strengthening procedures that emerged during Ronan Point's forensic demolition in 1986 also brings into question the adequacy of historic repairs in other blocks. Subsequent recommendations that local authorities reappraise and strengthen their large-panel-system blocks clearly were not comprehensively implemented.

Tower Blocks UK has called for a national safety audit for these blocks. In September 2017, the Department for Communities and Local Government encouraged local authorities and housing associations to check the structural integrity of their large-panel-system buildings and to determine whether they were fit to be supplied with piped gas, suggesting that they 'may wish to commission more intrusive forms of investigation'.[21] Tower Blocks UK remains seriously concerned that this has not been implemented. 'When the government wrote to [large-panel-system] owners and asked them to carry out checks, there wasn't any real pressure on them to do so,' Danielle Gregory said in 2023. 'No one was checking that they had done it.'[22] Peter Apps found, through a Freedom of Information request to the Building Safety Regulator in 2025, that at least 202 large-panel-system buildings in England had no record of strengthening work since the Ronan Point disaster and were still fitted with gas.[23]

We are living in the shadow of twin scandals: one over flammable cladding and another over large-panel-system faults. These problems are intertwined. They are the products of decades of state neglect, corporate wrongdoing, and inadequate regulation. They also reflect a systemic devaluation of the lives and voices of high-rise residents. Going forward, structural defects must not be used as a pretext for developer-led regeneration over the heads of local communities, nor for the erosion of desperately needed social housing – to which this book objects in the strongest possible terms.

The Ledbury Estate is located a short way south on the Old Kent Road from the sites of the Heygate and Aylesbury Estates. Danielle Gregory has been apprehensive about the potential fallout from her revelations, given the patterns of dispossession that have followed the demolition of social housing in the recent past:

> If a massive safety problem ends up leading to a massive loss of social housing, then it's a kind of double punishment. My worst fear is all these estates will eventually be demolished and replaced with mainly private apartments. After Grenfell and all the concern about the terrible housing inequality we have, what kind of response is that?[24]

We would do well to heed her warning.

Acknowledgements

I have received warm support and valued advice from a number of people in the course of this project, to whom I wish to extend my heartfelt thanks: Nick Bullock, Anna Davin, John Davis, Lucy Delap, Nick Garland, Miles Glendinning, Rebecca Goldsmith, Matt Green, Simon Gunn, Eve Houghton, Deborah Howard, Jessica Kelly, David Lawton, Matthew Lloyd Roberts, Peter Mandler, Helen McCarthy, Sofia Nivarti, Nick Ray, Leila Sackur, Ella Sbaraini, Andrew Seaton, Neal Shasore, Mark Swenarton, Simon Szreter, Christine Wall, and Olivia Warren.

I am especially grateful to Florence Sutcliffe-Braithwaite and Rebecca Jennings, who skilfully and sensitively supervised the PhD upon which a great deal of this book is based, at University College London. Also to Guy Ortolano and Barbara Penner, who were the superb examiners of a viva that brought forward fresh angles and new questions. I owe an unquantifiable debt to Otto Saumarez Smith for his counsel and unstinting encouragement over many years. I was lucky to receive assistance from the late Sam Webb, who spent five tireless decades campaigning on high-rise safety issues, before his death in 2022. Sam gave me access to his extensive personal archive, which has been invaluable for this project. Leo Hollis has been a superb editor, as has Jeanne Tao in production, and I extend my gratitude to the team at Verso.

Funding for this project has come from a variety of sources. I would like to thank the following bodies for their generous support, without which this book could not have been written. The Wolfson Foundation funded three years of doctoral research which makes up the backbone of this book. Pembroke College, at the University of Cambridge, granted me a studentship that covered the fees for my MPhil, allowing me to spend a year working on Ronan Point. A research fellowship at St John's College, Cambridge, has furnished me with time, space, and community during the final stages of this project. The College's support staff work tirelessly to look after researchers based there, for which I feel greatly indebted. I would like to thank the master, president, and fellows of St John's for financing the cost of illustrations for this book.

The Society of Architectural Historians of Great Britain, the editors of *Architectural History*, and the editors of *Modern British History* commended and published extracts of this research. They furnished me with much-appreciated guidance for improvement, buttressed by advice from their anonymous peer reviewers. My earlier writing about Park Hill was published in a journal article: 'Demythologising Park Hill, Sheffield', *Architectural History 66* (2023). I first wrote about Ronan Point in the journal article 'The Ronan Point Scandal: Architecture, Crisis, and Possibility in British Social Democracy, 1968–93', *Modern British History 34:4* (2023). Both journals have kindly permitted me to include revised material from these publications here.

The bread and butter of this research was made possible by countless hard-working staff at the Architectural Association Archives, the Bishopsgate Institute, the British Library, Cambridge University Library, the Churchill Archives Centre, Liverpool Central Library, the London Library, the London Metropolitan Archives, MayDay Rooms Archive, the National Archives at Kew, Newham Archives and Local Studies Library, the Piper Centre in Fulham, the RIBA Library at Portland Place, Sheffield City Archives, Sheffield Local Studies Library, Tower Hamlets Local History Library and Archives, and 56a Infoshop.

Beyond formal archives, a number of people have taken the time to share their stories and personal collections with me: Soryl

Angel, Sarah Benjamin, Hannah Brack, Sean Burns, Frances Clarke, Elaine Delay, Alan Dunn, Peter Gotham, Danielle Gregory, Mike Jempson, Chris Jones, Rachel Kirkley, Liz Lowe, Lyn Misselbrook, Barbara Phillips, Mark Phillips, Naomi Shaw, and Hannah Showler. I thank them for their trust. I am also grateful to Nicola Payne, for her kind permission to use the image of her grandmother, Ingeburg, and her mother, Diana, on the book's cover.

The title of this book was inspired by a community arts project of the same name which ran from 1999 to 2005 in Liverpool, during which artists and writers were invited to live in tower blocks slated for demolition, to develop art alongside their communities. The project was developed, managed, and curated by Neville Gabie, Leo Fitzmaurice, Kelly Large, and Becky Shaw.

Finally, my greatest thanks go to my family – most of all to my parents.

IMAGE PERMISSIONS

p. 9 Letchworth Garden City, Hertfordshire, November 1912 (Getty Images, 3289221 © Topical Press Agency/Getty Images)

p. 16 Christopher Tunnard's scheme for Claremont Park, Surrey, illustrated by Gordon Cullen, 1938 (Christopher Tunnard, 'The Case for the Common Garden', *Architectural Review* 84:502 [1 September 1938], p. 114 © Gordon Cullen Estate/University of Westminster Archive)

p. 18 Cartoon by William Heath Robinson, 1936 (W. Heath Robinson and K. R. G. Browne, *How to Live in a Flat* [London: Hutchinson, 1936], p. 3 © Look and Learn History Picture Archive)

p. 24 The Lawn flats, Harlow, Essex, photographed by Herbert Lionel Wainwright, 1951 (RIBA Collections, RIBA63886 © Architectural Press Archive/RIBA Collections)

p. 28 Showpiece housing, Alton West, Roehampton, London, photographed by Reginald Hugo de Burgh Galwey, 1954

(RIBA Collections, RIBA34553 © Architectural Press Archive/ RIBA Collections)

p. 30 Mural designed by Gordon Cullen in Coventry's Lower Precinct, photographed by Steven Baker, 2014 (Album, alb3986500 © Album/Heritage Images/Historic England Archive)

p. 35 Bush hammering in process at the Barbican Centre, photographed by Peter Bloomfield, November 1979 (© Barbican Centre Collection)

p. 41 Park Hill, photographed by Bill Toomey, 1960 (RIBA Collections, RIBA39918 © RIBA Collections)

p. 43 'Park Hill Estate, Sheffield', photographed by Roger Mayne, 1961 (Mary Evans Picture Library, 10514540 © Roger Mayne Archive/Mary Evans Picture Library)

p. 49 'Park Hill Estate, Sheffield, South Yorkshire', photographed by Roger Mayne, 1961 (Mary Evans Picture Library, 12021285 © Roger Mayne Archive/Mary Evans Picture Library)

p. 55 J. L. Womersley, site layout plan, 1953 (Sheffield City Council, Housing Committee Deputation to Europe, 'Multi-Storey Housing in Some European Countries', March 1955, p. 55; Sheffield Local Studies Library, Local Pamphlets, 205, no. 10, 042 S © Sheffield Local Studies Library)

p. 55 Park Hill's final site layout (A. E. J. Morris, 'Park Hill 1966: A Reappraisal', *Official Architecture and Planning* 29:2, 1966, p. 226 © Alexandrine Press)

p. 61 'Park Hill Estate, Sheffield – teenage boys larking about', photographed by Roger Mayne, 1963 (Mary Evans Picture Library, 11108367 © Roger Mayne Archive/Mary Evans Picture Library)

p. 62. 'Football on Long Henry Row', photographed by Mick Jones, 1969 (© Mick Jones)

p. 68 'View of the collapsed corner section of Ronan Point, a newly-built 22-storey tower block in Canning Town, East London', photographed by William Vanderson, 16 May 1968 (Getty Images, 2170347476 © William Vanderson/Fox Photos/ Hulton Archive/Getty Images)

p. 69 'Members of the Salvation Army hand out welcome cups of tea to rescue workers at the scene of today's partial collapse', 16 May 1968 (Alamy, 2Y70T8K © Smith Archive/Alamy)

p. 70 The front page of the *Evening Standard*, 16 May 1968 (© London Evening Standard Ltd.)

p. 80 Morris Walk flats, 1964 (London Metropolitan Archives, London County Council Photograph Library, 278674 © London Metropolitan Archives)

p. 88 Cartoon by Arthur Horner in the *New Statesman*, 29 November 1968 (British Cartoon Archive, University of Kent, AH0236 © Arthur Horner Estate)

p. 92 Poster for Joan Littlewood's play *The Projector*, 1970 (Sam Webb Collection, RIBA Archives, Piper Centre © RIBA Collections)

p. 93 Thomas and Selina McCambridge, photographed by Douglas Miller, 17 April 1973 (Getty Images, 16294 48749 © Getty Images/Douglas Miller/Keystone/Hulton Archive)

p. 99 'Stephen and Matilda Houses, Wapping', photographed by Jonathan Barker, October 1973 (© Jonathan Barker)

p. 100 'Children playing, Stephen and Matilda Houses, Wapping', photographed by Jonathan Barker, October 1973 (© Jonathan Barker)

p. 105 Stephen and Matilda Co-operative sign, circa 1976–77 (© Stephen and Matilda Tenants' Co-operative)

p. 111 'It's All at the Co-op Now!', *East London Advertiser*, 29 September 1978, p. 18. Text by Mike Jempson, photography by Tony Furby and Chris Johnson (© Newsquest Media Group)

p. 113 Members in the yard at the Stephen and Matilda Co-operative, photographed by Paul Barbara, early 1980s (© Paul Barbara)

p. 114 On the doorstep at Matilda House, photographed by Paul Barbara, early 1980s (© Paul Barbara)

p. 116 'Waiting for the performance of a play by the children at the playflat', photographed by Barbara Phillips, 1980 (© Barbara Phillips)

p. 131 'Sam Webb and His Crowbar and Club Hammer on the Roof of Ronan Point After Exploring Defects in the Structure', photographed by Bill Cross, 1 May 1984 (Shutterstock, 3064683a © Bill Cross/ANL/Shutterstock)

p. 136 The Community Links bus on the Brooks Estate, photographed by Frances Clarke, 1980 (© Frances Clarke/Tower Blocks UK)

p. 138 Dismantling of Ronan Point, 16 May 1986 (Newham Photos © London Borough of Newham Heritage Service)

p. 141 The National Tower Blocks Conference, 23 October 1983 (Bishopsgate Archive, TBUK/3 © Tower Blocks UK/Bishopsgate Archive)

p. 147 Front cover of Yorkshire Development Tenants Action Group, *High and Dry: A Unique Action Guide Based on Successful Campaigns by Tenants Against Damp and Defects* (London: Blackrose Press/Services to Community Action and Trade Unions, 1983) (by permission of Llyfrgell Genedlaethol Cymru/ The National Library of Wales © Brick/Annette Waterfield)

p. 151 Ocean Estate, 1953 (Tower Hamlets Local History Library and Archives, P14151, 331.3 © Tower Hamlets Local History Library and Archives, London Borough of Tower Hamlets)

p. 151 Ocean Estate, 1953 (Tower Hamlets Local History Library and Archives, P14155, 331.3 © Tower Hamlets Local History Library and Archives, London Borough of Tower Hamlets)

p. 163 'Pupils Getting Off the School Bus on the Ocean Estate Stepney', 12 September 1989 (Shutterstock, 1476039a © ANL/ Shutterstock)

p. 173. Marjorie Gallimore and the High Rise Tenants Group, photographed by Chenoa Parr, March 2001 (Liverpool Central Library and Archives, 363 HAT/4/2/7 b © Chenoa Parr/Liverpool Central Library and Archives)

p. 175 Demolition at Storrington Heys, photographed by Chenoa Parr, 2002 (Liverpool Central Library and Archives, 363 HAT/4/11/3 © Chenoa Parr/Liverpool Central Library and Archives)

p. 176 Porchfield Community Centre mural, photographed by Chenoa Parr, October 2001 (Liverpool Central Library and Archives, 363 HAT/4/1/2 d © Chenoa Parr/Liverpool Central Library and Archives)

p. 183 FACT Community Projects, 'Vera', photographed by Alan Dunn, 2003 (FACT Liverpool Flickr © FACT Liverpool/Alan Dunn)

p. 184 FACT Community Projects, 'Room 101', photographed by Alan Dunn, 2005 (FACT Liverpool Flickr © FACT Liverpool/ Alan Dunn)

p. 194 Tony Blair on the Aylesbury Estate, photographed by Stefan Rousseau, 2 June 1997 (Alamy, G47HE2 © Stefan Rousseau/ PA Images/Alamy)

p. 197 The Heygate Estate, photographed by Damian Grady, 2012 (Getty Images, 918905256 © Damian Grady/Heritage Images/Getty Images)

p. 199 Render by T. R. Hamzah & Yeang (Amanda Birch, 'A New Face for the Elephant', *Building Design* 1464 [10 November 2000], p. 18. © T. R. Hamzah & Yeang)

p. 205 The Strata SE1 Tower next to the Heygate Estate, photographed by Mickey Lee, 28 January 2013 (Alamy, 2BD99CH © Mickey Lee/Alamy)

p. 218 Furious jottings on a Costa napkin, undated (56a Infoshop Archive © Southwark Notes)

Abbreviations

BA	Bishopsgate Archives
CAC	Churchill Archives Centre
HRTG	High Rise Tenants Group
LA	London Archives
LCLA	Liverpool Central Library and Archives
LHAT	Liverpool Housing Action Trust
NALSL	Newham Archives and Local Studies Library
PCAD	Personal Collection of Alan Dunn
PCMJ	Personal Collection of Mike Jempson
PCSW	Personal Collection of Sam Webb, now held by the RIBA
SCA	Sheffield City Archives
SLSL	Sheffield Local Studies Library
THLHLA	Tower Hamlets Local History Library and Archives
TNA	The National Archives

Notes

Introduction

1. 'West Ham South Constituency-Polling District UU-Beckton Ward', *Electoral Register, London, England*, 1969, p. 6: LA GLC/PER/B/3498.
2. General Register Office, *Civil Registration Marriage Index, England and Wales* (1956), 5a, p. 1186; General Register Office, *Civil Registration Death Index, England and Wales* (1989), 18, p. 4; General Register Office, Death Certificate for Ingeburg Helen Payne, 2007, Register 1G001, Entry 154.
3. Vincent Mulchrone, 'Last Night on Floor 22', *Daily Mail*, 15 November 1968, p. 8.
4. 'Families Move to New Homes as Sky Flats Are Made Safe', *Daily Mirror*, 21 January 1969, p. 1.
5. Patrick Wright, *A Journey through Ruins: The Last Days of London* (London: Radius, 1991), pp. 89–90.
6. Patrick Dunleavy, *The Politics of Mass Housing in Britain, 1945–1975* (Oxford: Clarendon, 1981), pp. 354–5.
7. Peter Shapely, *The Politics of Housing: Power, Consumers and Urban Culture* (Manchester: Manchester University Press, 2014), pp. 2, 16.
8. They are compiled in the University of Edinburgh's fully searchable Tower Blocks Archive.

1. Why High?

1. Standish Meacham, *Regaining Paradise: Englishness and the Early Garden City Movement* (New Haven, CT: Yale University Press, 1999), p. 147.
2. Alison Ravetz, *Model Estate: Planned Housing at Quarry Hill, Leeds* (Abingdon: Routledge, 2013), p. 5.

3. Laurence F. Orbach, *Homes for Heroes: A Study of the Evolution of British Public Housing, 1915–1921* (London: Seeley, 1977), p. 139.

4. Christopher Addison, *The Betrayal of the Slums* (London: Herbert Jenkins, 1922).

5. Mark Swenarton, '"An Insurance against Revolution": Ideological Objectives of the Provision and Design of Public Housing in Britain after the First World War', *Bulletin of the Institute for Historical Research* 54:129 (1981).

6. Alan Powers, 'Models for Suburban Living', in Barbara Simms, ed., *Eric Lyons and Span* (London: RIBA Publishing, 2017), p. 24.

7. Julian Leathart, *Style in Architecture* (London: Thomas Nelson and Sons, 1940), p. 124.

8. Simon Pepper and Peter Richmond, 'Upward or Outward? Politics, Planning and Council Flats, 1919–1939', *Journal of Architecture* 13:1 (2008), p. 54.

9. Clough Williams-Ellis, *England and the Octopus* (London: Geoffrey Bles, 1928), p. 12.

10. Howard Marshall, 'A Rake's Progress', in Clough Williams-Ellis, ed., *Britain and the Beast* (Letchworth: Temple Press, 1938), p. 164.

11. Williams-Ellis, *England and the Octopus*, pp. 42–8, 28.

12. 'Balconies for Babies', *RIBA Journal* 42:2 (24 November 1934), p. 138.

13. 'Babies for Balconies', *The Times*, 1 November 1934, p. 15.

14. William Morris, 'The Housing of the Poor', *Justice*, 19 July 1884, pp. 4–5.

15. John Betjeman, 'What Would Wren Have Built Today?', *Financial News: Fiftieth Anniversary Number*, 22 January 1934, p. 34.

16. J. L. Martin and S. Speight, *The Flat Book* (London: William Heinemann, 1939), p. 7.

17. Elizabeth Darling, 'Kensal House: The Housing Consultant and the Housed', *Twentieth Century Architecture* 8 (2007), p. 107.

18. F. R. S. Yorke and Frederick Gibberd, *The Modern Flat* (London: Architectural Press, 1937), pp. 12, 8, 18.

19. Christopher Tunnard, 'The Case for the Common Garden', *Architectural Review* 84:502 (1 September 1938), p. 109.

20. Le Corbusier, *Towards a New Architecture*, trans. Frederick Etchells (London: John Rodker, 1927), pp. 60–1.

21. W. Heath Robinson and K. R. G. Browne, *How to Live in a Flat* (London: Hutchinson, 1936), p. 6.

22. Osbert Lancaster, *Homes Sweet Homes* (London: John Murray, 1939), p. 66.

23. Osbert Lancaster, *Pillar to Post* (London: John Murray, 1938), p. 70.

24. Richard Boston, 'A Few Home Truths for Dr Pevsner', *Guardian*, 18 November 1991, p. 36.

25. Reginald Blomfield, *Modernismus* (London: Macmillan, 1934), pp. 13, 82.

26. E. M. F., 'Modernismus', *Architects' Journal* 79:2042 (8 March 1934), p. 368.

27. 'Life in Flats Examined', *Town and Country Planning* 6:25 (October/December 1938), pp. 153, 156.

28. 'The President's Inaugural Address', *RIBA Journal* 40:16 (8 July 1933), p. 659.

29. Alison Ravetz, 'From Working-Class Tenement to Modern Flat: Local Authorities and Multi-Storey Housing between the Wars', in Anthony Sutcliffe, ed., *Multi-Storey Living: The British Working-Class Experience* (London: Croom Helm, 1974), p. 122.

30. Catherine Flinn, *Rebuilding Britain's Blitzed Cities: Hopeful Dreams, Stark Realities* (London: Bloomsbury, 2019), p. 30.

31. William Whyte, 'The Englishness of English Architecture: Modernism and the Making of a National International Style, 1927–1957', *Journal of British Studies* 48:2 (2009), pp. 455–6.

32. Thomas Sharp, *Town Planning* (Harmondsworth: Penguin, 1940), pp. 34, 45, 78.

33. Miles Glendinning and Stefan Muthesius, *Tower Block* (New Haven, CT: Yale University Press, 1994), p. 157.

34. Pepper and Richmond, 'Upward or Outward?', p. 84.

35. Elizabeth Denby, *Europe Rehoused* (London: George Allen & Unwin, 1938), p. 262.

36. Central Housing Advisory Committee, *Living in Flats: Report of the Flats Sub-Committee* (London: HMSO, 1952), p. 1.

37. Ministry of Housing and Local Government, *Flats and Houses: Design and Economy* (London: HMSO, 1958), pp. v, 3, 35.

38. Patrick Dunleavy, *The Politics of Mass Housing in Britain, 1945–1975* (Oxford: Clarendon, 1981), pp. 1, 44.

39. Simon Pepper, 'The People's House', *Architectural Review* 162:969 (1 November 1977), p. 270.

40. Peter Scott, 'Friends in High Places: Government–Industry Relations in Public Sector House-Building During Britain's Tower Block Era', *Business History* 62:4 (2020), pp. 552–4.

41. 'Chairman's Opening Remarks and Speech by Dame Evelyn Sharpe [sic]', in *High Flats: Report of a Symposium Held on 15 February 1955 by the Royal Institute of British Architects* (London: RIBA, 1955), p. 5.

42. Osbert Sitwell, *The Four Continents* (London: Macmillan, 1955 [1954]), p. 95.

43. Evelyn Sharp, *The Ministry of Housing and Local Government* (London: George Allen & Unwin, 1969), p. 84.

44. Ernö Goldfinger, 'High Flats', *Guardian*, 21 February 1968, p. 10.
45. Frederick Gibberd, 'High Flats in Medium-Sized Towns and Suburban Areas', in *High Flats: Report of a Symposium*, p. 14.
46. R. O. C. Hurst, 'The New Town of Harlow', *Highway* 46 (January 1955), p. 71.
47. 'Building Study: Shops and Flats in Basildon', *Architects' Journal* 136:25 (19 December 1962), p. 1383.
48. Sarah Williams Goldhagen, 'Something to Talk About: Modernism, Discourse, Style', *Journal of the Society of Architectural Historians* 64:2 (2005), p. 145.
49. Miles Glendinning, *Mass Housing: Modern Architecture and State Power* (London: Bloomsbury, 2021), p. 141.
50. 'Housing at Alton Estate, Roehampton', *Architects' Journal* 139:3 (15 January 1964), p. 132.
51. John Partridge, 'Roehampton Housing', *Twentieth Century Architecture* 9 (2008), p. 118.
52. James Gowan, 'Arthur Korn: In Memoriam', *Architectural Association Quarterly* 11:3 (1979), p. 49.
53. John R. Gold, *The Practice of Modernism: Modern Architects and Urban Transformation, 1954–1972* (London: Routledge, 2007), p. 171.
54. Colin St John Wilson, 'The Vertical City', *Observer*, 17 February 1952, p. 8.
55. Ministry of Housing and Local Government, *Homes for Today and Tomorrow* (London: HMSO, 1961), p. 3.
56. Reyner Banham, *Theory and Design in the First Machine Age* (London: Architectural Press, 1960), p. 220.
57. Le Corbusier, *Towards a New Architecture*, pp. 151, 153.
58. Susie Harries, *Pevsner: A Life* (London: Chatto & Windus, 2011), p. 451.
59. Nikolaus Pevsner, 'The Preservation of the Monuments of Victorian Commerce', *Journal of Industrial Archaeology* 2:1 (1965), p. 3.
60. Mark Girouard, *Sweetness and Light: The 'Queen Anne' Movement 1860–1900* (Oxford: Clarendon, 1977), p. 4.
61. Raphael Samuel, *Theatres of Memory*, vol. 1 (London: Verso, 1994), p. 123.
62. Walter Gropius, *The New Architecture and the Bauhaus*, trans. P. Morton Shand (London: Faber and Faber, 1935), p. 29.
63. Alison Stallibrass, *Being Me and Also Us: Lessons from the Peckham Experiment* (Edinburgh: Scottish Academic Press, 1989), p. 24.
64. Mark Crinson, *Alison and Peter Smithson* (London: Historic England, 2019), p. xv.
65. Christine Wall, Linda Clarke, Charlie McGuire, and Olivia Muñoz-Rojas, *Building the Barbican 1962–1982* (London: University of Westminster, 2012).

66. Mass Observation, *An Enquiry into People's Homes* (London: John Murray, 1943), pp. 218, 220.
67. Tom Harrisson, 'Houses or Flats?', *Town and Country Planning* 9:36 (Winter 1941/42), p. 117.
68. Mass Observation, *An Enquiry into People's Homes*, p. 52; Harrisson, 'Houses or Flats?', p. 119.
69. B. S. Townroe, 'What Do the Services Think?', *Architectural Design and Construction* 12:10 (1942), p. 202.
70. 'Human Needs in Planning: Discussion at Conference at RIBA', *RIBA Journal* 53:4 (February 1946), p. 126.
71. 'The Flat: Pride and Prejudice', *Architects' Journal* 81:2102 (2 May 1935), p. 653.
72. Margaret Willis, *Living in High Flats: An Investigation* (London: London County Council Architect's Department, 1955), p. 6.
73. Florence Sutcliffe-Braithwaite, *Class, Politics, and the Decline of Deference in England, 1968–2000* (Oxford: Oxford University Press, 2018).

2. Park Hill

1. Ivor Smith, *Architecture an Inspiration* (Kibworth: Matador, 2014), p. 201.
2. Henry Foster, 'Some Aspects of the Sheffield Development Plan', in David L. Linton, ed., *Sheffield and Its Region: A Scientific and Historical Survey* (Sheffield: Local Executive Committee for the British Association, 1956), p. 246.
3. Jack Lynn, 'The Development of the Design', in Jack Lynn and George Richmond, 'Park Hill Redevelopment, Sheffield', *RIBA Journal* 69:12 (December 1962), p. 449.
4. Sheffield City Council, Housing Development Committee, *Ten Years of Housing in Sheffield, 1953–1963* (Sheffield: Corporation of Sheffield, 1962), p. 3.
5. *Architectural Design*, September 1961, p. 388.
6. David Lewis, 'Criticism', *Architectural Design*, September 1961, p. 397.
7. Reyner Banham, 'Park Hill Housing, Sheffield', *Architectural Review* 130:778 (1 December 1961), p. 403.
8. 'Appraisal of Park Hill Redevelopment, Sheffield', *RIBA Journal* 70:7 (July 1963), p. 286.
9. Smith, *Architecture an Inspiration*, pp. 213–14.
10. Peter Blundell Jones, 'A Second Chance for Sheffield's Streets in the Sky', *Architectural Review*, 27 September 2011, architectural-review.com.
11. 'Legacy of an Architect', *Sheffield Telegraph*, 9 November 1990, p. 12.
12. Sheffield City Council, Housing Committee Deputation to Europe,

'Multi-Storey Housing in Some European Countries: Report of the City of Sheffield Housing Deputation', March 1955, pp. 36–7, 49: SLSL Local Pamphlets 205:10, 042 S.

13. J. L. Womersley, 'Park Hill Redevelopment Scheme, Development Area 1', March 1955, pp. 5–6, 1: SCA CA655/15.

14. Lynn, 'The Development of the Design', p. 448.

15. Ivor Smith, 'Park Hill, 1908–2008', lecture given to the Sheffield School of Architecture, 11 April 2008, available at Amazon Web Services, amazonaws.com.

16. Lynn, 'The Development of the Design', p. 448.

17. Joe Moran, 'Imagining the Street in Postwar Britain', *Urban History* 39:1 (2012), pp. 166, 173–8.

18. Michael Young and Peter Willmott, *Family and Kinship in East London* (London: Routledge & Kegan Paul, 1957), p. 166.

19. Central Housing Advisory Committee, *Moving from the Slums* (London: HMSO, 1956), p. 6.

20. Smith, 'Park Hill, 1908–2008'.

21. Jack Lynn, 'Sheffield', in David Lewis, ed., *The Pedestrian in the City* (London: Elek, 1965), p. 59.

22. Womersley, 'Park Hill Redevelopment Scheme, Development Area 1', p. 4: SCA CA655/15.

23. Smith, *Architecture an Inspiration*, p. 201.

24. Lynn, 'Sheffield', p. 59.

25. 'Park Hill Redevelopment', *Architects' Journal* 134:8 (23 August 1961), p. 271.

26. Banham, 'Park Hill Housing, Sheffield', p. 409.

27. Reyner Banham, 'The Vertical Community', *New Statesman*, 30 June 1961, p. 1056.

28. Phyllis Willmott, Diary from 2 May 1963 to 8 October 1963, entry for 5 September 1963: CAC WLMT 1/27.

29. 'First Park Hill Tenants in 21,000th New Home', *Star*, 5 November 1959, p. 11; 'No.1 Flat Tenant Gets Key', *Sheffield Telegraph*, 9 November 1959, p. 5.

30. 'First Park Hill Tenants in 21,000th New Home', p. 11.

31. 'Dr Patrick Nuttgens Speaks about Park Hill Flats', 21 January 1986: SCA ROM/109.

32. 'Appraisal of Park Hill Redevelopment', p. 284.

33. J. F. Demers, 'Social Survey', 13 September 1962, pp. 389, 392: SCA CA-HMC/2/1.

34. Chris W. Bacon, *Park Hill in Its Social Context* (Sheffield: University of Sheffield, Department of Town and Regional Planning, 1985), pp. 54–6: SLSL 331.833 SQ.

35. Jim Yelling, 'The Incidence of Slum Clearance in England and Wales, 1955–85', *Urban History* 27:2 (2000), p. 234.

36. Lynn, 'Sheffield', p. 60.
37. Foster, 'Some Aspects of the Sheffield Development Plan', p. 243.
38. Central Housing Advisory Committee, *Moving from the Slums*, p. 13.
39. Reyner Banham, 'Park Hill Revisited: English Public Housing That Broke the Rules (but Works Anyway)', *Architecture Plus* 2:3 (1974), pp. 110, 113.
40. Joan F. Demers, 'Park Hill – Part 1 – Sociological Report', 1960, p. 95: SCA CA-HMC/2/1.
41. Lynn, 'Development of the Design', p. 449; 'Multi-Storey Housing in Some European Countries', p. 55: SLSL Local Pamphlets 205:10, 042 S, p. 55.
42. Smith, 'Park Hill, 1908–2008'.
43. Ibid.
44. Letter from Henry Foster to Lewis Womersley, 'Park Hill – Redevelopment', 29 April 1959: SCA CA655/15.
45. Letter from Henry Foster to Lewis Womersley, 'Park Hill – Redevelopment', 8 August 1959: SCA CA655/15.
46. Letter from Lewis Womersley to Henry Foster, 'Park Hill – Redevelopment', 12 August 1959: SCA CA655/15.
47. Bacon, *Park Hill in Its Social Context*, pp. 29, 52–3: SLSL 331.833 SQ.
48. 'Appraisal of Park Hill Redevelopment', p. 283.
49. Demers, 'Park Hill – Part 1 – Sociological Report', p. 95: SCA CA-HMC/2/1.
50. 'Peter Harrison Reports from Park Hill Flats', November 1973: SCA ROM/109.
51. Peter Dunn, 'The Cliff Dwellers', *Sunday Times Magazine*, 3 April 1966, p. 40.
52. Smith, 'Park Hill, 1908–2008'.
53. 'Architectural Critics: I and II', *Town and Country Planning* 29:8 (August 1961), p. 338.
54. Jennifer Platt, *Social Research in Bethnal Green: An Evaluation of the Work of the Institute of Community Studies* (London: Macmillan, 1971).
55. Martin Pawley, 'Architects and the Philosopher's Stone', *New Society* 17:448 (7 January 1971), p. 720.
56. Jon Lawrence, 'Inventing the "Traditional Working Class": A Re-analysis of Interview Notes from Young and Willmott's *Family and Kinship in East London*', *Historical Journal* 59:2 (2016), p. 592.
57. Moran, 'Imagining the Street', pp. 176–7.
58. Banham, 'Park Hill Revisited', p. 110.
59. Reyner Banham, 'The Park Hill Victory', *New Society* 26:576 (18 October 1973), p. 154.
60. 'Human Needs in Planning: Discussion at Conference at RIBA', *RIBA Journal* 53:4 (April 1946), p. 126.

61. 'Appraisal of Park Hill Redevelopment', pp. 281–2.
62. Sheffield City Council, Housing Development Committee Minutes, 13 June 1963: SCA CA-HMC/2/2.
63. Sheffield City Council, Housing Management Committee Minutes, 12 September 1963: SCA CA-HMC/2/2.
64. Sheffield City Council, Housing Development Committee, 'Luncheon on the Occasion of the Official Opening of the Park Hill Redevelopment Scheme Part 1: Seating Arrangements', 16 June 1961, p. 4: SLSL MP1117 M.
65. Demers, 'Social Survey', p. 399: SCA CA-HMC/2/1.
66. Demers, 'Park Hill – Part 1 – Sociological Report', p. 98: SCA CA-HMC/2/1.
67. Sheffield City Council, Architect's Department and Housing Department, 'Park Hill Redevelopment Part 1 – Report on Amenities and Management (Joint Report by City Architect and Housing Manager)', 1959, p. 7: SCA CA-HMC/2/1.
68. Smith, 'Park Hill, 1908–2008'.
69. 'Appraisal of Park Hill Redevelopment', p. 285.
70. Demers, 'Park Hill – Part 1 – Sociological Report', p. 96: SCA CA-HMC/2/1.
71. Pat Starkey, 'The Feckless Mother: Women, Poverty and Social Workers in Wartime and Postwar England', *Women's History Review* 9:3 (2000).
72. Sheffield City Council, Housing Department, Annual Report, 1961, p. 26: SLSL 352.5 S.
73. Demers, 'Park Hill – Part 1 – Sociological Report', pp. 96–8: SCA CA-HMC/2/1.
74. Martin Harrison, *Young Meteors: British Photojournalism: 1957–1965* (London: Jonathan Cape, 1998), p. 46.
75. 'Member of the First Family to Live at Park Hill Flats (Son of the Caretaker) Recalls His Memories with Rony Robinson', March 2008: SCA ROM/109.
76. Demers, 'Park Hill – Part 1 – Sociological Report', pp. 94–8: SCA CA-HMC/2/1.
77. Lewis Womersley, 'Draft Report', February 1961, pp. 1–3: TNA HLG 37/20.
78. Selina Todd, 'Affluence, Class and Crown Street: Reinvestigating the Post-war Working Class', *Contemporary British History* 22:4 (2008), p. 502.
79. Womersley, 'Draft Report', pp. 1–2: TNA HLG 37/203.
80. Department of the Environment, Sociological Research Station, *The Estate Outside the Dwelling: Reactions of Residents to Aspects of Housing Layout* (London: HMSO, 1972), pp. 3, 24, 31, 43.

81. Sheffield City Council, Department of Planning and Design, 'Sheffield Inner City Area: Areas of Worst Deprivation', 1979, p. 1: SLSL 711.59 SQ.

82. Otto Saumarez Smith, *Boom Cities: Architect Planners and the Politics of Radical Urban Renewal in 1960s Britain* (Oxford: Oxford University Press, 2019), p. 16.

83. Jon Lawrence, 'Paternalism, Class and the British Path to Modernity', in Simon Gunn and James Vernon, eds, *The Peculiarities of Liberal Modernity in Imperial Britain* (Berkeley: University of California Press, 2011), pp. 163, 147.

3. The Ronan Point Disaster

1. 'How the Tenants Escaped', *The Times*, 17 May 1968, p. 1.

2. 'Tower of Terror', *Evening News and Star*, 17 May 1968, p. 1.

3. The Griffiths Inquiry denied that Carter's death was linked to the collapse, but this was contradicted in the local press: 'Ronan Point: Mystery Noise Heard before Explosion', *East London Advertiser*, 21 June 1968, p. 7; 'Flats Victim Dies', *Newham Recorder*, 30 May 1968, p. 1; Tony Hetherington, 'The Day Death Struck Ronan Point', *Stratford Express*, 5 May 1979, p. 26. Patrick Dunleavy puts the death count at five people, including Carter: Patrick Dunleavy, *The Politics of Mass Housing in Britain, 1945–1975* (Oxford: Clarendon, 1981), p. 242.

4. 'WHY? WHY? WHY?', *Evening Standard*, 16 May 1968, p. 1.

5. 'Medical Report on Miss Ivy Hodge', 10 September 1968, pp. 663–4: TNA AT 54/43.

6. 'Anxiety in High Places', *British Movietone News*, 20 May 1968: Associated Press Archive.

7. Lionel Esher, *A Broken Wave: The Rebuilding of England, 1940–1980* (London: Pelican, 1981), p. 80.

8. Dominic Sandbrook, *White Heat: A History of Britain in the Swinging Sixties* (London: Little, Brown, 2006), pp. 586–7. See also Paul Newland, *The Cultural Construction of London's East End* (Amsterdam: Rodpoi, 2008), p. 150; Charles Jencks, 'What Is Post-modernism?', in Lawrence Cahoone, ed., *From Modernism to Postmodernism* (Oxford: Blackwell, 1996), p. 472.

9. Charles, Prince of Wales, *A Vision of Britain: A Personal View of Architecture* (London: Doubleday, 1989), p. 37. Although reports varied between recording four or five fatalities, Charles puts the toll at two – certainly incorrect.

10. Nicholas Bullock, 'Building the Socialist Dream or Housing the Socialist State? Design versus the Production of Housing in the 1960s', in

Mark Crinson and Claire Zimmerman, eds, *Neo-avant-garde and Postmodern: Postwar Architecture in Britain and Beyond* (New Haven, CT: Yale University Press, 2010), p. 331.

11. C. L. Dunn, *The Emergency Medical Services*, vol. 2, *Scotland, Northern Ireland and the Principal Air Raids on Industrial Centres in Great Britain* (London: HMSO, 1953), pp. 212–16.

12. Nicholas Bullock, 'West Ham and the Welfare State, 1945–1970: A Suitable Case for Treatment?', in Mark Swenarton, Tom Avermaete, and Tom van den Heuvel, eds, *Architecture and the Welfare State* (London: Routledge, 2015), p. 99.

13. Simon Pepper, 'High-Rise Housing in London', in Peter Guillery and David Kroll, eds, *Mobilising Housing Histories* (London: RIBA Publishing, 2017), p. 137.

14. Bullock, 'Building the Socialist Dream or Housing the Socialist State?', p. 323.

15. 'Housing from the Factory', *Architects' Journal* 136:17 (24 October 1962), p. 949.

16. Miles Glendinning, *Mass Housing: Modern Architecture and State Power* (London: Bloomsbury, 2021), p. 153; Peter Scott, 'Friends in High Places: Government-Industry Relations in Public Sector House-Building during Britain's Tower Block Era', *Business History* 62:4 (2020), p. 558.

17. Taylor Woodrow-Anglian, 'Industrialised Building', April 1967, p. 1: LA GLC/AR/ENG/SE/01/002.

18. Walter Gropius, *The New Architecture and the Bauhaus*, trans. P. Morton Shand (London: Faber & Faber, 1935), pp. 40, 33.

19. Transcript of interview with Keith Joseph by Miles Glendinning, 13 April 1989.

20. Robert Smart, 'Bring Back the Environment', *Official Architecture and Planning* 35:1 (January 1972), pp. 33, 37.

21. Hugh Wilson, 'Britain's Failure to Make Use of Its Architects', *The Times*, 29 November 1968, p. 11.

22. 'Ronan Point: What Should Be Done?', *Architects' Journal* 148:50 (11 December 1968), p. 1367.

23. 'Ronan Point', *RIBA Journal* 75:12 (December 1968), p. 526.

24. Gavin Stamp, 'The Consequences of Le Corbusier', *Daily Telegraph*, 9 March 1987, p. 15.

25. J. M. Richards, *Memoirs of an Unjust Fella* (London: Weidenfeld & Nicholson, 1980), p. 263.

26. Malcolm MacEwen, *Crisis in Architecture* (London: RIBA, 1974), p. 16.

27. '"Cup of Tea" Clue to Disaster', *Daily Mail*, 17 May 1968, p. 1.

28. Harold Jackson, 'Flat Victims May Refuse to Return', *Guardian*, 17 May 1968, p. 1.

29. 'Tower of Terror', p. 1.

30. 'Flats Are Safe, Says Architect', *Daily Express*, 17 May 1968, p. 1.

31. 'Anxiety in High Places': Associated Press Archive.

32. Jackson, 'Flat Victims May Refuse to Return', p. 1.

33. Memorandum from Mr Chipperfield to Mr Osborn, 'Canning Town Flats', 17 May 1968, p. 145: TNA AT 54/30.

34. Memorandum from Mr Brain to Secretary, 'Canning Town Flats', 21 May 1968, p. 155: TNA AT 54/30.

35. Donald Keating, 'Ronan Point Inquiry', 24 June 1968, pp. 108–10: TNA AT 54/30.

36. 'Confidential Note for the Record', 15 August 1968, pp. 1–2: TNA PREM 13/2621.

37. Memorandum from G. H. Kirby-Smith, 16 August 1968, p. 1: TNA HLG 118/861.

38. Letter from Hugh Griffiths to the Minister for Housing and Local Government, 6 August 1968, pp. 1–2: TNA HLG 118/861.

39. Memorandum from Mr Brain to Mr Chipperfield, 7 August 1968: TNA HLG 118/861; 'Press Conference Held at the Ministry of Housing and Local Government', 15 August 1968, p. 9: TNA HLG 118/864.

40. Hugh Griffiths, Alfred Pugsley, and Owen Saunders, *Report of the Inquiry into the Collapse of Flats at Ronan Point, Canning Town* (London: HMSO, 1968), pp. 3–4, 52–3, 10, 37.

41. Memorandum from Mr Brain to Mr Chipperfield, 17 October 1968, p. 273: TNA AT 54/54.

42. 'Ronan Point Inquiry: Closing Speeches by Counsel: Days 19 and 20', 20 August 1968, p. 260: TNA AT 54/30.

43. Griffiths, Pugsley, and Saunders, *Report of the Inquiry*, pp. 4, 53, 62, 48.

44. 'Press Conference Held at the Ministry of Housing and Local Government', 15 August 1968, p. 9: TNA HLG 118/864.

45. 'Notice: Collapse of Flats at Canning Town: Public Local Inquiry', 21 May 1968, p. 28: TNA AT 54/30.

46. Letter from J&C Graham Consulting Mining and Civil Engineers, 31 July 1968, pp. 572–3: TNA AT 54/43.

47. Sam Webb, 'Obituary: George Fairweather, 1906–1986', *Building Design* 796 (18 July 1986), p. 8; Letter from George Fairweather, 7 June 1968, pp. 211–14: TNA AT 54/50.

48. Letter from George Fairweather, 26 July 1968, p. 534: TNA AT 54/43. Fairweather was permitted to formally submit evidence to the inquiry, but the tribunal declined to cross-examine him: 'Statement of Case for the Tribunal by George Fairweather', 15 July 1968, pp. 1–2: LA GLC/AR/ENG/SE/01/008.

49. Letter from D. D. French, 22 May 1968, p. 141: TNA AT 54/50.

50. Letter from C. C. Freedman, 28 May 1968, p. 181: TNA AT 54/50.

51. Letter from J. W. Carter, 17 May 1968, p. 71: TNA AT 54/50; Letter from Angus Hamblin, 17 May 1968, p. 65: TNA AT 54/50; Letter from E. W. Baigent, 19 May 1968, pp. 85–6; Letter from F. J. W. Courtney, 21 May 1968, p. 119: TNA AT 54/50.

52. Letter from Robert W. Lovegreen, 14 June 1968, pp. 321–2: TNA AT 54/42.

53. Letter from James McIntosh, 16 May 1968, p. 24: TNA AT 54/41.

54. 'Tower Block Cracks Are Not Dangerous – Say G.L.C.', *East London Advertiser*, 25 May 1973, p. 13.

55. Letter from James McIntosh, 23 July 1968, p. 521: TNA AT 54/43.

56. Letter from Citizens' Advice Bureau on behalf of Mr D. Cox, 16 May 1968, pp. 21–2: TNA AT 54/41.

57. Letter from George Charles Claridge, 19 May 1968, pp. 100–1: TNA AT 54/50.

58. Letter from Eric M. Wright, 28 May 1968, pp. 178–9: TNA AT 54/50.

59. 'Banners Reflect Fears of Tall Block Tenants', *East London Advertiser*, 15 November 1968, p. 1; John Smith, '"Move Us" Plea by 19th Floor Family', *East London Advertiser*, 27 November 1970, p. 20.

60. Quotations from Letter from K. McHugh, 20 May 1968, p. 23: TNA AT 54/50; Letter from J. R. Peters, 26 May 1968, p. 166: TNA AT 54/50. See also: Letter from G. W. Swain, 18 May 1968, p. 80: TNA AT 54/50; Letter from E. W. Baigent, 19 May 1968, pp. 85–6: TNA AT 54/50.

61. Letter from Mrs Cunningham, undated, p. 195: TNA AT 54/50.

62. Letter from Robert W. Lovegreen, 17 May 1968, p. 39: TNA AT 54/50.

63. Letter from A. Scott, 23 May 1968, p. 150: TNA AT 54/50.

64. Letter from Reg S. Christmas, 16 May 1968, p. 34: TNA AT 54/50.

65. Letter from Barrie L. Williams, 23 May 1968, p. 154: TNA AT 54/50.

66. Letter from J. Marlow to Barrie L. Williams, 24 May 1968, p. 155: TNA AT 54/50.

67. Letter from J. R. Peters, 26 May 1968, pp. 165, 168: TNA AT 54/50.

68. Letter from K. McHugh, 20 May 1968, p. 24: TNA AT 54/50.

69. Letter from A. H. Coyte, 20 June 1968, p. 380: TNA AT 54/43; Letter from James McIntosh, 16 May 1968, p. 24: TNA AT 54/41; Letter from S. Seil, 17 May 1968, p. 66: TNA AT 54/50.

70. 'Notice: Collapse of Flats at Canning Town: Public Local Inquiry', p. 28: TNA AT 54/30.

71. J. C. H. Marlow, 'Specimen Letter of Acknowledgement', May 1968, p. 7: TNA AT 54/41.

72. Ann Cvetkovich, *An Archive of Feelings: Trauma, Sexuality, and Lesbian Public Cultures* (Durham, NC: Duke University Press, 2003), p. 7.

73. Letter from A. H. Coyte, 20 June 1968, pp. 380, 382: TNA AT 54/42; Letter from E. E. Wynn, undated, p. 129: TNA AT 54/50; Letter from

B. S. Kelly, undated, p. 32: TNA AT 54/50; Letter from Eric M. Wright, 28 May 1968, p. 178: TNA AT 54/50; Letter from Dorothy Irving, 16 May 1968, p. 33: TNA AT 54/50; Letter from George Charles Claridge, 19 May 1968, p. 100: TNA AT 54/50; Letter from Robert W. Lovegreen, 17 May 1968, p. 40: TNA AT 54/50.

74. Sara Ahmed, *The Cultural Politics of Emotion*, 2nd edn (Edinburgh: University of Edinburgh Press, 2004); Stephen Brooke, 'Space, Emotions and the Everyday: The Affective Ecology of 1980s London', *Twentieth Century British History* 28:1 (2017).

75. Jackson, 'Flat Victims May Refuse to Return', p. 1; 'Disaster in Butcher's Road', *Daily Sketch*, 17 May 1968, p. 1.

76. Dunleavy, *The Politics of Mass Housing*, pp. 242–4.

77. '"We Live in Fear" – Tenants', *Newham Recorder*, 23 May 1968, p. 1; 'Ronan Point: Council Won't Discuss Petition', *Newham Recorder*, 13 June 1968, p. 4.

78. 'Skyscraper Flats Protest', *East London Advertiser*, 24 May 1968, p. 1.

79. 'Call for Halt on High Flats', *The Times*, 20 May 1968, p. 2.

80. Petition from 'the Tenants of Custom House Area' to Newham Borough Council, p. 221: TNA AT 54/50.

81. 'Call for Halt on High Flats', p. 2.

82. Petition from 'the Tenants of Custom House Area' to Newham Borough Council, undated, p. 221: TNA AT 54/50.

83. 'Ronan Point: Council Won't Discuss Petition', p. 4.

84. Peter Andrews, 'Tower Flats Meeting Boycott', *Newham Recorder*, 18 July 1968, p. 13; Ray Oates, 'Residents Fear Move to Tower Flats', *Newham Recorder*, 1 August 1968, p. 47.

85. Letter from F. Elwyn Jones to J. Marlow, 10 June 1968, p. 220: TNA AT 54/50.

86. 'Afraid of Life at the Top', *Newham Recorder*, 8 August 1968, p. 16.

87. Jeff Compton, 'Tower Flats Row: Residents Turn to Tories', *Newham Recorder*, 8 August 1968, p. 2.

88. Ian Ainsworth, 'Prison before Life in Sky Flats', *Newham Recorder*, 21 November 1968, p. 7.

89. Dunleavy, *The Politics of Mass Housing*, p. 253.

90. Memorandum from Anthony Greenwood to Harold Wilson, 'Flats – Disaster', 14 September 1968, p. 1: TNA PREM 13/2621.

91. 'Greenwood and TV Clash on Flats', *The Times*, 12 November 1968, p. 1.

92. Terence Bendixson, 'Ronan Point: Judgement in Doubt', *Guardian*, 9 November 1968, p. 11.

93. Paul Foot, 'Decline and Fall of Ronan Point', *Private Eye*, 30 August 1968, p. 193.

94. Ibid.

95. Letter from Edwin Hodge to J. Marlow, 9 June 1968, p. 219: TNA AT 54/50; Letter from J. Marlow to Edwin Hodge, 11 June 1968, p. 227: TNA AT 54/50.
96. Harry Brack, 'At Stake: The Safety of 100,000 People', *Evening Standard*, 7 November 1968, p. 11.
97. Harry Brack, 'The Plans That Gathered Dust for Three Ominous Years', *Evening Standard*, 23 September 1968, p. 7.
98. Memorandum from S. T. Cursley to Mr Summers, 'Ronan Point – Requests for Interview', 9 September 1968: TNA HLG 118/861.
99. Harry Brack, 'The Continuing Scandal of Ronan Point', *Evening Standard*, 13 November 1969, p. 19.
100. 'Cost of Strengthening High System Built Blocks Subject of the Tribunal's Recommendations', July 1970, p. 1: TNA HLG 118/1302.
101. GLC Housing Committee and GLC Finance and Supplies Committee, 'Appraisal and Strengthening of High Blocks – Government Grant', 19 February 1970, p. 1: LA GLC/AR/ENG/SE/01/004.
102. Letter from J. C. Swaffield of the Association of Municipal Corporations to R. Brain, 28 January 1970, p. 1: LA GLC/AR/ENG/SE/01/004.
103. J. Marlow, 'Strengthening of High Flats: Financial Implications', 3 June 1969, pp. 3–4: TNA HLG 118/1147.
104. Michael Cary, 'Appraisal and Strengthening of High Blocks', 17 November 1970, pp. 1–2: TNA HLG 116/1302.
105. 'Background Note: Grant for Strengthening High Blocks of Flats', November 1970, p. 1: TNA HLG 118/1302.
106. 'Appraisal of Large Concrete Panel Buildings of 6 Storeys and Below: Brief for Minister', undated, p. 1: TNA HLG 118/1147.
107. Judy Kirby, '"Whining Noise" Before Flats Disaster', *Evening Standard*, 18 June 1968, p. 22.
108. Peter Rankin, *Joan Littlewood: Dreams and Realities* (London: Oberon, 2014), pp. 203–4.
109. Letter from Joan Littlewood to Rev. Canon L. John Collins, 15 December 1969: PCSW.
110. Ronald Bryden, 'Mystery of Ronan Point', *Observer*, 6 December 1970, p. 25.
111. Emily Robinson, Camilla Schofield, Florence Sutcliffe-Braithwaite, and Natalie Thomlinson, 'Telling Stories about Post-war Britain: Popular Individualism and the "Crisis" of the 1970s', *Twentieth Century British History* 28:2 (2017), p. 278.
112. Alistair Cartwright, 'Landlordism on Trial: Rent Tribunals and Resistance in Post-war London, 1946–64', *Twentieth Century British History* 33:4 (2022), p. 609.
113. F. A. Osborn, 'Collapse of Flats in Newham', 16 May 1968, p. 138: TNA AT 54/30.
114. 'Back to a Tower', *Daily Mail*, 15 July 1968, p. 7.

115. 'Tower of Libel', *New Society* 24:551 (26 April 1973), p. 176.
116. Gavin Weightman, 'Ronan Observed', *New Society* 29:614 (11 July 1974), p. 70.

4. The Stephen and Matilda Tenants' Co-operative

1. Mike Jempson, 'It's All at the Co-op Now!', *East London Advertiser*, 29 September 1978, p. 18.
2. Letter from S. Woolf to Permanent Secretary, 'Housing Co-operative – The Stephen and Matilda Tenants' Co-operative', 27 July 1979, p. 1: TNA HLG/118/3178. In Scotland, Glasgow's Summerston Co-operative predated it: Memorandum from J. B. Cannon to Mr Teasdale, 'The Stephen and Matilda Tenants' Co-operative', 21 April 1978: TNA HLG/118/3178.
3. GLC Public Information Branch News Service, 'England's First Council Tenants' Co-operative', no. 280, 18 September 1978, p. 1: TNA HLG/118/3178.
4. Letter from A. S. Graham to R. A. Ambrose, 'Stephen and Matilda Tenants' Co-operative', 1 December 1977, p. 2: TNA HLG 118/3178.
5. Hansard, HC Deb, 14 January 1975, vol. 884, col. 385.
6. Guy Ortolano, *Thatcher's Progress: From Social Democracy to Market Liberalism Through an English New Town* (Cambridge: Cambridge University Press, 2019), p. 225.
7. J. P. Macey, 'Twilight Areas or Housing Deficiency Areas: Background to Proposed New Legislation', 6 December 1966, p. 1: LA GLC/DG/HG/11/57.
8. 'Wapping Parents' Action Group', *Open Door*, BBC2, 1974. A segment of this documentary is available at youtube.com.
9. Nigel Gansell, 'We See Row upon Row of Empty Flats', *East London Advertiser*, 6 December 1974, p. 33.
10. Mark Phillips, *Homelessness and Tenants' Control: Struggles for Council Housing in Tower Hamlets 1974–1976* (London: Dame Colet House, 1977), pp. 3, 8.
11. 'Developers in the Dock', *Community Action* 8 (May/June 1973), p. 30.
12. 'Stephen and Matilda Tenants Co-operative: Relations with the Trade Union Movement', November 1976, p. 1: THLHLA I/SPP/4/3/1/3; Mark Phillips, *Homelessness and Tenants' Control*, p. 62.
13. Tony Judge, 'Report of the Housing Management Committee', 1 July 1976, p. 1, LA GLC/DG/HG/11/158.
14. Tony Judge, 'Appendix: St Katharine's Estate', in 'Housing Co-operatives on the Council's Estates: Review', 9 February 1977, p. 12: LA GLC/DG/HG/11/158.
15. Tony Judge, 'Tony Judge on Housing Co-operatives: The GLC Experience', *Municipal and Public Services Journal*, 30 January 1976, p. 118.

16. Response by Tony Judge to Council Question by Lilias G. Giles, 29 March 1977, p. 1: LA GLC/DG/HG/11/158.
17. Mark Phillips, *Homelessness and Tenants' Control*, p. 70.
18. 'Existence in Sight', *SoMeTIMES* 1 (1978), p. 1: PCMJ.
19. 'Stephen & Matilda Management Committee Report A.G.M.', 16 July 1978, p. 1: TNA HLG 118/3178.
20. GLC, 'Model Agreement between the Council and the Stephen and Matilda Tenants' Co-operative', 31 March 1978, p. 1: TNA HLG 118/3178.
21. Letter from B. S. Quilter to S. Woolf, 'Housing Co-operative Agreement Between the Greater London Council and the Trustees of the Stephen and Matilda Tenants' Co-operative – St Katharine's Estate: Tower Hamlets', 30 March 1978: TNA HLG 118/3178; 'Stephen & Matilda Management Committee Report A.G.M.', 16 July 1978, pp. 1–2: TNA HLG 118/3178.
22. Colin Ward, 'It Won't Work Without Dweller-Control', *Town and Country Planning* 42:6 (June 1974), p. 300.
23. Colin Ward, *Tenants Take Over* (London: Architectural Press, 1974), pp. 8, 12.
24. Elizabeth Denby, 'Rehousing from the Slum Dweller's Point of View', *RIBA Journal* 44:2 (21 November 1936), pp. 63–5.
25. GLC Public Information Branch News Service, 'England's First Council Tenants' Co-operative', no. 280, p. 2: TNA HLG 118/3178.
26. John Davis, *Waterloo Sunrise: London from the Sixties to Thatcher* (Princeton, NJ: Princeton University Press, 2022), p. 229.
27. *SCOOP* 8 (November 1978), p. 3.
28. Hansard HC Deb, 14 January 1975, vol. 884, col. 381.
29. David Page, 'Housing Co-operatives: Options for Local Authorities', August 1975, p. 1: TNA HLG 118/2689.
30. Hansard HC Deb, 14 January 1975, vol. 884, col. 381.
31. Circular 8/76, January 1976: TNA HLG 118/2687.
32. Hansard HC Deb, 14 January 1975, vol. 884, cols 380–2.
33. Letter from George Wedd to R. Jones, 31 January 1975: TNA HLG 118/2689.
34. G. M. Wedd, 'Co-operatives', 6 February 1975: TNA HLG 118/2689.
35. Letter from Reg Freeson to Lord Goronwy-Roberts, 29 April 1975, p. 1: TNA HLG 118/2689. See also Page, 'Housing Co-operatives: Options for Local Authorities', p. 3: TNA HLG 118/2689.
36. Anthony Crosland, 'The Tenants' Hopeful Estate', *Guardian*, 16 June 1972, p. 14.
37. Hansard HC Deb, 12 April 1978, vol. 947, col. 1385.
38. Alison Matthews, *Management Co-operatives: The Early Stages* (London: HMSO, 1981), p. 3.
39. Memorandum from Mrs A. S. Graham to Mr Jackson, 'Stephen and

Matilda Tenants' Co-operative: Paragraph 9 of Schedule 1 to the Housing Rents & Subsidies Act 1975', 30 November 1977: TNA HLG 118/3178.

40. *(vacant lot)*, October 1976, pp. 4–5: PCMJ.

41. *Merry Xmas '76*, December 1976, p. 4: PCMJ.

42. *Newsletter*, 21 July 1978, p. 1: PCMJ.

43. Letter from S. Woolf to Mark Phillips, 'Matilda House: Redecoration', 17 January 1977: THLHLA I/SPP/4/3/1/3.

44. Mike Jempson, 'Return of the Old Pride', *East London Advertiser*, 29 September 1978, p. 18.

45. Stephen and Matilda Tenants' Co-operative, 'Supportive Document to the Application by the Spitalfields Project to the Manpower Services Commission', August 1977, p. 2: THLHLA I/SPP/4/3/1/3; GLC and Stephen and Matilda Tenants' Co-operative, 'Application to the Secretary of State', 28 February 1978, p. 1: TNA HLG 118/3178.

46. Stephen and Matilda Tenants' Co-operative, 'Supportive Document', pp. 1–2: THLHLA I/SPP/4/3/1/3.

47. Mike Jempson, 'Stephen & Matilda Tenants' Co-op 1975–2012', *Mike Jempson* (blog), 11 December 2023, mikejempson.eu. The legend 'WDFA' was emblazoned on the cover illustration of *(vacant lot)*, October 1976: PCMJ.

48. *Newsletter*, undated, p. 3: PCMJ.

49. 'Notes', *Newsletter*, 21 July 1978, p. 4: PCMJ.

50. 'Power and the Glory', *SoMeTIMES*, undated (circa late 1970s), p. 1: PCMJ.

51. 'Minutes of the Selection Committee Meeting to Discuss Its Policy', 2 February 1977, p. 1: PCMJ.

52. Stephen and Matilda Tenants' Co-operative, 'Supportive Document', p. 3: THLHLA I/SPP/4/3/1/3.

53. 'Stephen and Matilda', poster, undated (circa mid-1970s): PCMJ.

54. Richard Smith, 'Stephen and Matilda House (Rehabilitation Work)', 9 September 1977, p. 2: THLHLA I/SPP/4/3/1/3.

55. *(vacant lot)*, October 1976, p. 8: PCMJ.

56. *Newsletter*, 1978, p. 3: PCMJ.

57. Soryl Angel, email to author, 20 April 2024.

58. Memorandum from T. L. Jones to Mr Quilter, 'Stephen and Matilda Tenants' Co-operative', 25 September 1978: TNA HLG 118/3178.

59. Letter from S. Woolf to Permanent Secretary, 'Housing Co-operative – The Stephen and Matilda Tenants' Co-operative', 27 July 1979, pp. 1–3: TNA HLG 118/3178.

60. 'Graffitti', *SoMeTIMES*, 1980, p. 1: PCMJ.

61. *SoMeTIMES*, 'Special Republican Ed.', 24 July 1981, p. 2: PCMJ.

62. Soryl Angel, email to author, 10 April 2024; Soryl Angel, email to author, 20 April 2024.

63. 'Tenant Control', *Community Action* 25 (April/May 1976), pp. 27–8.
64. 'Tenant Co-ops – A Diversion', *Community Action* 31 (May/June 1977), pp. 15–19.
65. Letter from Linda Clarke, *Community Action* 33 (September/October 1977), p. 35.
66. Mike Geater, foreword to Julia Craddock, *Tenants' Participation in Housing Management: A Study of Four Schemes* (London: Association of London Housing Estates, 1975), p. iii.
67. Department of the Environment, *Final Report of the Working Party on Housing Co-operatives* (London: HMSO, 1975), p. 23.
68. Mark Phillips, *Homelessness and Tenants' Control*, pp. 94, 99.
69. Memorandum from N. L. Wicks to J. W. S. Dempster, 18 October 1976, p. 1: TNA PREM 16/2094.
70. Social Research Division, 'Difficult to Let Estates: What Can Be Done Cheaply in the Short Term?', 25 November 1976, pp. 1–4: TNA HLG 118/2643.
71. Judge, 'Housing Co-operatives on the Council's Estates: Review', p. 5: LA GLC/DG/HG/11/158. See this echoed in Page, 'Housing Co-operatives: Options for Local Authorities', p. 3: TNA HLG 118/2689.
72. 'Solving Their Own Problems', *Hendon Times*, 14 July 1977, p. 32.
73. *SCOOP* 8 (November 1978), pp. 8–9.
74. George Tremlett, *Living Cities* (London: Temple Smith, 1979), pp. 30, 24.
75. Horace Cutler, *The Cutler Files* (London: Weidenfeld & Nicolson, 1982), p. 13.
76. Tremlett, *Living Cities*, pp. 190, 180–1.
77. GLC Public Information Branch News Service, 'England's First Council Tenants' Co-operative', no. 280, p. 2: TNA HLG 118/3178.
78. 'Another Joke', *Summertimes* (1980), p. 3: PCMJ.
79. Jempson, 'It's All at the Co-op Now!', p. 18.
80. 'Stephen and Matilda Tenants Co-operative: Relations with the Trade Union Movement', p. 2: THLHLA I/SPP/4/3/1/3.
81. Mark Phillips, *Homelessness and Tenants' Control*, p. 10.
82. 'Air Time', *SoMeTIMES*, 1985, p. 3: PCMJ.
83. 'Which Way?', *SoMeTIMES*, 1980, p. 5: PCMJ; *SoMeTIMES*, 27 October 1985, p. 2: PCMJ.
84. 'Kids' Party', *SoMeTIMES*, 'Special Republican Ed.', 24 July 1981, p. 4: PCMJ; 'Sick of the Wedding?', *SoMeTIMES*, 'Special Republican Ed.', 24 July 1981, p. 5: PCMJ.
85. Mark Phillips, 'Tower Hamlets Federation of Tenants Associations', *SoMeTIMES*, 8 November 1980, p. 2: PCMJ.
86. 'Who Will Buy?!!!', *SoMeTIMES*, 1980, p. 1: PCMJ.
87. Cyril King, untitled document, 1986, p. 4: PCMJ.

88. Tremlett, *Living Cities*, p. 31.
89. Tower Hamlets Housing Co-ops Group, *Housing Co-ops in Tower Hamlets – A Future?*, September 1985: THLHLA LC7794, 331.4.
90. Matthews, *Management Co-operatives*, pp. 4, 31–3, iii.
91. 'Tenants' Co-ops Get DOE Backing', *Architects' Journal* 183:18 (30 April 1986), p. 23.
92. *SoMeTIMES*, 1985, p. 3: PCMJ.

5. The National Tower Blocks Network

1. Sam Webb, Chapter 1 of draft manuscript of *People in High Places*, 30 May 2014: PCSW.
2. Martin Hilditch, 'One Man's Battle to Improve Tower Block Safety', *Inside Housing*, 15 May 2018.
3. Sam Webb, 'A Small Child Might Ask Why . . .', *Architects' Journal* 161:2 (8 January 1975), p. 73.
4. Sam Webb, 'Letter: The Real Crisis in Architecture', *Architects' Journal* 160:27 (3 July 1974), pp. 9–10.
5. Sam Webb, 'Letter: Architectural Education in China: A Model for Us?', *Architects' Journal* 159:3 (16 January 1974), p. 123.
6. Sam Webb, 'The V Bomb of Peacetime', *Building Design* 574 (11 December 1981), p. 12.
7. 'Ronan Point: The Verdict', *Stratford Express*, 29 December 1979, p. 1; Christopher Warman, 'Builders of Ronan Point Must Pay Damages to Council for Explosion', *The Times*, 22 December 1979, p. 2.
8. 'Newham Tower Blocks Campaign', *Community Action* 58 (July–August 1982), p. 7.
9. 'Background to the N.T.B.T.C.', 1982: NALSL VF/NEW/728.
10. John McGhie, 'Faulty Towers', *Time Out*, 12 July 1984, pp. 8–9.
11. 'Possible Questions (for Parliament or Press Conference)', 5 November 1968, p. 7: TNA AT 49/7.
12. Robin Young, 'Evacuation Order for Ronan Point', *The Times*, 28 April 1984, p. 4; Aurora Percannella, 'The Tower Blocks Campaign', in *Community Links: Generating Change* (London: Community Links, 2017), p. 19.
13. McGhie, 'Faulty Towers', p. 8.
14. D. W. Varley, 'Visit to Newham LBC: Friday 4 May 1984', 12 April 1984: TNA AT 88/238.
15. Letter from Sue McDowell and Frances Clarke of the NTBTC to Sir George Young, 2 May 1984: TNA AT 88/238.
16. Hugh Muir, 'Conflicting Words of a Moving Story', *Newham Recorder*, 15 November 1984, p. 45.
17. Alan Thompson, 'Point Tenants Claim Cover-Up', *Building Design* 806 (3 October 1986), p. 32.

18. Charles Knevitt, 'Ronan Point Report "Altered"', *The Times*, 8 October 1984, p. 1; Sam Webb, 'Notes Taken from the Ronan Point Tribunal Inquiry Files Held in the Ministry of Housing and Local Government', April 1970: PCSW; Sam Webb, preface of draft manuscript for *People in High Places*, 17 November 2008: PCSW.

19. Letter from Hugh Griffiths to Minister for Housing, 14 October 1968, p. 257: TNA AT 54/54.

20. Sam Webb, 'WHY? WHY? WHY?', *RIBA Journal* 91:12 (December 1984), p. 42; Charles Knevitt, 'Ronan Point Inquiry Files Lost', *The Times*, 4 February 1984, p. 1.

21. Thompson, 'Point Tenants Claim Cover-Up', p. 32.

22. 'The Editors: Coming to Terms with Tower Blocks', *Architects' Journal* 179:20 (16 May 1984), p. 31.

23. Sam Webb, 'J'accuse', *Architects' Journal* 182:28 (10 July 1985), p. 23.

24. Paul Finch, 'Pointing a Finger', *Building Design* 710 (12 October 1984), p. 11.

25. London Borough of Newham Engineering and Surveying Service, 'Improving by Design: Ronan Point Dismantling', 16 May 1986, p. 5: BA TBUK/1.

26. Newham Council, 'Housing Committee Minutes', 15 November 1984, p. 934: NALSL VF/NEW/728.

27. Chris Huntley, '70 000 Tower Block Families in Danger', *Building*, 12 September 1986, p. 8; Charles Knevitt, 'Bad Workmanship Found', *The Times*, 5 September 1986, p. 2; Hugh Muir, 'Paper Used to Pack Joints after Collapse: Ronan Probe Set to Spark New Storm', *Newham Recorder*, 9 October 1986, p. 52.

28. 'Rubbish Joints Renew High Rise Fears', *Contract Journal*, 11 September 1986, p. 4.

29. Sam Webb, 'People in High Places', lecture, 24 May 1988: RIBA Library, RIBA Audio Collection, W.

30. Ibid.

31. Percannella, 'The Tower Blocks Campaign', p. 15.

32. 'Background to the N.T.B.T.C.': NALSL VF/NEW/728.

33. 'Newham Tower Blocks Campaign', p. 7.

34. London Borough of Newham News Release, 'New Houses Allocated to Young Families in Tower Blocks', 17 November 1983, pp. 1–2: BA TBUK/1.

35. 'Resolution from the N.T.B.T.C. to Be Placed Before the Annual General Meeting of: National System Built and Tower Block Housing Project Ltd Blackpool', 27 September 1986: NALSL VF/NEW/728.

36. 'Newham Tower Block Tenant Campaign: Renewal of Grant Aid', 19 October 1983, p. 1: LA GLC/DG/PRE/056/025.

37. Greater London Regional Council of the Labour Party, *A Socialist Policy for the GLC* (London: Greater London Council, 1981), pp. 5, 78–9.

38. 'Ronan Point Tower Block: Visit by Sir George Young', *Thames News*, 4 May 1984, youtube.com.

39. 'Good Riddance Ronan Point!', *Newham News*, June 1986, p. 1.

40. Sam Webb, 'Q&A for a Journalist', undated (circa 2008), p. 12: PCSW.

41. 'Housing Crisis Follows the Big Exodus', *Newham Recorder*, 15 November 1984, p. 18.

42. 'Minister Homes In on Tenants' Needs', *Newham Recorder*, 16 May 1991, p. 18.

43. Christine Webb, 'Back to Earth at Ronan Point', *The Times*, 26 May 1993, p. 28.

44. Sarah Boseley, 'Out of the Shadow of Ronan Point', *Guardian*, 13 February 1991, p. 23.

45. 'Ronan Point Redevelopment', *View* (Spring 1991), p. 6: BA TBUK/2.

46. Chris Partridge, 'In Place of Ronan Point', *Daily Telegraph*, 4 March 1992, p. 10.

47. Leslie Gillilan, 'Cracks in the System', *Guardian*, 7 May 1993, p. 21.

48. Webb, 'Q&A for a Journalist', p. 12: PCSW.

49. Frances Clarke, 'Confidential Minutes, Tower Blocks Meeting', 12 April 1984, p. 2: BA TBUK/1.

50. National Tower Blocks Network, *National Tower Blocks Directory*, 1987, p. 1: BA TBUK/2.

51. 'Webb Says "I Was Right"', *Architects' Journal* 180:41 (10 October 1984), p. 43.

52. McGhie, 'Faulty Towers', p. 8.

53. Charles Knevitt, '40,000 Flats Need to Be Structurally Surveyed After Ronan Point Report', *The Times*, 29 September 1984, p. 2.

54. 'Ronan Point to Be Evacuated', *London Housing: A Joint SHAC/ROOF Publication* (June 1984), pp. 1–2.

55. National Tower Blocks Network, 'Tower Block Faults: BRE's Findings Come Too Late?', 24 April 1985, p. 1: BA TBUK/1.

56. Basford Flats Tenants Association, 'Bison or Bull?', 12 July 1982, pp. 2, 7: Tower Blocks UK Online Archive.

57. National Association of Bison Tenants, 'National Week of Action', undated, p. 2: Tower Blocks UK Online Archive.

58. National Tower Blocks Network, 'Tower Block Faults: BRE's Findings Come Too Late?', p. 2: BA TBUK/1.

59. R. J. A. Sharp, 'Ronan Point and Docklands', 11 October 1984, p. 2: TNA AT 88/238.

60. Memorandum from N. W. Summerton to Mr Sharp, September 1984: TNA AT 88/238.

61. Sharp, 'Ronan Point and Docklands', p. 1: TNA AT 88/238.

62. Letter from Ian Gow to Nigel Spearing, 16 October 1984, p. 1: TNA AT 88/238.

63. R. J. Currie, B. R. Reeves, and J. F. A. Moore, *The Structural Adequacy and Durability of Large Panel System Dwellings: Part 2: Guidance on Appraisal* (Garston: Building Research Establishment, 1987), pp. 15, 1.

64. 'More Than Half of Britain's Tower Blocks Are a Fire Hazard', *View* (Winter 1990/91), p. 1: BA TBUK/2.

65. National Tower Blocks Network, 'Fire Safety Information Pack', 1991: BA TBUK/2; 'More Than Half of Britain's Tower Blocks Are a Fire Hazard', p. 1: BA TBUK/2; 'Profile on Fire Safety', *View* (Winter 1990/91), pp. 4–5: BA TBUK/2.

66. 'Showpiece Tower Block in Flames', *View* (Spring 1991), pp. 1–2: BA TBUK/2.

67. 'New Tower Blocks Bulletin', *View* (early 1984), p. 1: BA TBUK/6.

68. 'High-Rise Housing Can Be Turned Around', *Architects' Journal* 181:4 (23 January 1985), p. 32.

69. Webb, 'Q&A for a Journalist', p. 10: PCSW.

70. Daniel Stedman Jones, *Masters of the Universe: Hayek, Friedman, and the Birth of Neoliberal Politics* (Princeton, NJ: Princeton University Press, 2012), p. 293.

71. Sam Wetherell, '"Redlining" the British City', *Renewal* 28:2 (2020), p. 85.

72. 'Estate Sales', *Community Action* 65 (May/June 1984), p. 5.

73. Sam Wetherell, *Foundations: How the Built Environment Made Twentieth-Century Britain* (Princeton, NJ: Princeton University Press, 2020), p. 114.

74. Alice Coleman, *Utopia on Trial: Vision and Reality in Planned Housing* (London: Shipman, 1985), p. 184.

75. Safe Neighbourhoods Unit, *Ocean Estate Stepney, E1 (Tower Hamlets) – The Estate and a Plan for Action on Improvements*, 1983, pp. 17, 37: THLHLA LC7773, 331.3; Christopher Chamont, *The Ocean: A Short History of the Ocean Housing Estate in Stepney from 1937 to 2004* (London: Ragged School Museum Trust, 2005), pp. 15–24.

76. John Blake, 'They're Still Anxious on the Ocean Estate', *Hackney Gazette*, 15 November 1968, p. 1.

77. 'Banners Reflect Fears of Tall Block Tenants', *East London Advertiser*, 15 November 1968, p. 1.

78. 'Flats Tenants Order Workmen Away', *The Times*, 11 November 1968, p. 1.

79. 'Marchers Find Gas Cut Off', *Daily Telegraph*, 12 November 1968, p. 1.

80. 'Tower Flat Families Throw Out Workmen', *Daily Mail*, 11 November 1968, p. 9.

81. Mary White, *The Ocean Estate: Tenant Consultations Part 1. The Findings*, 1987, p. 27: THLHLA LCF00218, 331.3 WHI.
82. Councillor Chris Birt, 'Petition for James House Repairs', 26 April 1988: THLHLA LCP00232.
83. Gary Bird, 'Families "in Peril" Demand £1m Insurance', *Docklands Recorder*, 21 April 1988, p. 96.
84. Report of Neighbourhood Housing Manager, 'Ocean Estate – Progress Report', 11 October 1986, p. 10: THLHLA P/EVE/1.
85. 'Asbestos', Ocean Estate Tenants Association Newsletter, undated, p. 3: THLHLA LC7874, 331.5; 'Asbestos', *Ocean Breeze* 2 (May 1988), p. 3: THLHLA LC7869, 331.5.
86. Safe Neighbourhoods Unit, *Ocean Estate Stepney*, pp. 1, 72–3: THLHLA LC7773, 331.3.
87. This warning appears repeatedly in White, *The Ocean Estate*, 1987: THLHLA LCF00218, 331.3 WHI.
88. Dick Charlton, 'Ocean Estate', in Tower Hamlets Federation of Tenants, *Annual Report*, 1983–84, p. 21: THLHLA LC7863, 331.5.
89. 'Bengal, Bothnia, Malacca, Tunis', Ocean Estate Tenants Association Newsletter (April 1986), p. 2: THLHLA LC7874, 331.5.
90. Tower Hamlets Federation of Tenants, *Annual Report*, 1983–84, p. 11: THLHLA LC7863, 331.5.
91. *Tenant* 4 (February 1987), p. 6: THLHLA LC7864, 331.5.
92. 'The Great Estate Sale', *Tenant* 1 (Autumn 1985), p. 2: THLHLA LC7864, 331.5.
93. Rachel Woodward, 'Mobilising Opposition: The Campaign against Housing Action Trusts in Tower Hamlets', *Housing Studies* 6:1 (1991), p. 49; 'Refusing to Wear Ridley's HATs', *Architects' Journal* 187:33 (17 August 1988), p. 13.
94. Report of Neighbourhood Housing Manager, 'Ocean Estate – Progress Report', p. 6: THLHLA, P/EVE/1.
95. 'A Threat to Your Home', *Ocean Breeze* 3 (July 1988), pp. 4, 1: THLHLA LC7869, 331.5.
96. Michael Scorer, 'Blackmail', *Ocean Breeze* 5 (November/December 1988), p. 1: THLHLA LC7869, 331.5.
97. 'Gummer Sidles Round', *Ocean Breeze* 4 (September/October 1988), p. 1: THLHLA LC7869, 331.5.
98. 'Tenants Right to No Choice?', *Tenant* 2 (March 1986), pp. 4–5: THLHLA LC7864, 331.5.
99. Dick Charlton, 'The Government's Line', *Ocean Breeze* 4 (September/October 1988), p. 2: THLHLA LC7869, 331.5.
100. Scorer, 'Blackmail', p. 1: THLHLA LC7869, 331.5.
101. 'Minister Gets a Flat No!', *Tenant* 10 (November 1988), p. 1: THLHLA LC7864, 331.5.
102. Sheila Gunn, 'Times Diary', *The Times*, 19 October 1988, p. 14.

103. Dave Womersley, 'Raid!', *Ocean Breeze* 5 (November/December 1988), p. 3: THLHLA LC7869, 331.5.
104. 'Will Adams's HAT Song', *Ocean Breeze* 5 (November/December 1988), p. 2: THLHLA LC7869, 331.5.
105. Ocean Estate Tenants Association, 'Tenants Win Ballot over Trust Transfers', November 1988: THLHLA LC7869, 331.5.
106. Alan Travis, 'Ridley Forced to Cut Housing Trust Plan', *Guardian*, 17 March 1989, p. 3.
107. Andrew Seaton, *Our NHS: A History of Britain's Best Loved Institution* (New Haven, CT: Yale University Press, 2023), pp. 6–7.
108. Safe Neighbourhoods Unit, *Ocean Estate Stepney*, pp. 67–70: THLHLA LC7773, 331.3.
109. Ibid., pp. 37, 39.
110. Shabna Begum, *From Sylhet to Spitalfields: Bengali Squatters in 1970s East London* (London: Lawrence Wishart, 2023), p. 68.
111. Deborah Phillips, *What Price Equality? A Report on the Allocation of GLC Housing in Tower Hamlets* (London: Greater London Council Housing Research and Policy, 1986); *Homelessness and Discrimination: Report of a Formal Investigation into the London Borough of Tower Hamlets* (London: Commission for Racial Equality, 1988). See also Martin McEwen, 'Homelessness, Race and Law', *New Community* 16:4 (1990).
112. Deborah Phillips, *What Price Equality?*, p. 63.
113. Ocean Estate Tenants Association, 'Constitution', undated: THLHLA LCP00232.
114. *Tenants Tackle Racism: An Account of a Series of Experimental Workshops Held in Stepney* (London: Dame Colet House Community Centre, Limehouse Fields Tenants Association, Tower Hamlets Tenants Federation, 1986), p. 14.
115. 'Racist Attacks', Ocean Estate Tenants Association Newsletter, undated, p. 2: THLHLA LC7874, 331.5.
116. Douglas Broom, 'Buses to Take Asian Pupils to School to Prevent Race Attacks', *The Times*, 9 September 1989, p. 6.
117. Martin Newland, '£80,000 Bill for Busing Asians to School', *Daily Telegraph*, 12 September 1989, p. 3.
118. 'Tower Blocks Blown Sky High', *View*, Winter 1990/91, p. 8: BA TBUK/2.
119. 'Campaigning Workshop', 1983, p. 1: BA TBUK/3; 'Local Authority Improvement Programmes – Workshop Notes', late 1983, p. 1: BA TBUK/3.
120. Peter Malpass and Alan Murie, *Housing Policy and Practice*, 3rd edn (London: Macmillan Education, 1990), pp. 92–3.

6. The High Rise Tenants Group

1. Michael Heseltine, *Where There's a Will* (London: Hutchinson, 1987), p. 137.
2. *Liverpool Builds: 1945–65* (Liverpool: Public Relations Office, 1967), p. 42.
3. Liverpool City Council, 'Housing Action Trust Feasibility Study', 1991, p. 2: LCLA 363 HAT/2/3/1.
4. HRTG, *Final Report to Tenants*, 2005, pp. 2–3: LCLA 363 HAT/3/1/3 (a).
5. 'Liverpool HAT Facts and Figures' in document 'book.doc', March 2005, p. 5: LCLA 363 HAT/1/1/16.
6. Liz Lightfoot, 'Liverpool Leads the Way out of Council Towers of Decay', *Sunday Times*, 16 August 1992, p. 24.
7. Conservative Party, *The Next Moves Forward* (London: Conservative Central Office, 1987), pp. 11, 15.
8. Margaret Thatcher, *The Autobiography* (London: HarperCollins, 1995), pp. 558, 614.
9. Conservative Party, *The Next Moves Forward*, p. 14.
10. Ibid., p. 10.
11. Mary Langan, preface to Ian Cole and Robert Furbey, *The Eclipse of Council Housing* (London: Routledge, 1994), pp. ix–x.
12. 'Tenant Participation Review: Discussion Paper', 28 October 1992, p. 1: TNA AT 142/34.
13. R. A. Mills, 'Urban Housing Estates: Paper for the Secretary of State and Prime Minister', 24 August 1990, p. 1: TNA AT 142/30.
14. 'Urban Housing Estates: Note by the Secretary of State for the Environment, First Draft', 1990, p. 6: TNA AT 142/30.
15. 'Tenant Participation Review: Discussion Paper', p. 1: TNA AT 142/34.
16. 'Urban Housing Estates: Note by the Secretary of State for the Environment, First Draft', p. 1: TNA AT 142/30.
17. 'Diversification of Tenure', 17 August 1992, p. 3: TNA AT 142/34.
18. 'HAT Policy: Problems', 1990, p. 2: TNA AT 142/30; 'Questions of Principle', undated, p. 7: TNA AT 142/18.
19. 'Rundown Housing Estates: Meeting Renewal and Privatisation Objectives', 1990, p. 1: TNA AT 142/30.
20. 'Continuing with Waltham Forest', 1990, p. 1: TNA AT 142/30.
21. 'Rundown Housing Estates: Meeting Renewal and Privatisation Objectives', p. 1: TNA AT 142/30.
22. 'Housing: Brief for 12 September Meeting with the Prime Minister', 1990, p. 4: TNA AT 142/30.
23. 'Mori Survey Findings', *HAT News* 11 (December 1993), p. 3: LCLA 363 HAT/3/1/2.
24. 'Urban Housing Estates: Note by the Secretary of State for the Environment, First Draft', p. 5: TNA AT 142/30.

25. HRTG, *Final Report to Tenants*, p. 3: LCLA 363 HAT/3/1/3 (a).
26. 'Mori Survey Findings', p. 3: LCLA 363 HAT/3/1/2.
27. 'Tenant Board Member Marjorie Gallimore', *A Tall Order* 7 (26 July 1993), p. 3: LCLA 363 HAT/3/1/1:
28. 'Mori Survey Findings', p. 3: LCLA 363 HAT/3/1/2.
29. 'What's in It for Me?', *A Tall Order* 3 (6 July 1992), p. 1: LCLA 363 HAT/3/1/1.
30. 'Demolitions', *A Tall Order* 3 (12 March 1993), p. 4: LCLA 363 HAT/3/1/1.
31. *The Development Consultation Process, 1994–1995*, 1995: LCLA 363 HAT/5/1/6.
32. 'Sheil Park, Storrington Heys, Winterburn Heights, 1998–2002: Sheil Park', February 2002: LCLA 363 HAT/4/11/3.
33. *Half Way*, 2000: LCLA 363 HAT/5/1/7.
34. 'Notice Board', *HAT News* 21 (October 1995), p. 3: LCLA 363 HAT/3/1/2.
35. Brian Lewis and Paul Kelly, eds, *The 79 Bus to Childwall: A History of the Childwall HAT Development* (Pontefract: Pontefract Press, 2002), p. 15: LCLA 363 HAT/3/3/2 (h).
36. HRTG, *Any Other Business: The HRTG Story*, 2005, pp. 9, 8, 1, 11: LCLA 363 HAT/3/1/3 (b).
37. LHAT, *Annual Report*, 1993/1994, p. 3: LCLA 363 HAT/2/1/2.
38. *Liverpool Housing Action Trust: The Story. 1992–2005*, 2005: LCLA 363 HAT/5/1/9.
39. HRTG, *Any Other Business*, p. 4: LCLA 363 HAT/3/1/3 (b).
40. *Managing the Future*, 1993: LCLA 363 HAT/5/1/3.
41. *HAT Building Blocks for the Future*, 2005: LCLA 363 HAT/5/1/8.
42. 'Mori Survey Findings', p. 3: LCLA 363 HAT/3/1/2.
43. LHAT, *Annual Report*, 1998/1999, p. 25: LCLA 363 HAT/2/1/7.
44. *Liverpool Housing Action Trust: The Story*: LCLA 363 HAT/5/1/9.
45. HRTG, *Any Other Business*, p. 48: LCLA 363 HAT/3/1/3 (b).
46. *Half Way*: LCLA 363 HAT/5/1/7.
47. LHAT, *Final Annual Report*, 2004/2005, p. 20: LCLA 363 HAT/2/1/13.
48. '200th Homefinder Finds a Home', *HAT News* 25 (November 1996), p. 4: LCLA 363 HAT/3/1/2.
49. Interview with David Green in document 'adackregig.doc', 22 December 2005, p. 2: LCLA 363 HAT/1/1/16.
50. LHAT, *Annual Report*, 1993/1994, p. 1: LCLA 363 HAT/2/1/2.
51. HRTG, *Final Report to Tenants*, 2005, p. 2: LCLA 363 HAT/3/1/3 (a).
52. LHAT, *Final Annual Report*, 2004/2005, p. 15: LCLA 363 HAT/2/1/3; 'Exhibition Board 4' in document 'exhibbrds', December 2005, p. 4: LCLA 363 HAT/1/1/16.
53. LHAT, *Final Annual Report*, 2004/2005, p. 16: LCLA 363 HAT/2/1/13.
54. LHAT, *Annual Report*, 1998/1999, pp. 19, 5: LCLA 363 HAT/2/1/7.

55. *tenantspin workbook*, 2005, p. 2: LCLA 363 HAT/3/3/3 (c).
56. Report to HAT Board Meeting by Paul Kelly, 'An Arts Policy for Liverpool HAT', 28 January 2000, p. 11: LCLA 363 HAT/1/1/9 (a).
57. Report to HAT Board Meeting by Paul Kelly, 'The Superchannel Project', 14 July 2000, p. 2: LCLA 363 HAT/1/1/9 (f).
58. *tenantspin workbook*, p. 18: LCLA 363 HAT/3/3/3 (c).
59. HRTG, *Any Other Business*, p. 34: LCLA 363 HAT/3/1/3 (b).
60. Alan Dunn, 'Singing the Sound of Silence', *Corridor* 8:1 (2009), p. 57.
61. *The CHAT Files*, 2002: LCLA 363 HAT/3/3/3 (b).
62. Maria Brewster, ed., *Supermanual: The Incomplete Guide to Superchannel* (Liverpool: FACT, 2000), pp. 49–50: LCLA 363 HAT/3/3/3 (a).
63. *The CHAT Files*: LCLA 363 HAT/3/3/3 (b).
64. 'tenantspin in Malmö', October 2002: LCLA 363 HAT/3/3/3 (f).
65. *tenantspin workbook*, p. 25: LCLA 363 HAT/3/3/3 (c).
66. 'tenantspin, New York', 2002: LCLA 363 HAT/3/3/3 (d).
67. HRTG, *Any Other Business*, p. 35: LCLA 363 HAT/3/1/3 (b).
68. 'ALAN DUNN JEFF YOUNG SuperBlock.ppt', PowerPoint presentation, July 2016, slide 13: PCAD.
69. Jeff Young, 'SuperBlock', in Ben Parry, ed., *Cultural Hijack: Rethinking Intervention* (Liverpool: Liverpool University Press, 2011), p. 242.
70. All quotations from *SuperBlock* are from recordings filed under 'SUPERBLOCK EXTRACTS' on a personal hard drive to which Alan Dunn granted me access.
71. Young, 'SuperBlock', p. 242.
72. Ibid., p. 239.
73. James Hinton, *Seven Lives from Mass Observation: Britain in the Late Twentieth Century* (Oxford: Oxford University Press, 2016), p. v.
74. *tenantspin workbook*, p. 18: LCLA 363 HAT/3/3/3 (c).
75. HRTG, *Any Other Business*, p. 36: LCLA 363 HAT/3/1/3 (b).
76. 'TENANTSPIN ARCHIVE .rm FILES': 'docu intro.rm', undated: PCAD.
77. 'TENANTSPIN ARCHIVE .rm FILES': 'accordianista.rm', undated: PCAD.
78. 'TENANTSPIN ARCHIVE .rm FILES': 'areyoumoving.rm', 16 October 2002: PCAD.
79. Lewis and Kelly, *The 79 Bus to Childwall*, pp. 11, 58: LCLA 363 HAT/3/3/2 (h).
80. *Half Way*: LCLA 363 HAT/5/1/7.
81. *HAT Building Blocks for the Future*, 2005: LCLA 363 HAT/5/1/8.
82. Gerri Moriarty, Kevin McManus, and Lucy Horne, 'Giving Voice, Giving Dreams: Community Planned Projects for Liverpool's European Capital of Culture Bid', February 2003, p. 3: LCLA 363 HAT/3/3/1 (b).
83. Finn Gleeson, 'Memory, Community and the End of Empire on the Isle of Dogs, 1980–2004', *Historical Research* 95:270 (2022).

84. HRTG, *Any Other Business*, p. 36: LCLA 363 HAT/3/1/3 (b).

85. Roger Critchley, Jan Gilbertson, Geoff Green, and Michael Grimsley, 'Housing Investment and Health in Liverpool', Sheffield Hallam University, 2004, p. 51: LCLA 363 HAT/2/3/3.

86. *The Development Consultation Process*: LCLA 363 HAT/5/1/6.

7. The Heygate and Aylesbury Estates

1. 'Prescott Calls for Urban Renaissance . . .', *Architects' Journal* 208 (16 July 1998), p. 12.

2. Richard Rogers, 'An Urban Renaissance', *Guardian*, 26 June 2002, p. 9.

3. Will Self, 'Ghetto Blaster', *Building Design* 1385 (5 March 1999), p. 10.

4. Katherine Shonfield, 'Hard to Get a Grip on Virtual Labour', *Building Design* 1238 (13 October 1995), p. 7.

5. Tony Blair, 'Welfare to Work', 2 June 1997, Sky News via Getty.

6. Amanda Birch, 'A New Face for the Elephant', *Building Design* 1464 (10 November 2000), p. 16.

7. Bridget Cherry and Nikolaus Pevsner, *London 2: South* (Harmondsworth: Penguin, 1983), pp. 592, 562, 90, 595, 596.

8. Martin Mason and Finna Alexander, 'Future Slum?', *Building Design* 201 (17 May 1974), pp. 20–1.

9. Douglas Frank, 'The Greatest Happiness of the Greatest Number', *Architects' Journal* 151:21 (27 May 1970), p. 1288.

10. Ben Campkin, *Remaking London: Decline and Regeneration in Urban Culture* (London: IB Tauris, 2013), pp. 85–6.

11. Michael Romyn, 'The Heygate: Community Life in an Inner-City Estate, 1974–2011', *History Workshop Journal* 81:1 (2016); Michael Romyn, *London's Aylesbury Estate: An Oral History of the 'Concrete Jungle'* (Cham: Palgrave Macmillan, 2020).

12. Mark Tran, 'Anger Surrounds Demise of 1970s Estate', *Guardian*, 8 February 2011, p. 16.

13. MORI, *The Future of the Heygate: Research Study Conducted for London Borough of Southwark and Heygate Tenants and Residents Association* (1999).

14. Southwark Council, *The Aylesbury Estate: Revised Strategy*, 27 September 2005, p. 2.

15. Will Hurst, 'Official: Sixties Estate Risks Gas Blast Collapse', *Building Design* 1666 (24 March 2005), p. 3; Will Hurst, 'New Collapse Danger', *Building Design* 1657 (21 January 2005), p. 1; Sam Webb, 'LPS Exposed', *Building Design* 1659 (4 February 2005), p. 18.

16. Amanda Birch, 'The Towering Legacy of LPS', *Building Design* 1659 (4 February 2005), p. 19.

17. Keith Cooper, 'What Is the True Cost of Demolition?', *Architects' Journal* 242:20 (20 November 2015), p. 10.

18. Joe Penny, *The Promise of Cross-Subsidy: Why Estate Demolition Cannot Solve London's Housing Emergency* (London: Public Interest Law Centre, 2024), pp. 15–16.

19. Southwark Notes, 'Is This Our "Home" & "Community"?', undated: 56a Infoshop Archive, 'Heygate Estate' Box.

20. Christopher Jones, 'Pyramid Dead – The Artangel of History', *Mute Magazine*, 17 April 2014.

21. Southwark Notes, 'Is This Our "Home" & "Community"?': 56a Infoshop Archive, 'Heygate Estate' Box.

22. Heygate and Aylesbury Leaseholder Action Group, 'Market Value', 16 September 2011, p. 1: 56a Infoshop Archive, 'Heygate Estate' Box.

23. Allott and Lomax, *Heygate Option Appraisal Study* (1998), p. 25.

24. Campkin, *Remaking London*, p. 95.

25. Adrian Glasspool, 'Complaint Concerning the Conduct of Film Crews on Heygate Estate', 19 November 2010, p. 3: 56a Infoshop Archive, 'Heygate Estate' Box.

26. Emma Ailes, 'Filming on Heygate Nets Council £91,000', *Southwark News*, 2 September 2010.

27. Kirsty McNeill, 'All Profits Should Go to the Tenants', *Southwark News*, 12 November 2007.

28. John Prescott, 'Welcoming the "Wow" Factor', *Observer*, 27 June 2004, p. 5.

29. Duncan Bowie, *Politics, Planning and Homes in a World City* (London: Routledge, 2010), p. 30.

30. Ken Livingstone, 'London Needs Some More Clusters of Tall Buildings', *Independent*, 13 June 2001, p. 5.

31. 'Tories Blast at Urban "Hot Air"', *Architects' Journal* 211 (1 June 2000), p. 4.

32. Richard Morrison, 'High Anxiety', *The Times*, 28 November 2001, pp. 44–5.

33. Bowie, *Politics, Planning and Homes in a World City*, p. 94.

34. Ellis Woodman, 'Carbuncle Cup: The Winner Is . . . London's Ugliest Ever Tall Building', *Building Design* 1929 (13 August 2010), p. 6.

35. Better Elephant, 'Better Elephant – Campaigning for a Better Regeneration', 27 November 2011, p. 1: 56a Infoshop Archive, 'Southwark Notes Archives Group' Box.

36. Southwark Notes, 'Regeneration? Gentrification?', undated, southwarknotes.wordpress.com.

37. 'Has the Blair Decade Been Good for Architecture?', *Building Design* 1769 (4 May 2007), p. 11.

38. Rory Olcayto, 'A New English Architecture', *Architects' Journal* 230:11 (2009), pp. 23–33.

39. Owen Hatherley, *A Guide to the New Ruins of Great Britain* (London: Verso, 2010), pp. x–xxiv.

40. Owen Hatherley, 'After the Heygate Estate, a Grey Future Awaits', *Guardian*, 8 February 2011.

41. Otto Saumarez Smith, 'Defender of the Faith', *Apollo*, June 2022, p. 190.

42. Owen Hatherley, *Militant Modernism* (Winchester: Zero Books, 2008), pp. 42, 8.

43. Tony Blair, *The Third Way: New Politics for the New Century* (London: Fabian Society, 1998), pp. 15, 17.

44. Southwark Council, 'Elephant and Castle – Adoption of Supplementary Planning Guidance', 19 February 2004, p. 1, available at services.southwark.gov.uk/regeneration/elephant-and-castle?chapter=4.

45. Sherry R. Arnstein, 'A Ladder of Citizen Participation', *Journal of the American Planning Association* 35:4 (1969), pp. 210–24.

46. Southwark Council, 'Coping with Change – Stress Busters!', 15 October 2008: 56a Infoshop Archive, 'Heygate' File.

47. Southwark Notes, 'Southwark Notes – Whose Regeneration? Heygate Estate', 16 September 2011, p. 4: 56a Infoshop Archive, 'Heygate Estate' Box.

48. Heygate Was Home, 'Broken Promises', undated, https://web.archive.org/web/20150216000812/http://heygatewashome.org/displacement.html.

49. Sarah Knapton, 'Stressed Council House Residents Get £2,000 Happiness Gurus', *Daily Telegraph*, 9 October 2008.

50. 35% Campaign, 'Heygate Estate Happiness Therapy', 17 February 2013, youtube.com.

51. Mark Fisher, 'The Privatisation of Stress', *Soundings* 48 (2011), p. 124.

52. Southwark Council, *Core Strategy*, April 2011, pp. 82, 135.

53. Lend Lease, *The Heygate Masterplan: Outline Planning Application: Housing Statement*, March 2012, p. 21.

54. Elephant Amenity Network, 'Elephant Amenity Network Open Letter to Soundings', 28 July 2012, elephantamenity.wordpress.com.

55. Southwark Notes, 'Listening to No End: Regeneration, Consultation and Soundings Ltd at the Elephant', undated, southwarknotes.wordpress.com.

56. Southwark Notes, 'Gotta Be Ferral! A Cat Cornered!', undated, pp. 11, 6: 56a Infoshop Archive, 'Heygate' File.

57. Southwark Notes, 'Sound the Alarm!', pp. 1–6: 56a Infoshop Archive, 'Southwark Regens – to file' Box.

58. Southwark Notes, 'Gotta Be Ferral!'

59. Southwark Notes, 'Sound the Alarm!', p. 3: 56a Infoshop Archive, 'Southwark Regens – to file' Box.

60. Loretta Lees, 'The Urban Injustices of New Labour's "New Urban Renewal": The Case of the Aylesbury Estate in London', *Antipode* 46:4 (2014), pp. 931–2. See also James DeFilippis, 'The Emancipatory

Community? Place, Politics, and Collective Action in Cities', in Loretta Lees, ed., *The Emancipatory City? Paradoxes and Possibilities* (London: Sage, 2004); Guy Baeten, 'Regenerating the South Bank: Reworking Community and the Emergence of Post-political Regeneration', in Rob Imrie, Loretta Lees, and Mike Raco, eds, *Regenerating London* (Abingdon: Routledge, 2009).

61. London Tenants Federation, Loretta Lees, Just Space, and Southwark Notes Archives Group, *Staying Put: An Anti-Gentrification Handbook for Council Estates in London*, June 2014, pp. 10, 20: 56a Infoshop Archive, 'Southwark Notes Archives Group' Box.

62. Southwark Notes, 'Draft Report from the Siege of the Elephant: A Convergence Against the Gentrification of the Elephant & Castle', 18 January 2013, pp. 1, 3, 13: 56a Infoshop Archive, 'Southwark Regens – to file' Box.

63. Oliver Wainwright, 'How Developers Exploit Flawed Planning System to Minimise Affordable Housing', *Guardian*, 25 June 2015.

64. Rebecca Amato, 'On Empty Spaces, Silence, and the Pause', in Christoph Lindner and Gerard F. Sandoval, eds, *Aesthetics of Gentrification: Seductive Spaces and Exclusive Communities in the Neoliberal City* (Amsterdam: Amsterdam University Press, 2021), p. 247.

65. Felipe Lanuza, 'The Layered Absences of the Heygate Estate, South London (1974–2014)', *Architectural Research Quarterly* 24:1 (2020), p. 55.

66. 'Southwark Notes Archives Group Wishes You a Better Elephant for 2012!', 2012, p. 1: 56a Infoshop Archive, 'Southwark Notes Archives Group' Box.

67. Southwark Notes, 'Walking with the Elephant', 18 December 2011, southwarknotes.wordpress.com.

68. 'Southwark Notes Archives Group Wishes You a Better Elephant for 2012!', p. 3: 56a Infoshop Archive, 'Southwark Notes Archives Group' Box.

69. Southwark Notes, 'Regeneration Rip Off @ the Elephant Sat 19th July: Walk, Sound, Films', 6 July 2014, southwarknotes.wordpress.com.

70. Southwark Notes, 'Return of Walking the Rip-Off: Gentrification Walk of the Elephant', 19 February 2013, southwarknotes.wordpress.com.

71. Southwark Notes, 'Sound the Alarm!', p. 7: 56a Infoshop Archive, 'Southwark Regens – to file' Box.

72. Chris Wood, 'Heygate Heaven', July 2012, soundcloud.com; Chris Wood, 'NTS Scattershot: Aylesbury and Heygate Estates', 2013, soundcloud.com.

73. Michael Faraday School, 'Year 6 #Heygate Poetry', 2014, audioboom.com/posts/1840935-year-6-heygate-poetry.

74. Heygate Was Home, 'Press Archive', undated, https://web.archive.org/web/20150216012212/http://heygatewashome.org/press-archive.html.

75. Heygate Was Home, 'Nicola Redpath, Resident 1974–2000', undated, https://web.archive.org/web/20150216020821/http://heygatewashome.org/img/NicolaCarpenter.pdf.

76. Heygate Was Home, 'Doreen Gee, Resident 1974–2010', undated, https://web.archive.org/web/20150216041217/http://heygatewashome.org/img/DoreenGee.pdf.

77. Kate Eichhorn, 'Archival Genres: Gathering Texts and Reading Spaces', *Invisible Culture: An Electronic Journal for Visual Culture* 12 (2008), p. 1.

78. Fight for the Aylesbury, 'Statement from the Aylesbury Estate Occupation', 1 February 2015, fightfortheaylesbury.wordpress.com.

79. Fight for the Aylesbury, 'Even When We Lose in Court, We Win in the Streets. Victory to the Aylesbury!', 2 April 2015, fightfortheaylesbury.wordpress.com.

80. Southwark Notes, 'The Final Rip Off', undated: 56a Infoshop Archive, 'Southwark Notes Archive Group' Box.

81. Southwark Notes, 'Listening to No End'.

82. 'Take the Heygate Safari', undated: 56a Infoshop Archive, 'Heygate Estate' Box.

83. Southwark Notes, 'Southward Notes Attempts Regeneration Noir', 2012: 56a Infoshop Archive, 'Southwark Notes – blog' File.

84. Southwark Notes, *The Affordables* 1 (February 2012): 56a Infoshop Archive, 'Southwark Notes – blog' File.

85. 'Coming Soon: Waitrose', undated: 56a Infoshop, 'Southwark Notes to File' Box.

86. 'Seemingly Doing Well Yuppies', undated: 56a Infoshop Archive, 'Southwark Notes – blog' File.

87. Southwark Notes, '"No to New Prison" Say Locals', 6 October 2004: 56a Infoshop Archive, 'Southwark Notes – blog' File.

88. Southwark Notes, 'Heygate Pyramid: Artangel, Mike Nelson and Others Saga', undated, southwarknotes.wordpress.com.

89. Southwark Notes, 'Displacement Session', undated, p. 4: 56a Infoshop Archive, 'Southwark Notes – blog' File.

90. Marjolein 't Hart, 'Humour and Social Protest: An Introduction', *International Review of Social History* 52:15 (2007), p. 6.

91. James Fisher, 'A Peer of the Urban Realm', *Building Design* 1281 (11 October 1996), p. 11.

92. Sarah Schulman, *The Gentrification of the Mind: Witness to a Lost Imagination* (Berkeley: University of California Press, 2012), pp. 14, 49.

93. E. P. Thompson, 'The Moral Economy of the English Crowd in the Eighteenth Century', *Past and Present* 50:1 (1971), p. 79.

94. Amanda Baillieu, 'RIBA Should Take a More Critical Stand', *Building Design* 1753 (12 January 2007), p. 11.
95. London Tenants Federation, Loretta Lees, Just Space, and Southwark Notes Archives Group, *Staying Put*, p. 10: 56a Infoshop Archive, 'Southwark Notes Archives Group' Box.

Epilogue

1. Nicholas Boys Smith, 'True Blue – How Fair Conservatism Can Win the Next Election', *Conservative Home*, 25 November 2005.
2. Nicholas Boys Smith and Alex Morton, *Create Streets: Not Just Multistorey Estates* (Create Streets and Policy Exchange, 2013), pp. 25, 29, 30, 8.
3. Isabelle Carter, 'Youth, Race and the Inner-City Estate: Narratives of Everyday Life in Manchester's Hulme, 1970–1994', *Urban History* 50:2 (2023).
4. Sean Burns, *Dorothy Towers*, 2022 (documentary).
5. Lynn Abrams, Ade Kearns, Barry Hazley, and Valerie Wright, *Glasgow: High-Rise Homes, Estates and Communities in the Post-war Period* (London: Routledge, 2020).
6. Pearl Jephcott and Hilary Robinson, *Homes in High Flats: Some of the Human Problems Involved in Multi-storey Housing* (Edinburgh: Oliver & Boyd, 1971), p. 48.
7. John Boughton, *Municipal Dreams: The Rise and Fall of Council Housing* (London: Verso, 2018).
8. Pamela Johnston, ed., *Project Interrupted: Lectures by British Housing Architects* (London: Architecture Foundation, 2018).
9. Barnabas Calder, *Raw Concrete: The Beauty of Brutalism* (London: William Heinemann, 2016), p. 59.
10. Martin Hilditch, 'One Man's Battle to Improve Tower Block Safety', *Inside Housing*, 15 May 2018.
11. Sam Webb, 'Safety Last?', Fire Protection Association, 18 November 2022, thefpa.co.uk (published posthumously).
12. Oliver Wainwright and Peter Walker, '"Disaster Waiting to Happen": Fire Expert Slams UK Tower Blocks', *Guardian*, 14 June 2017.
13. Peter Apps, *Show Me the Bodies: How We Let Grenfell Happen* (London: Oneworld, 2022), p. 23.
14. Martin Moore-Bick, Ali Akbor, and Thouria Istephan, *Grenfell Tower Inquiry: Phase 2 Report*, vol. 2, part 3, *The Testing and Marketing of Products* (September 2024).
15. Apps, *Show Me the Bodies*, p. 293.
16. Arup, *Ledbury Estate: Structural Assessment of Bromyard, Peterchurch, Sarnsfield and Skenfrith House* (London: Ove Arup & Partners Ltd, 2017).

17. Arup, *Lewisham Homes, Lethbridge Estate: Structural Robustness Assessment* (London: Ove Arup & Partners Ltd, 2017); Arup, *London Borough of Hammersmith & Fulham, Hartopp Point & Lannoy Point: Structural Assessment* (London: Ove Arup & Partners Ltd, 2019); Ella Jessel, 'Haringey Set to Demolish Ronan Point-Style Blocks on Broadwater Farm Estate', *Architects' Journal*, 20 June 2018.

18. Adam Forrest, 'Hundreds of Tower Blocks Across UK at Risk of Collapse, Say Experts', *Independent*, 22 October 2018.

19. 'Cost of Strengthening High System Built Blocks Subject of the Tribunal's Recommendations', July 1970, p. 1: TNA HLG 118/1302.

20. J. Marlow, 'Strengthening of High Flats: Financial Implications', 3 June 1969, pp. 3–4: TNA HLG 118/1147.

21. Letter from Tamara Finkelstein to Local Authority Chief Executive, 'Safety of Large Panel System Buildings', 5 September 2017, available at 'Letters on the Safety of Large Panel System Buildings: 5 September 2017', gov.uk.

22. Martin Jones and Rhiannon Yhnell, 'Warning about Towers like Barton House in Bristol Made Years Ago', BBC News, 16 November 2023.

23. Peter Apps, 'Revealed: More than 200 Ronan Point–Style Blocks Still Have Gas and May Not Have Had Strengthening Work', *Inside Housing*, 13 March 2025.

24. Forrest, 'Hundreds of Tower Blocks across UK at Risk of Collapse'.

Index